Envisioning A New South Asia

ENVISIONING A NEW SOUTH ASIA

Edited by

T. Nirmala Devi
Adluri Subramanyam Raju

SHIPRA

Rs. 450; US$ 15

ISBN: 978-81-7541-447-1

2025 Impression
(2021, First Published 2009)

Envisioning A New South Asia

Published by:
SHIPRA PUBLICATIONS
LG 18-19, Pankaj Central Market
I.P. Ext., Patparganj, Delhi 110092, India
91 11 47322068; 9650028065, 9810522367
info@shiprapublication.com
www.shiprapublication.com

Foreword

It gives me great pleasure to write a foreword to this important volume, *Envisioning A New South Asia.* South Asia, one of the most important regional groupings in the world has 1.5 billion people with a number of languages and ethnic groups in the region. Yet there is unity in diversity and that is the most important and strongest aspect in South Asia. This region is the birth place for major religions, major civilizations in the world. It has its own civilizational processes. While existence of such historical narratives would make us proud, on the other hand the deep-rooted historical legacies may be obstacles when we try to transform the society into modernity. It is important to realize that these are parts of long historical and civilizational processes and therefore, we will be able to overcome all these difficulties.

SAARC has achieved significant and impressive records. When we compare achievement of SAARC for the last two decades, we need to keep in mind one of the important things, the 'sensitivity' in our region. Although we all have shared cultures, common cultural trends and then civilizational processes, the regional sensitivities do exist. These sensitivities are not quantifiable though. That is why we need to proceed with step-by-step approach.

No regional grouping will succeed, unless there is a proper 'connectivity' by road and by air. We need connectivity to increase regional trade and movement of goods and connectivity for the people to move from one place to the other in the region. Still we have not yet achieved the 100 per cent in connecting member States. The leaders of seven nations are very keen and they have repeatedly stated in their respective declarations and communiqués that SAARC capitals should be connected directly. It is very important to notice that people from seven Member-Countries are driving through 8,500 km starting from

Bangladesh ending SAARC Car rally in the Maldives. These activities would certainly bring people together.

We need to see that people of South Asia becoming rich in all senses and there should be a holistic way. We need to see that the region is without poverty. We need to provide good health and good education. I think this is how we need to proceed with creating a "New South Asia". I am sure that 1.5 billion people will be very happy in the years to come. We need to bring the message of regional cooperation to the people of South Asia.

In this connection, I appreciate the Centre for SAARC Studies, Andhra University, India, for bringing out a volume, which was the out come of a seminar, held in March 2007. This volume is a valuable addition to the literature on the subject. The book has to be commended for the contributors' competence provided on the subject. The editors–Prof. T. Nirmala Devi and Dr. A. Subramanyam Raju–deserve to be highly commended for their hard work in publishing the volume.

Sumith Nakandala
Sri Lankan Ambassador to Nepal

Acknowledgements

It is our foremost duty to express our deep sense of gratitude to the Ministry of External Affairs, New Delhi for extending the financial assistance to organise the seminar. We express our sincere thanks to the officials of the Ministry for their encouragement and help in organizing the seminar. We wish to convey our grateful thanks to Prof. K.C. Reddy, Chairman, Andhra Pradesh State Council of Higher Education, Hyderabad and to Prof. L. Venugopal Reddy, Vice-Chancellor of Andhra University, who have been kind enough in extending the moral and material support for organizing the seminar.

We are highly grateful to Amb. Sumith Nakandala, Sri Lankan Ambassador to Nepal and Amb. I.P. Khosla, Former Secretary, Ministry of External Affairs, New Delhi, for delivering the inaugural and keynote addresses respectively at the seminar. We thank all the paper contributors for their cooperation in bringing out this volume.

Contents

PART IV
SAARC – CHINA, ASEAN and BIMSTEC

Introduction

T. Nirmala Devi and Adluri Subramanyam Raju

South Asia is one of the very few regions in the world with geographical contiguity and linguistic and cultural homogeneity. The region, inhabited by more than one-fifth of global population, is afflicted by a number of social, political and economic problems compounded by political mistrust and suspicion. The South Asian states are plagued by inter-state conflicts over boundaries. Besides the inter-state disputes, intra-state conflicts are spilling over into neighbour's territories. There are hardly any pair of states in South Asia, which are not affected by trans-border spilling of ethno-nationalist, communal and militant activity. In addition, there is a sharp increase in unemployment, poverty, epidemics, drug trafficking, and environmental degradation etc. in the region. All these issues pose a far more serious and immediate challenge to the security of society. In spite of being home to nearly forty per cent of the world's poor, the region spends huge amount of money on military establishment, thereby prioritizing military security above human security. Competitive military spending has accentuated the historically derived mutual suspicions among the nations.

The South Asian states have begun realizing the importance of cooperation among themselves and are willing to address their problems collectively, as cooperation is the best alternative available for them in the era of economic globalization. The SAARC region has the potential to acquire a momentum of its own, leading to the total transformation of the region in the near future. Members have to set aside their disputes, in order to improve their economic relations. The India-Sri Lanka trade agreement is illustrative of subordinating differences to the goal of progress. They need to focus on creating a common South Asian market, transforming the region into a free trade area and promoting a dialogue between civil societies in the region. The governments of the South Asian states have to realize that it is high time to shift their focus from the security of the borders to regional cooperation.

The present volume is the outcome of an international seminar on *Envisioning A New South Asia* organized by the Centre for SAARC

Studies, Andhra University, Visakhapatnam during March 29-31, 2007. The papers not only focused on the problems being faced by the South Asian countries; but also suggested the amicable solutions to overcome these problems and the possible ways to reconstruct a new South Asia. Thus, the main focus of the seminar was to probe into various mechanisms to be adopted to make the South Asian region free from conflicts. This would enhance economic cooperation amongst the states and thereby improve the welfare of the people. While analyzing the conflicts and misunderstandings between/ among the countries in the region, the volume tries to underline the issues related to human development, traditional and non traditional security and the role of external powers in the peace process of South Asia.

There are sixteen papers in the volume, emphasizing on the various contemporary issues of South Asian region, which can be arranged into four sections. Part I surveys five papers on new horizons of South Asia and the role of connectivity in the globalized world and also the interlinked issues of peace process and conflict resolution. In his keynote address, I. P Khosla maintains that India, being the largest country in the region, must take unilateral provisions like duty-free access to its neighbouring markets and reduce trade barriers. He advocates that India has to take initiatives to improve structural capabilities like connectivity through road, rail, and maritime corridors and inland and maritime gateways within the region, in order to overcome physical and non-physical barriers and to attain the overall objective. Shibashis Chatterjee and Sulagna Maitra in their paper, argues that India perceives itself as a leading power of Asia and is more interested to adjust its role to a larger Asian theatre than investing seriously to repair its South Asian image. To this end, he maintais that India seeks to redefine SAARC to tie with its new 'Look East' policy, which is more accommodative of its economic and security concerns, even if it harbingers the tragic possibility of a geo-political and economic transcendence of the idea of South Asian cooperation. Gopalji Malviya's paper discusses how India-Pakistan relations reflect on cooperation at regional level. South Asia contends a stability- instability situation that is based on Kashmir, the core dispute and the nuclear weapons, the intervening variables that would alter the nature and dynamics of the dispute. He argues that the nuclear weaponization has provided India and Pakistan the will and motivation to display the statesmanship that is required for lasting peace and stability in South Asia. Noman Sattar, in his paper, addresses various issues which pose a challenge to the peace process. As terrorism is the major hindrance to the ongoing peace process between India and Pakistan, he advocates the steady peace process that is linked to development of the region. In his paper, Rajpal Budania discusses several conflict resolution strategies in the region and their prospects for success in the present situation. He argues that promotion of democracy and development, arms control, bilateralism and peaceful settlement of disputes, economic cooperation, interdependence, common security and common world view and confidence-building measures can provide useful insights into the conflict resolution strategies. He further maintains that both national and transnational developments will shape the prospects for conflict prevention, management and resolution in the region.

Part II devotes to the aspect of human security in the South Asian region. This section includes four papers, dealing with the core issues of the subject. T. Nirmala Devi, in her paper, emphasizes the need for inclusive growth by improving the human and economic security of South Asia's more than one-fifth global population through appropriate strategies and good governance. She further focuses on the priority in public spending, which should be diverted from defence to social sector, in order to strengthen the human security. She opines that India must share a common concern for peace process with other regional members, which would certainly project the whole South Asian region as a conflict-free zone with an improved standard of living. In his paper, Som P Pudasaini explains that the South Asian countries suffer from significant and mundane economic, political and diplomatic irritants. He maintains that poverty eradication, lasting peace and neighbourly diplomacy are indispensable to build a prosperous South Asia. Adluri. Subramanyam Raju's paper maintains that there is a sharp increase in drug trafficking, environmental degradation, unemployment, poverty, epidemics, ethnic or religious animosities and civil wars etc, which pose a serious challenge to the security of human beings than the military threats. Hence, he opines that there is a pressing need to focus on the humanistic aspect of the security debate. Finally, he analyzes three issues pertaining to human development, i.e. fishermen insecurity in South Asia, terrorist activities and energy security in the region. Nalini Kant Jha, in his paper, argues that contemporary discourse on peace and human security hardly take into account the thoughts of Indian thinkers. He discusses the relevance of traditional Indian approach to human security for addressing contemporary issues of South Asian peace and security.

Part III deals with the non-traditional security and other core issues of South Asia , as contained in the following four papers. M.J.Vinod, in his paper, explains how non-traditional issues affect relations between communities, peoples and states in South Asia. He feels that this could perhaps provide a better understanding of the problems afflicting the region, which could help promote alternative visions, options and approaches to the conflict resolution in the region. J. Laxmi Narasimha Rao argues that the states of the region are liberalizing their economies in recent years and showing more interest in greater intra-regional trade by reducing tariffs and non-tariff barriers and inviting investment. However, he maintains that the region has to go a long way in reaching integration in the true sense and spirit. He explores various means and mechanisms in realizing a South Asian Union in the region. Syed Ali Mujtaba, in his paper, tries to visualize a common South Asian Union and discusses the prospects for such a regional grouping. V. Sreemannarayana Murthy explains how the social processes are in operation in different countries of South Asia. He examines the scope for accommodation between rival ethnic groups in different countries with a special focus on Sri Lanka, where the ethnic crisis snowballed into a violent confrontation between the Tamils and the Lankan forces by taking a heavy toll on its social fabric.

Part IV examines the role of external powers in the peace process of South Asia. Three papers are included in this section, reflecting the shadow of China, ASEAN and BIMSTEC on the member countries. In his paper, Srikanth Kondapalli argues that China's interaction with South Asian countries expanded its role in the region to make it perhaps the third largest external factor in the policies of these countries, next only to the United States and the former Soviet Union. Although China's interaction with the region are rooted in history, he argues that the present state-to-state relations have emphasised the aspects of protecting territorial boundaries and sovereignty issues, given the geographical proximity of most of these countries. In his paper, A. Lakshmana Chetty examines the process of India's integration with the regional cooperative frameworks. He evaluates the prospects of Northeastern India's joining in the national mainstream and its emergence as an economically potential centre. He strongly advocates the integration of Northeastern region with the rest of India, not only to overcome its poverty and ethnic strife but also to make it a solid springboard for the globalization process. Finally, Y. Yagama Reddy argues that India acts as an anchor for the countries in the Bay of Bengal region, not only on account of its age-old cultural and trading contacts with its immediate eastern neighbours, but also due to the similarities based on geology, land forms, climate, biotic life and agricultural typology—all signifying the character of a macro-region. He opines that India need not get itself strained in swimming in the pool of South Asian politics and instead it must set out itself for sailing across the Bay of Bengal. In such an event, SAARC would get itself salvaged from the state of being wrecked, he adds.

PART I

South Asia: Connecting to a Globalized World

1

South Asia: Connecting to a Globalized World

I.P. Khosla

Long before the European colonialist came on the scene, South Asia was at one time a world centre of economic growth, trade and wealth. One estimate of the South Asian region puts its GDP at purchasing power parity calculations at nearly twenty five per cent of the global total in the year 1700; this was also the case for the year 1500 and the year 1600. The picture for the Asian economy is equally startling. In 1600 this accounted for sixty three per cent of world GDP and the figure for 1700 was not much lower, at fifty eight per cent. The figure was down to five per cent by the end of the twentieth century for South Asia, though, of course, for Asia as a whole it was at thirty per cent, which is still significant. This is one of the standard estimates of the world economy over the centuries made by Angus Maddison for the Organization for Economic Cooperation and Development. There are, of course, many other studies that have established the close convergence between growth and prosperity, on the one hand, and the development of domestic as well as international trade, on the other.

So, in large measure, the high levels of income in South Asia and Asia in general in earlier centuries were due to the trading links that existed between South Asia, Asia in general and the rest of the world and these links, in turn, could be fostered by the excellent connectivity that the transport linkages in those historic times provided. Along the great trade and travel routes by sea and by land, such as the Silk Road, went its manufactures and other products, textiles, spices including pepper. In ships and ship-building it led every other region. Its exports were such as to be found in the major markets of the time, so much so that from the Roman Empire to the eighteenth century Europeans, the loss of gold and silver in payment for these goods was bemoaned. The trade routes from Central Asia and China, from the Mediterranean and Africa, criss-crossed the Indian Ocean. Ancient roads and rivers criss-crossed the region itself and linked up with the Indian Ocean seaports that were the gateways to the world.

On land, corridors and hubs linked every part of undivided India: the Grand Trunk road leading up to the borders of Afghanistan on one side and the Bay of Bengal on the other; other roadways radiating inland from the great international seaports like Calicut, Cochin, Quilon and Cannanore; they were used for export and import from the empires inland. The ports of South Asia, especially those located on the coast of Gujarat, attracted large numbers of foreign traders because of the immense variety of their markets and the apparent wealth of the cities.

Not only roads, but river systems such as the Ganga-Brahmaputra-Meghna were used for such transport. And from the ports radiating outwards there were the sea routes which linked South Asia to a comprehensive trading network across the Arabian sea and the Bay of Bengal. The Indian Ocean, in fact, was for practical purposes a single maritime entity and people knew they could sail from one end to the other on trading or other expeditions.

Before large parts of Asia were colonized, and apart from the trade routes and the intricate system of transport networks mentioned above, South Asia was also internally well connected as a single unified administrative and financial unit, for instance, during the great empires, the Mauryans, the Guptas and the Mughals among others. This continued, of course, even after colonization. This meant that, for several thousand years, with some gaps, the countries of the region also shared a single governing and administrative culture, a habit of working together, an infrastructure of roads, canals, shipping and, more recently, rail and telecommunications.

Colonial Policy

The colonial powers did two things in this respect. They cut the former international routes in order to ensure that the connections were exclusively from the colonies to their own home lands; As one author says, "it is good to be reminded ... how the ancient Indian Ocean 'world' of maritime trade and commerce, sustained and strengthened by human-cultural flows and intercourse at regional and sub-regional levels, was deranged by the imperial-colonial metropolitan economies..."[1]

Secondly, they developed and greatly expanded the existing transport and communications networks within their own colonies, so that the components of each of the empires were internally even better connected than they had been, as they were to the colonial power, but all the other connections that had been built up over the earlier centuries were severed. In this way, for example, British India became one economic entity, one network of communications, one market with a single currency and a common external economic policy. After 1947 these networks were cut over the years due to the political division of the region.

Hence the logic of regional cooperation within South Asia seems not to require restating. Of all the regions in the world going for regional cooperation this is the one with longest history as a coherent political, economic and administrative entity. All that is required is to restore that which we have had over the centuries, which should not be too difficult to envisage. This does not mean it can actually be achieved or concretized, in contrast to visualization, without effort. Herein lies one of the problems that the region faces that there is a plethora of 'Vision' documents but few of them are able to suggest how that vision is to be concretized.

The Forces of History

Today the forces of history have pushed the South Asian region to the periphery of the world economy, with a total GNP which amounts to about five per cent of the world total, though no doubt in recent years economic growth rates have been impressive, especially in the case of India. But, in general, the centres of growth and wealth, of industry and technology, have moved to North America, Europe and East Asia and the major trade routes have shifted to the Atlantic and Pacific oceans. One of the primary reasons for this decline appears to be the loss of connectivity induced by colonial policy. The global economic weight of South Asia has gone down to insignificant proportions because connectivity, trade and financial flows contribute importantly to economic growth and these have been severed for nearly three hundred years.

For the region, therefore, a much bigger effort is needed to develop and grow economically, for it amounts to reversing a historical trend.

It is not being argued here that transport and communication networks, or connectivity in general are the most important factors for economic growth and progress, nor of course that they are the ones to which exclusive attention needs to be paid. But their importance has always been considerable: in the growth and prosperity of Venice in the years after 1100, of Holland in the seventeenth century and of Britain in the nineteenth, expanding trade was crucial. This importance has actually increased over time due to all the things that have been happening to the global economy and particularly the phenomenon known as globalization.

This word has a confusing number of meanings attached to it. Conservatives in the US talk about capitalism being the ultimate solution to all problems. Hence globalization becomes linked to endist thinking: the end of history or of the state; the end of modernity and of ideology; the end of everything that is not part of the neo-liberal and capitalist agenda. And progress will, in this new globalized world, be marked by global governance implemented through the United Nations, the World Trade Organization, the World Bank and the International Monetary Fund, regional and sub-regional associations in order to bring about a new world order based on market civilization. This is the widest meaning of the term; it includes the coming together of peoples, their political institutions, the spread of democratic pluralism, a free press and an independent judiciary; and the spread of the benefits of science and technology, the mass media and the internet, the hybridization or homogenization of culture; the proliferation of NGOs and professional associations with transnational connections as well as other supranational groups. These are just a few of the manifestations of this phenomenon.

The World Bank talks of three waves of globalization: the first from 1870 to 1914; the second from 1950 to 1980; the third from 1980 to 2000 and which is still going on. Each wave was accompanied by an expansion in the international movement of goods, capital and people, and by unusually high growth rates of national products among those countries which took part in the expanded movement. In a 2001 study called "Globalization, Growth and Poverty: Building an Inclusive World Economy" the World Bank reports that the twenty four developing countries that increased their integration into the world economy from 1980 to 2000 achieved higher growth in incomes – five per cent per annum per capita compared to two per cent in the developed world – longer life expectancy and better schooling than the others. China, India, Hungary, Mexico are among them. But two billion people in the countries of sub-Saharan Africa, the Middle East and the former Soviet Union are being left behind because they have not been able to integrate; these countries must improve their investment climate, have better social protection, so that they can avail the benefits of globalization. In order to help the process the rich must open their markets, slash agricultural subsidies and increase development aid.

Economist Jagdish Bhagwati is a hyper-globalist who agrees that this is not the first time rapid world economic integration is taking place;

it occurred in the late nineteenth and early twentieth centuries, and the expansion of "trade, capital flows and migration were no less then than they are today".[2] Others agree. "The period of globalization preceding World War I was quite similar to the one we are living through today"[3] But today's globalization, they do not fail to add, also has something new about it.

There are some who have a different take on this phenomenon. One of the leading theorists of globalization does not agree that there have been waves of globalization earlier; he asserts that it is completely new and says, it is "the overall process by which the entire world becomes increasingly interdependent, so as to yield a 'single place' ".[4]

In general globalists of all varieties agree that globalization is unstoppable; that it is a force for good; and that, though it is manifest everywhere, it is to be seen most palpably in economic transactions. The fact is that the globalization of economies is now a universal phenomenon that has resulted in the integration of national economies at both regional and sub-regional levels.

The foundation for the central role that economic transactions occupy in the process of globalization is provided by the changes that have happened over time and as a result of technological advances, in production systems. These changes have gradually happened since 1945, but after 1990 they have definitely accelerated. They can be encapsulated in one word: integration. Integration is the reason that connectivity is so important today.

Paradoxically, this has occurred through dispersal. There is today, especially for the large multinational company, a new division of labour through which production of the single item that the consumer buys is, as far as the producer is concerned, broken up into a number of components; and the components are not always produced in the same place; they could be farmed out among several production centres and these could be located in different countries, may be even different regions. In other words, the production and consumption of goods and services is increasingly multi-national in character and individual economies increasingly interdependent.

Econometric studies into intra-industry trade gives one insight into the extent of this phenomenon. In the UK, for instance, trade at the three digit level within industries grew from 0.22 to 0.38 or by seventy two per cent over the period 1964 to 1980 in food and live animals, while in a product which is technologically more advanced like chemicals, where it was already at the level 0.56 in 1964 it grew to 0.69, over twent three per cent, by the year 1980. So the degree to which a product is technologically advanced determines that the level of such trade will be higher. In general it has been found that where there is a greater involvement of trans-national corporations the levels of intra-industry trade are higher; this is the second factor. Furthermore it is also found that there are several distinct factors other than the two cited above which account for a larger level of intra-industry trade. A product where large scale economies are available has more of intra-industry trade; also where foreign investment is there and particularly if the market structure is tending towards monopolistically competitive conditions.[5]

A more liberalized regime of trade and transport coupled with advances in international logistics, information technology, electronic documentation, cross-border facilitation measures, streamlined customs procedures, to mention only the most important ones, have greatly expanded the scope for international trade in goods and services with consequent increased demand for movement both within and across the national boundaries.

So we need the instruments which will facilitate integration: the different components of a single product have to be brought together, transported to one great assembly line. This means, first of all, zero tariff and non-tariff barriers; secondly the best that transport systems can offer.

Measures to Globalize: Removing Trade Barriers

Free trade areas and customs unions are envisaged in Article XXIV of GATT (General Agreement of Tariffs and Trade), 1994. This provides, regardless of the general commitment to grant most favoured nation treatment to all contracting parties, for the formation of either of these, or the adoption of an interim agreement necessary for their formation. Article XXIV (7) of GATT provides that the contracting parties (meaning all those who are part of GATT) shall be notified about such an interim agreement.

There are other provisos to this article. One is that the duties and other regulations of commerce maintained and applicable within the free trade area at its formation should not be higher or more restrictive than the corresponding duties and so on existing prior to its formation. This means, of course, that since within the framework of WTO there is a mandatory lowering of tariffs and non-tariff barriers over time, the earlier any region wishing to do so forms a free trade area followed by a customs union, the better. The other important proviso is that in the case of an interim agreement there must be a plan and schedule for the formation of the free trade area or customs union "within a reasonable length of time".

This means around ten years. The South Asian Free Trade Area (SAFTA) provides for ten years for the least developed and eight for the others.

Free trade areas and even more so customs unions violate the most favoured nation principle that has been accepted by the GATT contracting parties since 1947. These are not the only violations: Article XXIV itself provides that the provisions of the agreement shall not prevent advantages accorded to the trade by any contracting party to an adjacent country to facilitate frontier traffic; in principle even the preferences given to developing and least developed countries and the trading regimes set up for the textile and garment sectors are violations, but all these are taken to be beneficial to the poorer countries and in any case to be temporary. Article XXIV is, in any case, a major exception that benefits the developed countries most and looks like becoming permanently part of world trade. However, this only recognizes a reality that the so-called Regional Trading Arrangements (RTA's, which include free trade areas and customs unions) have proliferated since 1947. By 2002 there were some 240 in force and the number is likely to go up to 300 and beyond. Bilateral RTA's are included in this.

The RTAs formed by the developed countries have sought different means to discriminate against the products of developing countries. This does not include all developing countries, since privileged access to certain of the major RTAs has been given to a selected few among them. This involves the diversion of trade away from those developing countries who have not been given this benefit, thus creating another category of GATT contracting parties, those who do not have to be members of RTAs but yet avail of specific advantages. The treatment by the European Union of certain North African and other African countries in the franco-phone zone is one example.

They have not only resorted to such trading diverting methods, but "RTAs also tend to distort investment patterns. The regional champions are protected by common external tariffs and a variety of non-tariff measures such as voluntary export restraints, screw driver and local content regulations and anti-dumping levies."[6]

Measures to Globalize: Transport

Furthermore, transport costs have become a significant determinant of competitiveness; an integrated and efficient transport system is an essential element to compete at any level, and therefore to globalize. The provision of physical infrastructure in the form of an integrated transport network is essential, but not sufficient. It is essential in addition to have adequate facilitation measures to address all the non-physical barriers so that goods, vehicles and people can move freely across international borders. Among all the various measures to be taken would be included transport and the infrastructure for building this up by land, water and air, as well as telecommunications and generally the electronic means of connectivity. It would also include knowledge connections. In particular, given the problems that the South Asian region is facing, and will increasingly face in this regard, it would include energy. Now that Afghanistan has joined SAARC as the eighth member, it can serve a vital function as a bridge for connecting Central Asia with this region.

But above all, it means that the roads and road transport, the air, sea, rail networks, the ports and container services, must be efficient.

The importance of efficient and cheap transport and communications as an essential input for greater economic productivity and more rapid growth has been recognized since ancient times. These factors are particularly significant for South Asia today as it endeavours to connect better to a globalized world; but they were always indispensable.

During the course of the centuries and even in ancient times ports and other centres of trade rose or fell depending on their efficiency; and today this is happening on a much larger scale. Colombo comes up because it is efficient and fast; Mumbai goes down because of shipping delays; and so there is talk of a land bridge which "could become a connecting link between the national highways in South India and those in Sri Lanka. It would facilitate a continuous road and ferry link from Madurai to Trincomalee for cargo and passengers."[7] This suggests that cargo for Indian destinations can be unloaded in Colombo and taken across to India. This example suggests the ways in which total transport integration can be envisaged: the development of every method of transport, road, rail, river and maritime, air, of hubs and corridors across South Asia, linking the region with Asia and with the world beyond that in such an integrated way that the producers' dream of 'just in time' delivery can become a reality. What this needs is not just the physical infrastructure, but also bilateral, regional and multinational agreements and national measures for trade facilitation, such as stream lined customs procedures.

Trade and Growth

With all these changes in the way the world economy functions new relationships have started emerging: new divisions of labour, of collaboration and competition.

A major implication is that world GNP growth is now more closely than ever before tagged to the growth of world trade. The former has been growing at three per cent per annum in the 1990s, while trade was growing at six per cent, and financial flows are growing the fastest at twenty two per cent per annum. So the growth of the economy is closely tied to trade and finance growth; this is shown by the experience of India where the rate of growth of the economy increased from 3.5 per cent in the sixties and seventies to 5.5 per cent in the eighties, over six to seven per cent in the nineties, and then over eight per cent with the coming of the new millennium in close harmony with the increased percentage of trade in GNP. In all the countries of South Asia these increasing rates of growth went with an even more rapid expansion in the share of trade in GNP and in FDI inflow.

So this is what is making globalization happen. And it has seen the emergence of three economic megablocs: NAFTA, the EU, and the East Asian group. The three groups account for eighty five per cent of world GNP. This is an answer to the rules governing the world trading system, the effect of which is to bolster the competitive positions of those who are members of one or other of the blocs, expand their internal markets and mobilise large internal resources for R&D and investment. The freeing of trade in itself creates R&D resources; free trade leads eventually to a Customs Union, which in turn leads to investment regimes, and to harmonization of macro-economic parameters; as we have been able to see in Europe and North America, this results in enhanced bargaining power in regional and global negotiations. There are other benefits, too. Regional and non-regional companies have an incentive to invest to take advantage of the protected and larger market; regional companies have a larger market for growth which can also be encouraged by intra-regional investment.

So while there is a great deal of discrimination against those outside the groupings, the direct and spill over benefits for those who are insiders are tremendous. And this tariff reduction and trading system, introduced originally to help Europe reconstruct after the war through economic integration, now discriminates against those outside.

The Asian Level

The Asian level has particular importance; there has been a shift in the balance of economic power to Asia during the last two decades, where savings rates are high, and most future growth is expected, despite the recent crisis. This has spill-over effects through production, trade, finance, and global interdependency.

The East Asia summit has already discussed the shape likely to be taken by the evolving architecture of regional cooperation at the Asian or sub-Asian levels. The latter includes several organizations in which India has played a leading role, such as BIMSTEC (the Bay of Bengal Initiative for Multi-Sectoral Technical and Economic Cooperation), the Mekong-Ganga cooperation, ARF, the ASEAN Regional Forum and others. SAARC itself is linked to ASEAN and has growing ties with others like ECO and the GCC. Asian Economic Integration has been widely discussed and studied and details of an Asian currency worked out. These can all be regarded as building blocks for an Asian community or an Asian Union.

As an example the intra-regional multimodal transport connectivity in Europe has provided foundational support to the convergence of economies, growth and development of trade amongst the EU member countries. Various initiatives for promotion of intra-regional transport connectivity taken in other regions also like ASEAN, GMS and ECO of Central Asia have had remarkable success.

The Greater Mekong Sub-region was constituted with support from the Asian Development Bank in 1992, with the main focus on road and transportation linkages between the six members.[8] Another useful example is offered by ASEAN, where the member states have adopted a long term vision for an integrated and harmonized trans-ASEAN transportation network. An ASEAN Framework agreement has already been signed on the facilitation of goods in transit and a number of protocols are being developed in order to implement the trade facilitation measures.[9]

These experiences could be useful for SAARC in its efforts to strengthen transport links across their region.

The South Asian Context

But it is first of all important that South Asia thinks further forward, beyond SAFTA, towards the establishment of a customs union at the earliest possible date. This would be within the context of the consensual approach that characterizes the WTO. "Because of the consensus approach adopted in the WTO negotiations, a coordinated response of South Asian countries would be more effective in realizing their objectives...."[10] Note that the SAFTA agreement contains no hint of such a union, or of a common external tariff. But SAFTA in itself has great potential both for increasing intra-regional trade as well as for the efficiency seeking restructuring of industry and the creation of supply capacities in the lesser developed member states. Transport connectivity is essential for this.

It has been rightly noted that "much of the advantages of geographical proximity among SACs (South Asian Countries) is lost owing to the absence of satisfactory transport and communication linkages. Besides, whatever transport linkages that existed under an unified administrative set up was depleted with partition of the Indian subcontinent."[11]

One expert in the subject pointed out that in South Asia "the need for transport integration remains perhaps the most urgent since it is integral to the operationalization of a free trade area."[12] This is particularly so since the countries of the region "are paying a tremendous price for the present deplorable conditions of their transport infrastructure and linkages."[13]

SAARC and Transport Integration

For several years SAARC had shown little interest in transport or even other forms of connectivity. The importance of transport was recognized; a technical committee on transport was set up within the Integrated Programme of Action (IPA) in 1983, even before the formal launch of the regional organization in 1985. Under its auspices data bases and directories were compiled, seminars and workshops were organized and training courses were conducted. However this entire subject did not figure as a separate item in the SAARC summit level declarations until the twelfth summit, held at Islamabad in January 2004, which recognized the importance of the subject by asserting that it was essential for accelerated and balanced economic growth, to strengthen transportation, transit and communication links across the region. This was reiterated at the next summit, which also noted the ongoing SAARC Regional Multimodal Transport Study (SRMTS) to enhance transport connectivity among the members.

Manmohan Singh explained in his statement at that summit that what we are today witnessing is 'nothing short of an Asian resurgence based upon the rebuilding of the pre-colonial arteries of trade and commerce that created a distinct Asian identity in the first place'; so the question is whether South Asia is prepared to be an integral part of this resurgence or will it be marginalized? If it is not to be the latter it is necessary to take the first decision 'to reconnect the countries of the sub-continent on the one hand and then reconnect the sub-continent to the large Asian neighbourhood on the other' if this region is to reclaim the prosperity that is its due.

Then the fourteenth summit reiterated the importance of connectivity in fulfilling the major objectives set out in the SAARC Charter; and it was agreed that better connectivity within South Asia comes first. This means physical connectivity, economic connectivity as well as people to people contacts, with a smooth flow of goods, services, peoples, technologies, knowledge, capital, culture and ideas within the region. The importance of cultural diffusion and interaction should not be under-rated for, as has been noted, maritime trade, which is one form of connectivity, "provided the means, and often was the stimulus, for interaction between various indigenous civilizations of the Indian Ocean".[14]

As a follow up specific decisions were also taken on extending the SRMTS to include Afghanistan, the new member from that summit onwards. Another important set of decisions, closely linked to the idea of connectivity, was in regard to trade facilitation. The summit underlined the importance of implementing trade facilitation measures, especially standardization of basic customs nomenclature, documentation and clearing procedures. It directed that a comprehensive agreement on harmonizing customs procedures be finalized; that harmonization of technical and phyto-sanitary standards and their implementation in a trade-friendly manner is important in boosting intra-regional trade; and that a SAARC Standards Coordination Board should function.

And in August 2007 the first meeting of SAARC Transport Ministers was held in New Delhi, at which a number of ideas were floated: a rail corridor between Chennai and Colombo; a road from Agartala to Chittagong; a ferry service from Colombo to Cochin; direct air connections among all the SAARC capitals.

The SRMTS

Following up on the Islamabad SAARC summit decision and recognizing the importance of transport integration in South Asia, SAARC, with financial and technical support from the ADB, initiated the SRMTS with the main objective of enhancing multi-modal transport connectivity among SAARC member states, so as to promote intra-regional trade. The SRMTS report was completed in June 2006 and is now with the SAARC Secretariat and the governments of the member states. It has not yet been made public, but several of the members of the team that compiled it have been speaking about their views on the subject both before writing the report and have also spoken on the same lines after it was completed; thus there is enough knowledge about the particulars that are reflected in it.

An initial identification of corridors/gateways has been done by the team, which resulted in the selection of ten Regional Road Corridors, five Regional Rail Corridors, two Regional Inland Waterways Corridors, ten Maritime Gateways and sixteen Aviation Gateways. Further assessment of these corridors/gateways revealed their physical and non-physical barriers and specific measures were suggested to address them.

On road transport, the team found that there were no significant physical barriers on the road corridors identified; in fact quite a good quality road network exists and ninety per cent of the road corridors totalling around 8,800 kms have two or more lanes and a large chunk of regional road corridors in India and Pakistan are in fact four-lane divided highways. It was also found that less than five per cent of the corridors need physical improvement and another less than five per cent, mostly near the border areas, needs widening up to two-lanes. But the non-physical barriers were many and included the lack of bilateral transport agreements to facilitate uninterrupted movement of goods and vehicles across the borders between India and Bangladesh, as well as between Pakistan and India. So goods are required to be transhipped at the border between the trucks of neighbouring countries. Other important physical/non-physical barriers identified included the lack of parking, immigration and customs offices, baggage scanning equipment, telephone and warehousing at several border posts, as well as EDI/IT and standardization of working hours and weekly holidays, as well as use of complicated customs procedures and lack of transparency in inspection.

On rail transport, the picture was similar; South Asia has one of the largest railway networks in the world, over 77,000 route kilometres of which Indian rail network alone covers 63,465 route kilometres. About seventy per cent of this network is broad gauge largely in India, Pakistan and Sri Lanka. Although the railway network historically played a significant integrating role in the socio-economic development of this part of the world, over the years it has been losing its market share to the road transport. This trend is being reversed by infusion of huge investments in railway development plans in India, Bangladesh and Pakistan. Once the integrated transport system of South Asia becomes operational and the rail network is available for movement of intra-regional trade, rail should be able to capture most of its lost traffic, particularly the long distance traffic in which it has a cost advantage.

For the regional rail corridors the major physical barriers include the lack of standardization of technologies, operation and maintenance practices including different types of gauges, braking systems, incompatibility of rolling stock, inadequate loop lengths, some missing links of shorter lengths in the border areas, lack of physical infrastructure at interchange points, load restrictions on bridges, lack of coordination for gauge conversion programmes on different railway systems and capacity constraints in certain sections of the identified corridors.

But, again it is the non-physical barriers which may create a bigger problem; the most crucial one was the lack of a multilateral rail transport agreement. Other non-physical barriers included manual handling of documentation, duplication of customs checks, limited working hours, restrictions on movement of open wagons and oil tankers, uni-directional traffic and the suspension of rail-cum-ferry services between Sri Lanka and India.

Inland waterways corridors serve the interest of only Bangladesh and India, where levels of traffic both intra-country and transit had been reducing over years, although during certain periods bilateral traffic has been substantial. But inland waterways transport has great potential to provide a cost effective transport service between India and Bangladesh, and one of the most crucial non-physical barriers identified was that the renewal of the protocol between India and Bangladesh only on a monthly basis, instead of a more rational, say five years.

With regard to maritime transport, South Asia is endowed with about twenty five major ports, of which ten were selected as gateways of regional significance. In 2003, these twenty five ports together handled 366.22 million tonnes of traffic, including 5.85 million TEUs of containers.

The major barriers identified in regional maritime gateways included likely capacity constraints at many of the gateways, together with heavy siltation at channels where depths fluctuate with tide. Channel markings were also not adequate and suffer from poor maintenance. Cargo and ship handling equipment, as well as floating craft were found to be quite old in many gateways. Poor road and rail connectivity, lack of ICDs and CFS were other major physical barriers, besides lack of roro ferry vessels and passenger handling facilities at Cochin and Tuticorin.

The non-physical barriers were again the most crucial and include lack of professional management and computerization, as well as EDI/IT to link up stakeholders. Customs procedures are too complicated, cumbersome port documentation was still in use. The absence of a bilateral agreement for ferry service between Colombo and Tuticorin/Cochin is a major non-physical barrier.

For air transport around 251 weekly flights were operating between different regional destinations, and in 2004 they carried around 2.23 million passengers and 36,602 tonnes of freight. The overall passenger growth in intra-regional travel has been one of the highest in the world at twelve per cent per annum, while for freight it has been an equally impressive 7.5 per cent per annum over the period 2001-04.

It is of special urgency, therefore that steps should be taken for improved connectivity in this field. Some of the major physical barriers that could impact the sixteen identified gateways included likely capacity constraints at several gateways for both passengers and cargo in terms of runways, parking areas for aircrafts, passenger handling areas, cargo processing facilities (green channel, cold storage, etc), as well as security and baggage handling facilities. The non-physical barriers included the limited number of direct flights resulting in the need for transfers and involvement of travel even outside the region, the low use of air travel compared to economic conditions, the high air fare and airport charges compared to other regions and visa restrictions.

There are so many physical and non-physical barriers that have to be overcome that it is useful to prioritize. The team found it possible to agree on the kind of prioritization that should be attempted and the following steps were recommended.

Road Corridors

- Transport and transit agreements between India, Bangladesh and Pakistan to allow through movement of freight;
- Improvements of the roads through Bihar, West Bengal, and Bangladesh to assist Nepal, Bhutan and Bangladesh in reducing transit costs, as also the last few kilometres of road up to the international borders, which should be treated as part of national highways;
- Modern border crossings between India and its neighbours (both sides) in order to facilitate transit of both passengers and freight;
- Facilitation measures and simplified customs procedures for efficient clearance of goods across the border points.

Rail Corridors

- Augmentation of sectional capacity along the identified corridors to handle the projected and potential growth of intra-regional traffic;
- Coordinated standardization of technologies including track and gauge, rolling stock and signalling.
- Provision of identified physical infrastructure at inter-change points, yards, terminals and transhipment hubs;
- Construction of missing links on the corridors;
- Strengthening of bridges and permanent way to enable through movement of loaded broad gauge freight trains in the region; and

- Development and adoption of a multilateral rail transport agreement by the SAARC member states to facilitate barrier-free movement across the region.

Inland Waterways

- The existing protocol between Bangladesh and India to be renewed, each time, for longer periods, say up to five years;
- Investment in dredging and vessels replacement; and
- To make inter-country traffic movement by IWT attractive, more ports of call in Bangladesh should be allowed.

Maritime Gateways

- Need to expand port capacity, especially to handle more container traffic, particularly at Colombo (as the regional hub), Chittagong, Haldia and Male;
- Plan and augment rail, road and pipeline connectivity at all ports;
- Improved port and trade facilitation measures needed to reduce dwell times;
- Improved dredging to maintain water depths as well as channel marking, especially at Chittagong, Colombo, Kolkata/Haldia and Port Qasim; and
- Introduce professional management capability, and encourage private sector involvement in port development and operations.

Maritime Corridor (Passenger)

- Re-commissioning of Passenger Ferry Service between India and Sri Lanka.
- Aviation Gateways
- Promotion of low cost carrier concept by each country;
- Development and redesign of international passenger terminals, especially at Bhutanese, Indian and Nepalese airports; feasibility of new airports, especially in Bhutan;
- Improvements in radar systems/ILS to increase runway capacity to international maximums; and
- Introduction of commercial practices in airport management and encouraging private sector in development and management of airports.

Conclusion

Finally, it goes without saying, of course, that it is the coordinated and focused commitment of SAARC member states to resolve and overcome the identified physical and non-physical barriers which will get connectivity into place; this is more important than the rather nominal investments needed.

Indeed, while the list of things to be done is much longer than given above and the report goes into nearly 200 pages of detailed recommendation, it is possible to conceptualize and then to categorize it quite neatly into three:

First, the physical or infrastructural work, which includes roads, the railways, shipping, airlines, which do not even require much in the way of funds since not much has to be done. Second, the creation of facilities, easier crossing of the borders, getting visas, simpler documentation for customs and such like. This is dependent on the desire of governments to provide the conditions under which people, goods, electronic data, messages and other things like energy can move across borders in our region. This is more important than the first, but even easier, and it requires less funds, but there must first be a decision by governments that they would like to do it, which seems at present to be far away.

The third is the most important and the easiest, the meeting of minds which results in real connectivity, as distinct from transportation, transit or communication; it involves the movement of ideas and of knowledge and the kind of genuine exchange which leads to shared thinking. No expenses are needed for this purpose; it only requires that the existing barriers be dismantled.

In this entire process India, as by far the largest state in the region, has necessarily to take longer steps in building region wide cooperation than the others and this will have to include unilateral steps such as giving duty free access to its markets even before being required to do so by the SAFTA regime, bringing down non-tariff barriers as well as reducing as far as possible the negative list, which is at present far too long in the case of all the signatories to SAFTA. The easing of capital flows so that Indian investment in the region is facilitated, initiating trade facilitation measures such as required at the land border crossings, customs clearance and so on, should all be designed to give an upward thrust to the flow of goods and other traffic between the countries of the region, and to create a demand for better connectivity in a self-reinforcing process.

India will also have to bear the major cost of the physical infrastructure which will be required towards the overall objective.

References

1. Sanjay Chaturvedi, "Resurrecting Maritime South Asia: Critical Perspectives in the 21st Century", in Adluri Subramanyam Raju (ed.), *Reconstructing South Asia, An Agenda*, New Delhi: Gyan Publishing House, 2007, p. 297.
2. Jagdish Bhagwati, *In Defence of Globalization,* New York: Oxford University Press, 2004, p. 10.
3. Thomas L. Friedman, *ibid,* p. xiv.
4. Roland Robertson, *Internationalization and Globalization*, in University Centre for International Studies Newsletter, University of Pittsburg, Spring 1989, p. 8.
5. Bo Sodersten and Geoffrey Reed, *International Economics*, London: Macmillan Press, 1994, pp. 178-83.
6. Research and Information System for the Non-Aligned and Other Developing Countries, *World Trade and Development Report 2003: Cancun and Beyond*, New Delhi: Academic Foundation, 2003, p. 27.
7. A. Subramanyam Raju, "Maritime Issues in South Asia", in Raju (ed.), n. 1, p. 162.
8. Withaya Sucharithanarugse, "Concept and Function of ACMECS", *South Asian Survey*, vol.13, no. 2, July-December 2006, p. 293.
9. See M. Rahmatullah, "Integration of Transport Infrastructure: A Key to Economic Dynamism in South Asia", in K.K.Bhargava and Sridhar K. Khatri (eds.), *South Asia 2010, Challenges and Opportunities*, New Delhi: Konark Publishers, 2001, p. 138.
10. Nagesh Kumar, "Emerging WTO Issues and Challenges: Imperatives for South Asia", *South Asia Economic Journal*, vol. 1, no. 1, March 2000, p. 13.
11. I.N.Mukherjee, "Regional Trade Investment and Economic Cooperation among South Asian Countries", in K.K.Bhargava et al., (eds.), *South Asia, Towards Dynamism and Cooperation*, Bombay: Popular Prakashan, 1994, p. 19.
12. Rehman Sobhan, "The Twelfth SAARC Summit: Charting a Road Map for South Asian Cooperation", *South Asian Survey*, vol.12, no.1, January-June 2005, p. 9.
13. Muchkund Dubey, "The Twelfth SAARC Summit: Deeper Integration in South Asia", *South Asian Survey, ibid,* p. 32.
14. Kenneth McPherson, *A History of People and the Sea*, Delhi: Oxford University Press, 1993, p. 272.

2

Space and Regional Cooperation: The SAARC Story

Shibashis Chatterjee and Sulagna Maitra

The success of any regional organization can be explained, in conceptual terms, by any of the three ways. First, as the literature on functionalism and neo-functionalism had shown in the past, and Adler's exciting use of norms suggested recently, a powerful precondition of a regional organization is the making of a security community, a concept which is remarkably flexible and therefore adaptable by both constructivist and liberal paradigms. Second, free trade and liberal policies and institutions may also bind a region together by creating a nexus of mutual cooperation and interdependence such that political or militaristic conflicts would eventually become obsolete and be discarded as counterproductive to the peace and prosperity of the region as a whole. Third, a region could also be formed by forging a community over and above the distinctive national identities of its members. All these processes may contribute in creating a successful region, but the dynamics of each would remain distinct. This paper accordingly builds on this framework in the first three sections. It argues that the South Asian Association for Regional Cooperation (SAARC) has remained a virtual non-starter since none of these frames of regional identity formation and cooperation seems powerful or effective in the sub-continent. The idea of security community is trumped by the strategic disunity of the sub-continent owing both to the generic conflict between India and Pakistan and India's disputes with other South Asian states on various issues. The idea of redefining South Asia as a cooperative free market area flounders due to the economic asymmetry between India and the other members on the one hand, and the pull of globalization on the other. Finally, South Asia fails to evolve a new regional identity based on community due to its very own historical dynamics that has sought to prioritize its idea of citizenship and territoriality over the idea of an overarching, deterritorialized community, which rules out the distinction in allegiance towards citizens and outsiders (South Asians).

The South Asian regional experiment under SAARC commenced with certain structural limitations and for analytical clarity, it is imperative to highlight these underpinnings of the organization. First and foremost, the SAARC Charter since its inception was a compromise, a testimony to the reluctance of its actors to engage in forging South Asia as either a strategic, economic or a communitarian space. Thus, the basis for cooperation under SAARC was conceived along the most generalized terms of "promoting peace, stability, amity and progress in the region through strict adherence to the principles of the United Nations Charter and Non-Alignment, particularly respect for the principles of sovereign equality, territorial integrity, national independence, non-use of force and non-interference in the internal affairs of other States and peaceful settlement of all disputes."[1] With the New Cold War in its backyard failing to provide any compelling converging agenda for cooperation among the seven South Asian nations, SAARC envisaged to engage itself with promoting "the welfare of the peoples of South Asia and to improve their quality of life to accelerate economic growth, social progress and cultural development in the region and to provide all individuals the opportunity to live in dignity and to realize their full potentials; to promote and strengthen collective self-reliance among the countries of South Asia; to contribute to mutual trust, understanding and appreciation of one another's problems; to promote active collaboration and mutual assistance in the economic, social, cultural, technical and scientific fields; to strengthen cooperation with other developing countries; to strengthen cooperation among themselves in international forums on matters of common interests; and to cooperate with international and regional organizations with similar aims and purposes."[2] However, a complementary set of mechanisms to realize these SAARC objectives were conspicuous by their absence. Ironically it sought to promote mutual trust and understanding but intentionally precluded deliberations on all contentious and bilateral issues of the region by the notorious Article X of the Charter.

Second, by excluding Afghanistan and Myanmar, the organization did not in its initial stages incorporate the entire geographical space denoted by the term South Asia. This has been rectified to a certain extent with

Afghanistan joining the organization at its fourteenth summit (New Delhi) in April 2007.

Thus, SAARC was envisaged as a platform based on the lowest common denominator to accommodate the major regional actors. In this sense, SAARC was an attempt to initiate cooperative mechanisms in a region torn by historical feuds, contested territorial and resource entitlements and divergent tacit Cold War allegiances on certain pervasive humanitarian and developmental issues that plagued one fourth of humankind inhabiting South Asia.

Deprived of a compelling agenda, specific timeline, a serious 'trust deficit' among its actors and binding principles of unanimity and exclusion of contentious issues, it is no surprise that the growth of SAARC has been slow and painful. At birth SAARC members identified five common areas of interest namely agriculture, rural development, tele-communications, meteorology and health and population. The organization established its Secretariat in 1986. The scope of SAARC was expanded at the Kathmandu summit (1987) to include wider economic cooperation. Subsequently, South Asian Preferential Trade Arrangement (SAPTA) was ratified in 1995 at New Delhi and eventually advance was made towards achieving a South Asian Free Trade Area (SAFTA) at Colombo in 1998. The Colombo summit also gave SAARC a mandate to build extra regional dialogues. Eventually, the articulation of a joint SAARC 'voice' at international fora was also desired.

While these agreements remain on paper as landmarks in South Asian cooperation, achieving these goals has proved to be an uphill task. SAARC and its action-list has been hostage to the region's volatile peace and security quotient. Ironically the organization itself has remained incapable of making significant positive contributions to this end. Thus, what demands attention is that how far SAARC, now twenty two years and fourteen summits old, has been able to transgress its endemic deficits in favour of forging a comprehensive South Asian cooperative space.

The paper finds that Indian vision of graduating into a major power is a crippling detriment to the idea of a thriving SAARC. Since the unresolved problems of its immediate neighbourhood are largely held responsible for sapping India's vitality, it is increasingly becoming receptive to the idea of an extended community that involves a conscious process of transcending its South Asian identity. Unless the idea of SAARC attaches more meaningfully to a wider frame of both geo-political and commercial interests, its prospects does not appear to be salvageable from its current state of in significance.

Security Community, Regionalism and Geo-politics of Space

In simplest terms, security community connotes a shared perceptional space that betrays a broad agreement amongst partners that all differences would be resolved short of armed conflict or use or threat of use of violence. The concretization of the perceptual space depends on an incremental growth of institutions and practices that build on the available body of trust in the region. Institutions formalize expectations, rewards and sanctions. Strong institutions are thus most powerful investments to peace. The making of a security community is a direct affront to the theoretical claims of realism in two senses. First, a security community espouses the idea of cooperative security, whose actors define security with rather than against others. Second, the idea of security community is critically anchored in perceptual or ideational considerations rather than material factors. Both these attributes are unacceptable to standard realist theories that define security in competitive and material terms.

The making of a security community is a historical rarity, with Western Europe being the classical paradigmatic case, and the Association of Southeast Asian Nations, as originally constituted, being its closest approximation. In the case of the former, the unprecedented wreckage and devastation of the two world wars provided a strong impetus to create a security community as a basic precondition for self-sustaining growth and redemption of its civilizational heritage. The ideological polarization of Europe and the brooding shadow of war between the Soviet Union and the United States that fell on the continent contributed vastly to the making of a security community. In the case of Southeast Asian states, it was the threat of communism that united the ruling elites in their commitment to forge the regional organization as an engine of growth in a condition of peace and stability. In case of South Asia, the idea of a regional organization force shape in conscious separation from the idea of security and power, since contentious bilateral issues are by definition kept outside the frame of operations. In brief, the idea of a security community never caught the imagination of the South Asian elites. The absence of a consensual idea of security in the sub-continent undoubtedly limits the scope of SAARC as a regional organization. It explains the inability of SAARC to develop as a security community, one that could transcend the recursive, competitive security dynamics by a cooperative framework that could encourage peaceful modes of conflict resolution at thresholds far below from direct mobilization. The absence of war in the sub-continent since 1971 is no evidence disputing the said proposition; despite lack of declared wars, the South Asian states have deliberately decided to stay away from developing regional conflict resolution mechanisms and security institutions that would ameliorate the sources of conflict persisting between them.

The central realist argument is that the prevailing geo-political dynamics of South Asia still continues to be the chief component of the region's make-up and the continuity of that dynamics is primarily responsible for trumping the macro-transformational consequences of globalization in the sub-continent. Unlike most other regions of the world, military expenditure in both absolute terms and as percentage of Gross Domestic Product (GDP) increased in South Asia between 1990 and 2000 and there is no sign of any drastic alteration in this trend. In more specific terms, realists offer three reasons why South Asia is unable to transcend its self-identity, or rather, fails to evolve an identity at the regional level, which is commensurate with the needs of a security community, particularly in terms of evolving apposite institutions and practices.

First, nationalism remains rather wide-spread and strong in South Asia with a large number of unsettled cultural, ethnic, historical, and status issues stoking the fires of nationalist passion. Second, South Asians continue to assign high value to sovereignty and independence, which can be attributed to their memory of birth through partition and having lived under long colonial occupation by an alien power. It is not a mere coincidence that some of the strongest resistance against any dilution of sanctity of the principle of non-intervention in the domestic affairs of the state, as inscribed in the Charter of the United Nations, came from the South Asian states. South Asian states continue to betray extraordinary sensitivity to the idea of border control or physical occupation of territory as top prerogatives of sovereign states. The unresolved issues of sub-nationalism of ethnicity have only reinforced the resolve of the state (in South Asia) to reconfirm its territorial dominance. The same fear underlies South Asian concerns for 'illegal' migration and/or clandestine border crossing; in fact, South Asian states seldom recognize the existence of migrants and refugees, and betray a strong hostility towards the immigrant population. Third, the identity of South Asia still continues to be drawn along strategic lines. South Asia emerged as a critical regional security complex during the Cold War and continues to be so after the demise of systemic bipolarity.[3] The nuclearization of the subcontinent has further reinforced this strategic configuration. In strategic terms, South Asia remains divided by the status-quoist integration of the subcontinent by India and the revisionist account held by Pakistan. While India has always emphasized the geo-strategic unity of the subcontinent, Pakistan has worked for extra-regional involvement or engagement to offset the strategic advantage held by India. These contradictory efforts have generated complex interactional problems in the sub-continent. While the two other larger South Asian states, Bangladesh and Sri Lanka have stayed neutral to this fundamental divide, they have also by and large refrained from joining with India, being mistrustful of the intentions of a hegemonic India. For both Sri Lanka and Bangladesh, sub-national issues have prevented normalization of bilateral relations with India, exposing the enormous salience of internal security considerations within the sub-continent. The binary of the inside/outside, citizen/people, hierarchy/anarchy, and friend/foe, progressive (within) /necessitous (without) continue to mark South Asia's existential reality. The borders do not show any signs of retreat; identities do not appear to be broad or inclusive. This neither means that people-to-people contact or civil society initiatives are absent in South Asia nor does it indicate absence of trade, commerce and other modes of communication amongst the South Asian states. What it shows is the overwhelming dominance of the strategic configuration as the constitutive norm of the sub-continent that automatically results in the valorization of the principle of differentiation and the concomitant strong legitimation of the territorialized practices of sovereignty that together rule out the formation of a security community in South Asia.

The entitlement crisis of states in South Asia, owing to neo-liberal globalization and the weakening of the social commitments of the welfare state, is also empirically true, and the identification between the state and its citizens continues to be problematic. But the bond between the state and its citizens was never strong in South Asia. Globalization has spurred on the trend, leading to a multiplication of sub-nationalist demands in India and other South Asian states. But to reiterate the point made earlier, regions are ineffective locales for fresh identities in South Asia and there is little indication of global sensibilities over human rights scrutiny of national law in any state within the region. Globalization might have created or diffused a new rights consciousness, but there is very little institutional architecture available in South Asia or in India to use this realization as a potential tool for reforming the notion of citizenship or statehood in the region.

The state has in fact become more xenophobic about its frontiers in the east despite the promise of the Look East magic and there is little domestic support to a new politics of regionalism, which might redefine South Asia in a mode more consistent with the demands of globalization. There is little evidence of any concrete problematization of territoriality or sovereignty other than in the critical narratives of a group of social scientists. The state has undoubtedly become more contested and fragmented, but there is nothing visible by way of politics of deterritorialization or any imagination of a form of political community that transcends the framework of the nation-state, notwithstanding the claims to the contrary.[4] More people and communities have become sensitive about their claim to political specificity or particularity and actively demand their homeland as either autonomous or independent of the existing state. But they all continue to imagine in the territorial metaphor within the existing framework of limited possibilities for the satisfaction of the political aspirations (territorially conceived) of a host of communities that are forced to cohabit the bounded space of existing structures.

On the other hand, it appears that globalization is embraced more in the interest of national vitality or national power. Neo-liberal policies are often explained along geo-political axes. The argument here is that if India needs to realize its potential of being a genuine great power, an ambition that is no longer utopian owing to India's successful economic policies of greater free trade and more extensive marketization, it has to pursue neo-liberal economic policies of greater free trade and more extensive privatization. Strategic depth and economic non-interventionism coincides according to this view. Successful globalization is then a mean for state empowerment, the best path for the country's inevitable graduation to a pantheon of great powers.[5] One need not ascribe to this (neo) realist-liberal mix to deny claims of globalization in the South Asian /Indian context. But the argument is useful in as much as it shows that there is no inevitable contradiction between the pulls of geo-economics and the pressures of geo-politics, co-existence is at least as conceivable as mutual opposition.

The regional dynamics of South Asia, as a continuity of domestic trends, emphasizes the element of continuity rather than change. The primary reasons behind India's wars with Pakistan or the fundamental issues under dispute remain unresolved, despite the marked improvement in bilateral ties between the two states in recent years. India is still to sort out its territorial disputes with China and the Kashmir issue is yet to be addressed.[6] On top of India's territorial dispute (over Kashmir) with

Pakistan, other aspects of their conflict include societal/identity issues (communal versus secular) and a general or broad dynamics of arms competition, particularly over nuclear warheads and missiles. The last decade has witnessed continued rivalry on defence related matters, despite big increases in the quantum of trade and business, and notwithstanding the sustained process of dialogue and normalization. The issue of intervention and support to secessionist forces or insurgent groups also persists as a major bone of contention. Till the territorial issue over Kashmir is not satisfied to the mutual consent of both states, the use of low-key violence or support to terrorist groups (in Kashmir) would continue to remain a viable policy option for Pakistan, to which India would need to respond in 'statist' terms. A closer look into India's problem with Bangladesh, the other major sub-continental state, also reveals growing anxiety over the border, illegal migration, fundamentalist Islam, and cross-border terrorism. This is *not* to suggest that an alternative regionalism cannot grow in South Asia. Nor is this argument an investment in geo-political determinism. By available evidence, no such alternative vision seems to be gaining over the prevailing politics of alienation and fear in South Asia. But this does not mean that an alternative politics of reflexivity cannot emerge in the sub-continent. By surveying the trends that prevail on ground, globalization, once more, seems impervious to the pattern of inter-state relations in the sub-continent.

The asymmetric power relations in the subcontinent evoke a fractured perception of security which, in the absence of a common external threat, prohibits the growth of a security community. On the one hand, India, the evident major power in the region, "identifies its security with the security *of* the region"[7] thus seeking to ward off any external influence upon the region that could potentially upset the status quo. On the other hand, the rest of the members seek to define their security in the region through external power intervention to thwart any potential hegemonistic ambitions of India. In fact, Pakistan has always consciously weighed its commitments to South Asia with its obligations in West Asia. The statement of Pakistan President Gen. Zia, made prior to the first SAARC summit brings out his views regarding SAARC and Pakistan's relations with West Asia. He said that Pakistan's participation in the summit would not in any way affect its relations with the Muslim countries and that it would maintain its national identity at all costs and continue to play a positive role in the Middle East, since Pakistan enjoyed an important place in South Asia as well as Western Asia. Further, according to an observer from Pakistan, the regional advantage of participating in the

SAARC was that the arrangement could, if the need arose, "come to deflect the weight of India" vis-a-vis its smaller South Asian partners.[8] It was emphasized that Pakistan, Bangladesh, Sri Lanka, Maldives, Bhutan and Nepal had very good, if not ideal relations with each other. However none of the six states could be said to be enjoying tension free relations with New Delhi.

Previously, Nepal faced internal unrest led by movements which evoked some sympathy in India. While the former entered into a Treaty of Peace and Friendship with India in 1950, it has made conscious attempts to increase its maneuverability especially with respect to security affairs. Bangladesh, on the other hand, has problems with India regarding its Chakma ethnic group in the Chittagong hill areas. The issues of illegal immigration into India, terrorism and border disputes have been sore points of Indo-Bangladesh relations.

The second issue that belies the idea of a security community is the principle of bilateralism championed by India. As the most powerful nation in the region, the country also has the dubious distinction of being involved in the most number of inter-state conflicts with its neighbours. However India has steadfastly refused to evolve a multilateral conflict resolution mechanism with the SAARC, choosing instead to deal with the issues bilaterally. This arrangement in the SAARC is unique considering the dispute resolution mechanism adopted in the neighbouring ASEAN. Thus, India has refused to discuss its political conflicts with its neighbours at the SAARC forum, despite the best efforts of the other member states. Nevertheless, these issues have cast a dark cloud over cooperation within the SAARC itself.

The Indian doctrine of bilateralism was eloquently defended in the following words:

> "Will the UN General Assembly session not be held because there is a situation between India and Pakistan? We will both be there. Similarly, we can be there anywhere in the world, including in South Asia, and not allow, with a little wisdom on our part, to let bilateral issues cloud the SAARC process,"[9]

External Affairs Minister Yashwant Sinha said.

> "India is fully committed to the SAARC process. We want SAARC to prosper and become a powerful instrument of regional cooperation. It has been our endeavour not to allow bilateral contentious issues to thwart or cloud the SAARC process."[10]

On another occasion, External Affairs Minister Jaswant Singh conveyed to Bangladesh Foreign Minister M Murshid Khan that India today categorically rejected Bangladesh's suggestion to involve the SAARC in the Indo-Pakistan conflict, saying that there was no room for any regional grouping to play any role in settling the dispute between the two countries.

However, the remaining member states point out the impossibility of growth of South Asian regionalism without resolving the bilateral issues. The obvious example is of course the Indo-Pakistan conflict centering on Kashmir that has sabotaged numerous summit deliberations officially as well as unofficially. The Islamabad SAARC summit is one of the instances where the summit took on a bilateral colour, with India and Pakistan deciding to hold a composite dialogue in India to take the peace process forward.

"There is no problem with other countries of the region. The pace of the SAARC is slow because of tensions between India and Pakistan. We had a vision of economic development of the region. However, it could not gain momentum due to conflicts between these two countries."[11]

Kathmandu Post, a daily from Nepal, bemoans:

> "In its new role, the regional body has become an `akhara' (ground for physical bouts) for wrestling matches between India and Pakistan, two of the largest members of the group... Isn't it then high time to re-examine the role of the SAARC? If it is to be hijacked by the Indo-Pakistan agenda each and every time any significant meeting is held, then why hold such meetings at all? And why keep the SAARC going, in its current ineffective role? ...As long as Indo-Pak hostilities remain, the SAARC will not be able to achieve any progress.''[12]

The News Today, a daily from Bangladesh, writes:

> "As is widely known, the SAARC has not been able to make any noteworthy progress in promoting regional cooperation and partnership due to Indo-Pakistan political confrontation ..... one of the ways to make this regional forum stronger is to remove misunderstandings among the member-nations and to hold summit meetings and consultation regularly. The South Asian leaders should realize the imperatives and move forward to mend their differences."[13]

The Indian action of air dropping food and relief and sending the IPKF to Sri Lanka to combat the LTTE crisis in 1987 presents an additional dimension to the problem of evolving a security community. India's action under Prime Minister Rajiv Gandhi was seen as hegemonic and in many ways antithetical to the doctrine of non-interference in domestic matters. Eventually, the act spurned fears of interventionism among the smaller nation states of the region. While India has subsequently sought to allay such fears by propounding the *Gujral Doctrine*, it has done little to facilitate confidence building in the region.

Liberalism, Free Trade and Regionalism

The second possible route to a study of regional organization could be liberal institutionalism, a framework based on liberalization, open communications and an array of functional cooperation. Apparently, the spurt of new regionalism, occurring along with globalization, is based on the logic of free trade induced cooperation leading to a thick web of interdependence within a region configured in conventional geographical terms. There are quite manifest contradictions involved in this process. First, the configuration of the idea of a region along conventional geographical lines is clearly problematic given the revolutionary changes in the technologies of communication that sought to redefine the meaning of space and time across the globe. Given the fluidity of technology and the increasing irrelevance of settled borders to the transaction of a whole series of goods and services, the region, as conventionally understood, is not necessarily the most productive site for trade, commerce and economic exchanges. Modern technology has revolutionized the notion of scale, and the idea of the region as a geographical category cannot be immune to its effects. Second, the whole idea of liberal institutionalism hinges on the logic of Pareto optimality, where states are willing to forgo relative differences in their benefits if all gain in absolute terms. The problem with this idea is not merely its apparent simplicity – the belief that economic calculations are necessarily independent of security and political considerations – but also its inability to factor in grossly asymmetric situations where the larger party lacks incentive to engage the lesser counterpart, while the latter lacks the capability to reciprocate the former in terms of both positive benefits and negative penalties. The South Asian case is a classic representation of this anomaly. India demonstrates lukewarm interest in the South Asian Preferential Trade Arrangement (SAPTA) since it has little incentive to dismantle the tariff structures all at once and prefers bilateral free trade agreements instead. The structural asymmetry between India's economy and the rest of South Asia quite naturally makes multilateral arrangements more favourable to the smaller states, but their deep-set fear of being swamped by Indian goods holds them back. The conventional appeal of Pareto optimality fails to satisfy them or assuage their fears of being overwhelmed by the stronger economy despite guarantees of much higher positive fields arising out of free trade. Pure free trade considerations have little value in expanding the width or depth of regional cooperation in South Asia; the very dynamics of globalization and the scale of expansion of the Indian economy rules out unconstrained economic expansion within the region. On the contrary, it brings into being the logic of transcendence, the spatial extension of the organization to link it with Southeast Asia and Asia Pacific states, by way of India's Look East initiative. The very idea of deepening the SAARC qua the liberal route is erroneous, since it does not take sufficient cognizance of the structural disparity within the region, which remains a major argumentative blind spot of the whole liberal or neoliberal thesis.

The inability of member states to cooperate along the lines of Pareto optimality coupled with the disassociation of economic regionalism from the concept of territoriality by virtue of technology have reinforced each other to hinder the growth of economic cooperation. The neoliberal logic of regional economic communitarization or fragmentation of the global trading system (as seen by the WTO regime) has failed in South Asia on account of certain specificities.

First, almost all the nations carved out from the region's British colonial empire, since the 1940s, abided by policies of protectionism and promoted import substitution to advance self-reliance and development. In effect these measures promoted both trade diversion from South Asia and duplication of commodities (like jute and rubber) across the region thereby limiting intra-regional trade. Until 1990, when South Asia, notably India, introduced systematic economic liberalization, average intra-regional trade constituted only two per cent of the region's total trade. Thus, the growth of trade in the region has not coincided with a corresponding increase in intra-regional trade. While trade in South Asia has grown from $1.2 billion in the 1980s to $7 billion in 2004 and the region is one of the fastest growing in the world (in terms of GDP).[14] The SAARC ranks very low in terms of intra-regional trade, which remains below 5 per cent of South Asia's total trade with the world. This is in comparison with intra-bloc trade in the EU that stands at a robust 55 per cent or within ASEAN at about 20 per cent. Furthermore, intra-SAARC trade is also skewed heavily in favour of bilateral trade between India and the other member countries. Bilateral trade between the member states excluding India is miniscule.[15] The 'characteristic features' of South Asian economic relations like restrictive trade policies, lack of information, resource constraint and dependence on external aid also contradict the idea of cooperation for absolute gains.

Second, South Asia being essentially a developing region suffers from the endemic problems of South-South cooperation. The 'direction of trade' illustrates that most nations, especially India and Pakistan, trade essentially with the developed countries. It is only Bangladesh and Sri Lanka that import a substantial proportion from South Asia, primarily India. Ironically, these form only a small fraction of India's exports. Further, the countries have chosen to behave as competitors in the international export market rather than as a comprehensive bargaining group like ASEAN.

Third, intra-regional trade has also been hostage to inadequate infrastructural facilities in terms of road, rail and air services. Despite being geographically contiguous, the region is one of the least integrated in terms of existing rail/ road/air infrastructure and safe passage. Further growth of the logistics sector over the past decades in these countries has been uncoordinated with no effort to promote compatibility of the various transport systems, especially railways. Eventually it has inhibited intra-regional trade movement by increasing costs and security of delivery. The lack of infrastructure is a major blind spot in the SAARC initiatives to launch SAFTA. Further, despite the apparent enthusiasm for a free trade area, the SAARC nations have failed to provide transit facilities through their territory for goods coming from neighbouring countries. As it is rightly pointed out, free trade for the new member Afghanistan has little meaning if it is denied transit facilities through Pakistan into India and Bangladesh.[16] The criticality of transport in facilitating economic integration has been admitted by SAARC leaders. To quote the Indian Prime Minister Manmohan Singh:

> "We all know when we talk of great integration, the transport costs, transaction costs, can become a problem to closer trade integration. So, it is quite obvious that in this region we have to ensure that means of transport and communication do not become a bottleneck to expanding mutually beneficial economic cooperation. We want trade expansion to become a win-win game. Therefore, easier transit rights, access to each other's transportation and communication systems can facilitate that process and that is what I was referring to."[17]

The hurdles faced by the SAARC's flagship programs like SAFTA may be traced along these factors. "There are number of positives outside the ambit of trade in goods like investment and common energy grid that SAFTA would facilitate. Bhutan and Nepal have surplus power and there could be import of energy into India. But, the possibility of having a quantum jump in trade in goods is not very encouraging," Ajai Sahai, Director-General of the Federation of Indian Export Organizations (FIEO), said.[18] India has as many as 884 items on the sensitive list where the SAFTA norms would not be applicable. Pakistan on the other hand, has implemented the SAFTA with India only along the lines of the existing bilateral trade policy. This implies Pakistan would allow only 773 items to be imported from India while there are as many as 2646 items common on Pakistan's import and India's export list.[19] Further trade liberalization in the region has been a prisoner of political conflicts. Pakistan's refusal to implement the norms of the SAFTA fully is based on the argument that liberalization of trade has to be linked to progress on the resolution of long standing disputes between the two countries, the core issue being that of Kashmir.[20] Cooperation at the SAARC has often been held hostage to such differences between member states, especially India and Pakistan. It is observed that by the time the SAFTA goal of reduced tariff of zero to five per cent is finally realized by 2016 it may well become irrelevant on account of multilateral FTAs negotiated under the WTO regime and bilateral free trade agreements.[21] Another severe omission of SAFTA is trade in services despite the fact that South Asia is fast emerging as an exporter of services to the developed world. Further, SAFTA pays little attention to non-tariff and para-tariff barriers imposed by member countries.

While economic cooperation at the SAARC remains hostage to bilateral, political and historical issues, India and other member states have sought to redefine the South Asian economic space in a manner that facilitates transcendence to adjacent economic zones and avoids the inter-state conflicts that besiege the SAARC. Thus, the BIMST-EC has been conceived as a bridge between South and Southeast Asia and also to foster economic consolidation by avoiding the rhetoric of the Indo-Pakistan conflict.

Most scholars opine that the onus for triggering off regional integration lies heavily with India owing to its physical prominence, economic predominance and potential strategic aspirations in the region. It is argued that just as intra-regional trade has been circumscribed by political misgivings in the region, India's leadership in announcing unilateral trade liberalization vis-à-vis its neighbours could infuse trust and reap strategic dividends. Further it would also facilitate economic integration of India's geographical fringes like the Northeast. The issue of energy security also provides a point of convergence among the SAARC members. While these factors are likely to prompt greater economic linkages, it may be a while before they crystallize into economic integration. This is reflected by the hurdles in securing the oil pipeline from Iran through Pakistan. Ironically, while SAARC remains the most prominent regional organization, crucial economic projects have seldom taken the SAARC route and have crystallized overwhelmingly through bilateral or multilateral agreements.

Community, Space and Regionalism

The third possible way to build a regional organization could take the form of community, by encouraging cultural bonds that dilute the coarseness of territoriality. But such communitization requires a politics of reflexivity and a constant accumulation of trust, which in turn demands the growth of social power structures given to a radical redefinition of the identity of the region. Communitization is the most demanding of regional imaginations, for it requires a denaturalization of the conventional wisdom prevalent for decades together. Communities require denaturalization of settled borders and a denial of the politics of exclusivity that post-colonial national states breeds. The nation is remarkably strong in South Asia as a spatial imagination, despite innumerable contestations to its claims or privileges. One need not, however, misread the nature of such contestations, no matter how strong they appear. Threats to real nations do not threaten the imagination of the nation in modular forms. Each contestation encapsulates new claims to nationhood, with little political imagination to the contrary. All South Asian states are beset with serious legitimacy claims and states like India, Pakistan and Sri Lanka suffer from endemic secessionist movements that are ethno-national in inspiration. The inherent weaknesses of the nation-building projects have turned the South Asian states increasingly xenophobic towards each other when it comes to the definition of citizenship and the articulation of political community. South Asia continues to build on the statist model of *otherization*, where the secured, progressive domain of the rights-bearing and duty-bound citizen is contrasted with the regressive and necessitous realm of the external, reflected in the kid glove treatment meted out to neighbours in a climate of mistrust and fear. Tight border control mechanisms, rigid and effective differentiation between the insiders and outsiders, the citizen and the outsider, the hysteria over migration and people's movement, still continue to define the normative and cultural architecture of the South Asian sub-continent. The politics of difference remains an existential necessity for the autonomy of South Asian states. Exclusions are, thus, compulsive for the states. Such exclusionary practices tend to undermine the alternative communitization of the sub-continent, a fringe project that lingers on margins. Given the modular compulsions of nationalism in

South Asia, its regional identity is hostage to the politics of will as exemplified by each member state. The idea of an overarching community threatens the very articulation of the sub-continent along the principles of sovereignty, territoriality and citizenship; communitization, therefore, confronts both memory and the present at once. While it seeks to deny the legitimacy of difference as a condition of historical possibility of separate nation-states, the transcendence of these differences in a new political project of late modernity threatens the sovereignty of particularity as expressed in the body of the nation. The weakness of the idea of a regional people-hood, one that rises above citizenship and the implied distinction of us and they, explains the superficiality of SAARC as a regional organization. Its prime weakness remains its inability to espouse any alternative identity, a failure that further strengthens the logic of transcendence. For people in South Asia imagine pan-communities along deterritorialized but transcendent lines – India mainland embracing a discriminative diaspora, emulated by Pakistan, Bangladesh and Sri Lanka all over the globe.

The community imagination of South Asia as a theatre of cooperation continues to be fragile, owing to the legacy of state-centric configuration of the sub-continent. Against this the proponents of regionalism may argue that nationalism has weakened in the last ten years in the sub-nationalist or ethnic mobilization in different parts of South Asia owing to the effects of globalization. In what way globalization has played the trigger here? By most accounts, the cultural narrative of globalization is essentially homogenized – it is culture of Western cosmopolitanism that finds an unprecedented opportunity for global dissemination qua modern technological means. If the global cultural narrative is singular, then it is a threat not merely to the culture of nationalist particularity, but also to the cultural forms below the nation, which the nation subsumes by way of representation. The argument here is that globalization produces an unintended effect – homogenization deforms into fragmentation. Ethnic communities or sub-national groups find new opportunities for accentuating their difference from others and articulating the same. The specificity of the nation in terms of its value-articulation is not necessarily a threat unto itself unless the value (on which the nation is based) is directed against the framework itself,[22] In fact, even communitarian writers concede that ethnic sub-nationalism in South Asia is unable to transcend the imagination of the nation-state as a spatial category. They replicate or mirror the nation-state in their secessionist discourses, demanding their own nation-states by exercising their right to self-determination on ethnic grounds. There is little evidence of any imagination of network communities or a politics of deterritorialised people-hood, where the exercise of political authority would not be co-terminous with a given territory but extend to people or communities identified by a given criteria. There is no sign of any movement towards neo-medievalism in South Asia, towards the creation of political communities unattached to discreet territorial locales. The argument of sub-nationalism or ethnic mobilization as triggered by globalization is *non sequitur*. The argument can make sense only if the transformation attests to the spatial imagination of the framework of the nation-state. Anti-state activities and secessionist tendencies are, therefore, logically unrelated to the relevance of the sovereign state as a political framework.

There are several reasons why South Asia has not evolved as a community. The foremost of these is most certainly the unexceptional tenacity of the nation-state as a container of political community. Successful territorial nationalism requires the neat binaries of inside/outside, rights/force, community/outsiders, order/anarchy, etc. The configuration of a political community within a specific territorial container would, therefore, require harsh references with others. The orderly, rightful and prosperous life of a body of citizens enjoying the protection of a legitimate sovereign requires the others to be defined as opposites. This, however, is a myth, a dangerously false representation. For, "While political boundaries may be continuously readjusted and redrawn, social boundaries are taken to be sacrosanct and immutable. The right to like in one's community, an indispensable plank in the agenda of human rights, is both self-evident and an evil-in-itself. I want to live in my community not because it delivers certain goods but because it defines my identity ... Insofar as the state appropriates the social space of community, it forces the latter to come into conflict with itself".[23] Given the complexity (if not complete untruth) of each of these attributes that threatens to subvert the political project of national building from within, the oppositional character assumes even more ferocity. For the national security imaginary is required to make the states what they are not. The dominant discourse is above all a silencing strategy, a move to configure the territorial nation despite its ethnic incompatibility. Borders become crucial for the consolidation of the artifice, despite the routine transcendence and historical abnormality. The South Asian states, therefore, display the obvious distortion of a coercive construction, a perverse tendency to define identity at the margin. As Samaddar alleges, "Whatever may be the actual figures of migration across the border, the reality of trans-border human flow has been so perennial and persistent and hence so overwhelming and real that the state has had to succumb to it. The state realizes that this is not only the territorial border, but the margin of the nation too. Either the glorious nation is today a thing of the past along the border, or this is a border village, thana, subdivision, district and province which does not respect the nation".[24]

Moreover, to desperately preserve the stability effects of territoriality and nationalism, in the face of multifarious struggles within, scape-goating the neighbour becomes an indispensable aid. Referring to the state strategies pursued in the northeast, Das argues, "It becomes possible for the state to argue that any doubt expressed in this regard is externally engineered and manipulated by a foreign country ... This also makes it possible for the state to treat the internal 'enemy' much in the same manner as it treats an external enemy".[25] Surveillance, counter-insurgency techniques, superior intelligence, augmented military capacity perpetuates the problem rather than settling it. But even such routine tactics are believed to be insufficient or ineffective. They fail to divide and keep the lines intact. They compromise with the flow, deflate and succumb. Hence, the national security imaginary in South Asia invests in a strategy of total negation, an attempt to deny communication to people on the plea of security, order and identity. In Samaddar's words, "Out of this lament has come a reluctant acknowledgement that people on the border cannot be prevented from interacting with each other, that trade will continue, that brutal methods against the migrants will incur great displeasure on this side. Hence a method more than merely policing the border has to be found to tackle the problem. The state has indeed decided on such a policy: not on one policy, in fact, but three : *total demarcation of the border, issuing of photo-identity cards to villagers near the border and border fencing*. Truly, a deadly combination".[26]

The imagination of region as community demands the transcendence of the identity of the state and its politics of territoriality by a new politics of reflexivity, for modernity cannot heal the psychology of fear. The promise of modernity and its "exorcism of the demon of tradition", the reification of the state as the embodiment of the heroic man and a sacred site of his 'mancraft', the incessant homogenization of identities and denial of differences, are problems and not solutions for security. Samaddar cautions, "States in South Asia have gone mad over migration, refugees, exiles and migrants. The state system is being subverted at will along the Indo-Bangladesh border, Bhutan-India-Nepal border, Indo-Pakistan border in Kashmir, Indo-Burma border and Burma-Bangladesh border ... It is said, whom the gods would destroy, they first make mad."[27]

The promise of security lies in tapping the forces that ignore, subvert and defy the territorial markers of control and power and refuses to accept the received wisdom of the familiar historical narrative that silences any possibility for change. South Asia remains a theatre of conflicts, being hostage to a maximalist model of accommodation, one that requires total friendship from the other. Differences and asymmetries have no role here. The reflectivist model of accommodation, on the contrary accepts, allows and accommodates differences, by negating the normative desirability and practical feasibility of total friendship. Total friendship is the convenient ploy to defer real friendship, one that allows meaningful differences to be negotiated without any arbitrary affirmation/negation based on a mythical idea of a common good. Reflexivity, in contrast defines the self by some element of the other, thereby sublating both the rigid distinction between subject and object and identity and difference (such dichotomies being deliberately biased towards specific categories). India's security then lies in its conscious recovery of a contra-history – a history that goes against the received narrative of territoriality, arms race, alliances and crippling force postures. Only a politics that redefines the neighbourhood and reconfigures the innate pessimism of frontiers and margins can provide meaningful security to the people and communities. Democratization and heterologue, pluralism and communication, rather than balance of power, border surveillance and deterrence are the real investments to South Asian peace.[28]

Contrary to the expectations of radical visionaries like Samaddar or communitarian scholars like Ashis Nandy, the peculiar historical configuration of the sub-continent, therefore, tends to rule out trust or community as models of cooperative regionalism in South Asia. The sub-continent remains one of the most territorialized parts of the world, with all states aspiring for exclusive models of nationhood and ruling out the idea of extended neighbourhood that melts the distinction between right-bearing citizens and the outsiders. The contrasting responsibility of citizens towards each other and the South Asian peoples spells out the problem of evolving a regional identity transcending the modular or territorial notion of state-based identity in the sub-continent. The South Asian region is, thus, premised on a paradox: extraordinary sensitivity of state leaders to any intervention in domestic affairs from the neighbours persists alongside routine abrogation of the non-interventionist norm. Given the intensity of the citizen/non-citizen divide in the sub-continent, the definition of space as community does not even appear to be a remote possibility within a meaningful time horizon.

Conclusion

The problems with SAARC as a regional organization are multifarious. But the moot point remains the structural asymmetry that India has vis-à-vis its South Asian neighbours. Indian role conceptions of power, wealth and community are at variance with the present material parameters of South Asia. India's aspired power projection goes beyond South Asia, and it clearly wants liberation from the South Asian quagmire to play a more assertive role in Asian, if not global, affairs. Indian security thinking is clearly dominated by a status-quo vision of unifying the South Asian sub-continent strategically as a precondition to expand its influence elsewhere.

When it comes to commercial policies and the economic imagination underlying it, the logic of transcendence assumes even more clarity. South Asia as an economic space is too claustrophobic for a growing Indian economy and the logic of scale, more than anything else, demands rapid integration of India with Southeast Asia and the Asia Pacific with or without the existing South Asian states. The structural difference between the Indian economy and those of its neighbouring states of South Asia is a strong impediment to establish a free trade regime in South Asia that would be truly remunerative and economically attractive for all the states of the region. India clearly prefers bilateral economic deals with its South Asian neighbours rather than genuine economic multilateralism for obvious reasons. The relatively weak and smaller neighbours want just the opposite. The pull of globalization has further compromised the chances of success for a liberal regional economic arrangement. The logic of the market, to which the liberal imagination is inextricably wedded and the present direction of India's foreign and domestic economic policies, militate against the idea of sub-optimal gains in the interest of altruistic considerations. There is yet to be any compelling counter economic reasoning that makes regionalism at the level of the SAARC, as it is presently constituted, an attractive option for India, in keeping with the meta-assumption of self-interest or egoism as the driver of the liberalization policies pursued in the different spheres of the economy as a whole.

Finally, the SAARC is structurally and historically incapable of transcending its self-image as a collective of sovereign nation-states as the only form of community having a claim to legitimate political arrangement. The fixity and exclusionary nature of South Asian borders rule out its transmogrification into a looser form of political community that would radically question the inside/outside or citizen/others distinctions. India suffers from grave difficulties in its capacity for identity-transformation within the sub-continent since the principle of territoriality as a container of national specificity trumps attempts at redefinition over and above the state. The neighbours have problems of community vis-à-vis India and these cannot be ignored in fashioning a vision for regional cooperation along communitarian lines. In simple words, South Asia remains too state-centric to allow itself to be redefined as a community of people. India arguably has little incentive in such a move since its existing conflicts over community remain intense and often violent and any attempt by New Delhi to espouse a vision of a community is liable to be translated as socially hegemonic by the neighbours. The dilation of the state and the contested nature of community-state ties trump the community imagination of South Asia. Given the centrality of India in the sub-continent and the unsettled claims of nationhood in virtually all South Asian states, there is little realistic possibility of carving out a new South Asian identity at the level of a community that might provide a fresh conceptual basis to build a strong regional organization here. At least, India's unsettled historical residues of conflicts over community vis-à-vis its neighbours rule out such a vision as serious paradigm for regionalism in South Asia.

References

1. *SAARC Charter*: 1985
2. Article I: Objectives, *SAARC Charter: 1985*
3. Barry Buzan, and Ole Waever, *Regions and Powers: The Structure of International Security*, Cambridge: Cambridge University Press, 2003, p. 94
4. Ranabir Samaddar, *The Marginal Nation: Transborder Migration from Bangladesh to West Bengal*, New Delhi: Sage, 1998; "The Failed Dialectic of Territoriality and Security, and Imperative of Dialogue", *International Studies*, vol. 35, no. 1, 1998; *The Marginal Nation : Transborder Migration from Bangladesh to West Bengal*, New Delhi, Sage, 1999; "Friends, foes and Understanding", *Economic and Political Weekly*, vol. 36, no. 10, 10 March 2001; (ed.), *Space, Territory and State*, Hyderabad: Orient Longman, 2002 and Samir Kumar Das, *Ethnicity, Nation and Security: Essays on Northeastern India*, New Delhi: South Asian Publishers, 2003.
5. Baldev Raj Nayar and T.V. Paul, *India in the World Order: Searching for Major Power Status*, Cambridge: Cambridge University Press, 2001 and

Baldev Raj Nayar, *The Geopolitics of Globalization: The Consequences for Development*, New Delhi: Oxford University Press, 2005.

6. Brahma Chellany, "Preface", in Brahma Chellany (ed.), *Securing India's Future in the New Millennium*, New Delhi: Orient Longman and the Centre for Policy Research, 1999, pp. XVIII- XX.
7. Baljit Singh, "Regional Cooperation in South Asia: Problems and Prospects", *South Asian Survey*, vol. 12, no. 2, 2005, p. 181.
8. Padmaja Murthy, "Relevance of SAARC", *Strategic Analysis*, vol. 23, no. 10, January 2000, pp. 1782-1783.
9. *The Tribune*, August 2002.
10. *Ibid.*
11. Hussain Muhammad Ershad, the former Bangladesh President, *The Hindu*, 18 July 2003.
12. *The Hindu, ibid.*
13. *Ibid.*
14. Madhvi Bhasin, "South Asian Cooperation: Myths and Realities", *India Quarterly Journal*, vol. 62, no. 1, January-March 2006, p. 10.
15. Singh, n. 7, p. 178.
16. Muchkund Dubey, "SAARC and South Asian Economic Integration", *Economic and Political Weekly*, vol. 42, no. 14, 7-13 April 2007, p. 1238.
17. Indian Prime Minister Manmohan Singh, at Press Conference at the SAARC Summit, Dhaka, 13 November 2005- http://meaindia.nic.in/pressbriefing/2005/11/13mi01.htm, accessed 21st May, 2007.
18. *Hindu Business Line*, 2 January 2006.
19. *Ibid,* 31 July 2006.
20. *Ibid.*
21. Dubey, n. 16.
22. Das, n. 4, p. 107.
23. *Ibid,* p. 41.
24. Samaddar, *The Marginal Nation*, n. 4, p. 58
25. Das, n. 4, p. 87.
26. Samaddar, n. 24, p. 59.
27. *Ibid,* p. 63.
28. Samaddar, n. 4, 2001.

3

New Horizons in South Asia: A Focus on Indo-Pak Relations

Gopalji Malviya

The overriding reality of the twenty first century is now striking differently from the strongly held perceptions – political, strategical, economical as well as technological – as seen at the beginning of the twentieth century. The dichotomy is compounded by settled mindsets who clutch to old irrationalities and are baffled by new realities. At the dawn of twenty first century, South Asia offers an ambivalent picture; various changes in international strategic environment had a deep impact on this region. The South Asia is rightly called 'a region of chronic instability'. The development at the international, regional and domestic levels also brought the changing notions of security. While the military threats of cold-war dynamics has disappeared, and the regional conflicts, ethnic violence, militancy and terrorism have surfaced along with a possible nuclear flash point. A South Asian canvas of the emerging security agenda provides the basis of analysis of the host of challenges and threats that confront the nation-states of the region. On a common denomination, the range of military and non-military threats faced by all the nation-states have been primarily due to the state centric issues of insecurity with the intensity of regional rivalries, inter-state border disputes, communal antagonisms, unresolved boundary issues and possible nuclear exchange. The next tier of security threats and challenges emanate from human issues of insecurity that feature cross-border movements of refugees, illegal migrations, religious fanatism, ethnic cleansing, human rights violations and secessionist activities along with infiltration of terrorists, insurgents, etc. The third tier of insecurity has emerged from transnational challenges to security emergent from environmental pollution, rapid depletion of water resources, loss of biodiversity wealth, energy resources depletion, resource scarcity resulting from environmental degradation, ecological threats and its cumulative impact on the society and state system in South Asia. Absence of civil society and poor governance are indicators for a very dim hope of improving the status quo.

The region confronts the serious problems of internal security vulnerabilities, challenges to regime legitimacy and hence regime insecurity. The complexity of the region's security had been further compounded by two perilous challenges, viz, the heightened nuclear thresholds of India and Pakistan intertwined with the relentless pursuit of terrorist activities that had gained even greater lateral space since the nuclear weaponization of the two powers since May 1998. The implications of terrorism and the new war in the region have serious consequences for the fundamental stability of the region. The relentless pursuit of terror and armed conflict in the form of cross- border terrorism and low intensity conflicts had aggravated the prevalent tense bilateral relations between India and Pakistan to new levels of crisis escalation resulting towards a possible nuclear exchange too.

The concept of security has traditionally encompassed military security. Its broadened canvas now includes the realms of environmental and human security. In the face of global integration of economics and governance, and growing violence and terrorism the world over, security paradigms have diversified in approach and strategies. Diplomatic channels, promotion of Track II diplomacy, role of civil society and non-state actors in security has seemingly enhanced. Most security issues and problems are often the products of global, regional and domestic developments; the major sources of South Asian security problems are the regional countries' threat perceptions and security pursuits. Global and domestic developments have only added undesired complexities. The involvement of great powers directly affected the military balance within the region and introduced further complications. The balance of military forces remains an important determinant in the context of South Asian relations, influencing both perceptions of security and the conduct of diplomacy.

Because of great divestitures in religion, race, language, caste, cultural heritage and ethnic bondage, South Asia is historically a fertile ground for conflicts. The complex ethno-religious dispersion defying geographical boundaries has resulted in tension and conflicts in inter-state relation in the region. Most of the sub-national conflicts exist in Punjab, Kashmir, Jaffna, Assam, Kathmandu and Chittagong Hill Tracts, etc. One of the remarkable features of the regional ethno-religious conflicts is that India shares at least one important ethno-religious group with each of its neighbours. Any ethnic and religious conflict in any country has cross border influence. In many cases, the ethno-linguistic and religious bondage have transcended national boundaries and as a result, the ethnic problem in one country has created instant repercussions in another. As such, existence of a number of ethno-religious conflicts in the region is likely to pose constant threat to regional peace and stability.

In South Asia, there are a number of disputes, the causes of which are deeply rooted in its history. The partition of British India is considered as the core of conflicts, which had started driving both the 'Key players' on the path of confrontation. India's thrust for regional hegemony is evident in New Delhi's defence and security calculations which draw its legacies from the British Raj. In maximum number of cases, India is the common counterpart of bilateral disputes in the region and most of the conflicts are basically political in nature.

Bilateral disputes generate tensions and create unnecessary hurdles for the regional peace and stability. But progress on issues of regional concern should not be held hostage to the resolution of all bilateral disputes. Settlement of disputes can facilitate cooperation by generating greater confidence. The reality is that all contentious issues can be addressed within the cooperative framework and in no way challenge cooperation.

The security paradigm of South Asia underwent a structural change with the nuclear tests of India and Pakistan in May 1998. As the two countries entered into a missile race, serious concern was expressed in the world's strategic circles about the risk of a nuclear holocaust in the region. Though the agreements reached at Lahore in February 1999 as a result of the bus summit between the two Prime Ministers were welcomed, their impact was rapidly dissipated as a result of the Kargil conflict in Kashmir three months later. This structural change was followed by the event of 9/11. This totally altered the existing status quo. Post 9/11, Operation Enduring Freedom had an overwhelming impact on the South Asian environment; the existing role of the US is very significant not only in the operation but also in bringing the South Asian states into a closer working relationship. It has given the status of the 'major non-NATO ally' to Pakistan and is working towards forging a 'greater India' through defence pacts, which pose serious ramifications for peace in South Asia.

Current Initiatives

There can be no denying that India is a large country that is poised to overtake many of its former competitors in the global economy. Accepting that India could be a better neighbour by show of greater sensitivity towards its small neighbours, it needs to be pointed out that India's smaller neighbours can also contribute to better relations in the region by learning to accept geopolitical realities and be more pragmatic about India. India's security concerns in the region must be duly understood by them, and whatever independent decisions they take should not jeopardize India's interests. It must be realized by all countries of South Asia that the destinies of all countries are tied together. Surely, in India's prosperity rests the hope of economic upliftment for the rest of the region.

Peace, prosperity, security and stability of South Asia largely depend on strategic equations between New Delhi and Islamabad. Last sixty years have shown that a prolonged adversarial perception has only dampened the spirit of cooperation and development in the region. The rigid stand on identified areas of respective concern and military solutions to resolve the dispute is highly improbable and no longer the preferred form of options. The leadership in respective capitals at all levels communicated this realization. This echo is also heard in Western capitals. The pathways to achieve regional stability and peace have been vexations due to the high temperature in emotional adversity and communal parochialism. However, the efforts of various channels of communication and recent creation of 'new environment' generated since January 2004 has paid the peace dividends. In April 2005, Indian Prime Minister Manmohan Singh and Pakistani President Pervez Musharraf have reaffirmed their commitment to carry forward the peace process. The 'Political Will' demonstrated by the two leaders to sustain the dialogue on all issues has been quite encouraging to provide robust hope and confidence towards prospects for peace between India and Pakistan.

Since the time the sub-continent was partitioned in 1947, India and Pakistan have been archrivals. During the six decades gone by, they have fought four wars. After a long era of mutual animosity and hatred, both countries have only recently decided to jointly embark on a voyage of mutual trust and confidence. Of late, tensions have cooled down, and in their joint statement issued in the wake of President Musharraf's visit to New Delhi in April 2005, both parties have said they would boost business ties and cross-border travel, set up a joint economic commission and open consulates in Mumbai and Karachi. Both have agreed to open up the heavily militarized frontier dividing Kashmir and encourage cultural exchanges.

The January 2004 SAARC summit in Islamabad marked a historic breakthrough, with India and Pakistan agreeing to resume a composite dialogue on all issues including Kashmir. Referring to relations with

Pakistan, the Indian Prime Minister said India wanted to engage itself in a sustained and comprehensive dialogue with Pakistan. There is now a reservoir of goodwill between the people of India and Pakistan. Time is now conducive to develop a political, social and economic interlink that can sustain the difficult journey ahead. Announcing a series of measures to enhance people-to-people contacts, India and Pakistan have pledged not to let terrorism impede the 'irreversible' peace process. They have also agreed to address the Jammu and Kashmir issue in a "purposeful and forward looking manner" for a final settlement. The fresh confidence building measures (CBMs) including the decision to increase the frequency of bus service between Srinagar and Muzaffarabad; to allow trucks to use this road to promote trade, are part of the joint statement.

CSBM – A Dim Hope

The viability of Confidence and Security Building Measures (CSBMs) has been yet another source of conflict de-escalation and had provided vital hope for regional stability and security. In the context of the emerging security paradigms in South Asia the imperative is to analyze the relevant issues and concern between New Delhi and Islamabad in their strategic, political and economic dimensions is significant. South Asia contends a stability-instability situation that is based on Kashmir as a main dispute and nuclear weapons the intervening variable that is likely to alter the nature and dynamics of the dispute. The nuclear weaponization had provided the two nuclear-armed states the will and motivation to display the statesmanship that is required for lasting peace and stability in South Asia. In fact, all issues have been quite encouraging to provide the robust hope and confidence towards prospect for peace between India and Pakistan.

Recent efforts to fill the trust deficit between India and Pakistan have a huge potential for the progress, prosperity and development of the entire South Asian region. The process of confidence-building measures that has been instituted between India and Pakistan particularly since 2004 has enlarged the constituency of peace and cooperation. Probably, both the countries have realized that in the changed global scenario, they cannot change the border but they can certainly change the nature of borders. The soft instead of hard borders had great promise for the people of this region. Now India and Pakistan are trying to convert their hard borders into soft by facilitating the movement of people and goods across the boundaries.

Some of the other important CBMs are establishment of Khokrapar-Munabao Rail link by 1 January 2006, bus routes to be introduced from Poonch and Rawlakot in PoK; early start of Amritsar-Lahore bus service;

allow movement of trucks across the LoC to enhance trade; more trade consulates will be opened in Mumbai and Karachi; mechanism to resolve Sir Creek and Siachen issues; explore cooperation for gas pipeline through Pakistan. Both the sides have addressed the issue of Jammu and Kashmir and agreed to continue these discussions in a 'sincere and purposeful and forward looking manner for a final settlement.' The Indian President Abdul Kalam has forecast more confidence building measures between India and Pakistan in the near future, saying this could lead to greater economic cooperation between them. Addressing a joint session of parliament, Kalam said that India was engaged in a serious dialogue with Pakistan and good relations between the two countries were vital to peace and prosperity in the region. Recently Indian Prime Minister has suggested that 'the Line of Control' could become a 'Line of Peace' with 'freer flow of ideas, goods, services and people.' This is a bright idea and needs a reciprocal statesmanship from Pakistan.

Role of Democracy and Civil Society

South Asia's democratic transition is incomplete and is facing rough weather. These countries have limited understanding about democracy. It is primarily understood as a form of government in South Asia. Even as a form of government, it is reduced to the majority rule, which is described and largely known as a 'tyranny of the majority' meaning thereby that democracy is not understood as a broader canvas in South Asia. Democracy has generally been understood and even practiced in terms of political superstructure. It has not been related to socio-economic structures and the cultural dynamics of the South Asian societies. Consequently, there exists a clear hiatus between the political superstructure and social-economic base of democracy in South Asia. Hence, democracy has failed to bring about fundamental socio-economic and political change in the society. Democracy has empowered the elites rather than the masses in this region.

Although the structures of governance in South Asian region are being diversified and differentiated, governance is still the last priority. This region has witnessed too much government and too little governance. The past couple of decades have witnessed the rise of democratic movements in every South Asian country but the feudal mindset and authoritarian tendencies do not allow them to bring about fundamental change in the society. Post-colonial South Asian states have pursued a modern agenda in building nation state and popular interactions are, for the most part, shaped by 'state driven choices'. The single-minded approach of the nationalist discourse in building a nation state has marginalized civil society. The drive for preserving a state sovereignty, national security and search for national identity has resulted in emasculating people-to-people contacts in this region. Though it is a western concept but it is linked with the concept of democracy. Civil society is a new terrain of democratization. In recent times, concept of civil society has emerged as the primary focus for the expansion of participative democracy in both authoritarian and liberal democracies. South Asian states are multi-ethnic and multi-cultural society. Hence, a participative democracy could expand the role and significance of civil society.

Civil society does not exist in South Asia because prevailing geo-political and geo-strategic environment do not permit this. The region lacks any political culture suitably needed for a civil society. Deliberate attempts have been made to weaken the civil structure by the forces of status quo and power hungry ruling elite. The realization of the fact among the states in South Asia is that political solution is the only way of resolution of any dispute that is possible through dialogue and understanding. Hence, South Asian states have to bring their houses in order and learn to live with peace and tranquility with neighbours that are required for harmony.

Conclusion

The logic of neighbourhood existence and civilization links among the developing countries of South Asia has provided constructive background conditions for cooperation in the region. South Asia is considered as a geo-strategic by some and as a geo-economic unit by other; and as a single civilizational whole by many. Such assessments create positive possibilities regarding regional cooperation in South Asia. Despite differences over the modalities and strategies of cooperation, all states in the region subscribe to its beneficial impact.

Regional cooperation can strengthen the building of a lasting edifice of peaceful co-existence through initiatives and interactions in the fields like the cultural, scientific, technological and economic spheres. SAARC was expected to be an instrument for the promotion of peace, progress and stability in this part of the world. It can also enhance our sovereignty and foster peace, freedom and social justice among the member states. It will, above all, be a framework for promotion of the welfare and prosperity of our peoples and the improvement of their quality of life. With trade and investment being guided by trans-national factors, economic regionalism has emerged as the driving force for sustaining economic networking around the globe. In this background, lack of cooperation in

South Asia is attributed to the poor rate of economic development and absence of economic complementarities among the states of the region.

The South Asian Free Trade Area could bring about desired result and as a first step in the evolution of SAARC as a regional trade block and an economic union. Regional economic integration, however, is more about finding an engine of growth rather than test for trade promotion activity. The new found interest in such regional arrangements would also help to exploit potentials of efficiency-seeking restructuring of industries on a pan regional basis. Energy cooperation among South Asian countries presents immense potential. To promote regional cooperation in this area, South Asian energy dialogue could be initiated. There are other areas for greater cooperation like education, medical tourism, disaster management, environmental degradation, water resources, human trafficking and small arms proliferation, etc. SAARC could evolve mechanism for a dialogue and discussion at appropriate levels for mutual advantage.

The economic transition is also in progress in the South Asian region. Since late 1990s, the majority of South Asian countries have introduced globalization as a measure to address their economic crisis by way of reducing poverty and thereby improving governance. However, globalization has accelerated the process of growth but development is still a mirage. The impact of globalization indicates that it has not been accompanied by a reduction in poverty or improvement in human security and development through the formation of social capital. The South Asian countries have begun to realize that politics in the region cannot be pursued through conflict and confrontation. Though, it is the dominant but not the only mode of politics, economic cooperation is also a significant mode of politics that could be pursued along bilateral as well as multilateral channels.

South Asia is a region of vast potential. It is also a region of multiple diversity. It has shown in the past its potentials and achievement capability in its world class wisdom, rich civilization, literature and cultural heritage and its immense reservoirs of natural resources and extensive reserves of capable people. However, if South Asia is to evolve its own path of progress from poverty to prosperity, it is necessary to restructure the traditional mode of cooperation, reconsider the existing paradigm of regional governance, and revitalize the roles that states have so for been able to play in cultivating their mutual ties and relationship vis-à-vis the region as also at the international level. All these demand a new vision, new missions, new goals and strategies – goals that can be achieved and strategies that deliver.

4

The Peace Process: Challenges and Prospects

Noman Sattar

South Asia has seen more conflicts than cooperation since the partition of the subcontinent. This has been the result of adversarial relations between the two major regional powers, India and Pakistan. SAARC was conceived to promote peace in the region and enhance cooperation. Many view it as not fulfilling its objectives and feel its role has been hobbled by India-Pakistan rivalry. It is unable to face the political challenges and conflict situations that arise in different parts of the region.

India and Pakistan remain major players in the region. They have added to their 'power status' after nuclearization in 1998. It is debatable whether it made South Asia more or less secure. The 9/11 attacks in the US brought about a qualitative change in the regional environment. On the one hand, the two became partners in the US war against terrorism, on the other hand India's new global role changed its regional role. The two sides are continuing a composite dialogue, addressing a host of issues, but many challenges remain. These directly affect the region and SAARC.

Is the Indo-Pakistan peace process leading somewhere? How would its failure or success affect the regional situation? How and where does SAARC lack? How could SAARC be made more effective in achieving its objectives? The above questions do not relate to Indo-Pakistan relations alone. Fruitful outcome of the peace process would give a boost to regional peace and integration, rejuvenating SAARC. The paper addresses the above issues and links political developments and challenges to regional peace and the future of SAARC. The point being made is that SAARC has the potential to become a vibrant regional organization, but it needs a strong will and effort on the part of its members.

India-Pakistan Context

India-Pakistan rivalry is seen as a given in South Asia. For many people, for a long time it was seen as a constant, as inevitable. In the historical context, it is punctuated by three major wars, minor conflicts, occasional tensions, as well as nuclear crises – even when the two were not nuclear powers. Any discussion about the region refers to the above context.

Pokhran tests in 1974 brought India and South Asia to the nuclear threshold. This embarked Pakistan on the nuclear path (apart from a growing sense of insecurity after the1971 debacle). Thus the Indian nuclear tests of 1998 did not come as a surprise. Nor was Pakistan's prompt response. This completed the nuclear equation; this was the new South Asia reality at the close of the twentieth century.

Given the political-military landscape of the region, this made the region a nuclear flashpoint, and being termed as the most dangerous place on earth. After 1998, nuclear dimension was added to the historical adversarial relationship of India and Pakistan, raising the inevitable and tricky question of security. To the optimists, deterrence would work as it did since the mid eighties, as recessed or non-weaponized deterrence.

The worst fears were materialized in 1999 when Kargil took place. The limited conflict took a heavy toll in terms of sense of insecurity and loss of goodwill; it put a strain on South Asian security and deterrence. The pessimists were almost proved right. Fortunately, the optimists had the last laugh. After a deal in the White House, the conflict was resolved: deterrence was made to work. Deterrence and stability have engaged the strategists and scholars alike in South Asia. While strategic stability is seen in terms of deterrence, stability, STABILITY has many connotations, General stability, Crisis stability, Missile stability, etc.

Kargil raised questions about the stability of deterrence in South Asia, while it led to a downturn in Pakistan's relations with both the US and India. 9/11 came as a defining moment, a watershed in the US relations with South Asia, and Indo-Pakistan relations. War against terrorism took the form of active US engagement in the region as Pakistan became a willing coalition partner in view of its security predicament.

More importantly, for the first time India and Pakistan were on the same side of the fence, de facto partners in the war against terrorism. Post-9/11 chaos adversely affected the stability of the region. Terrorist attack on the Indian parliament in December 2001 triggered a severe crisis. This brought the two rivals eyeball to eyeball in a tense military standoff that lasted for more than a year. This was another test of deterrence stability. Amid posturing and rhetoric, deterrence was salvaged, through diplomacy (and good sense). The standoff ended in 2003, when the two sides gave in the interest of peace. The SAARC summit in Islamabad (2004) became a watershed, paving the way for a composite dialogue that continues amid apprehensions and cautious optimism. It has led to:

'A stable cease fire along the LoC;
'Bus service between Muzaffarabad and Srinagar;
' Involvement of Kashmiri leadership in dialogue;
'Train service on Kokrajhar-Monabao route;
'An agreement on pre-notification of missile tests;
' Nuclear risk reduction measures.

All these have served as CBMs, strengthening the peace process, improving the political climate of the region. The Islamabad summit proved to be a shot in the arm for SAARC as well.

Apart from the above, the two sides signed an agreement on pre-notification of missile tests in 2005; have addressed nuclear risk reduction and unauthorized use of nuclear weapons. They have addressed Siachin issue and have apparently bridged differences.

Recently they agreed to an Anti-Terrorism Mechanism. (SAARC countries signed the Convention on Suppression of Terrorism at the Kathmandu summit in 1987.) Such positive developments have been followed by missile tests – the most recent was the Pakistan's test of BABAR Cruise missile in March. It tested surface to surface (200 km range) Hatf III ABDALI; in February it tested (2000 km range) SHAHEEN II, soon after signing an agreement to cut nuclear accidents. This is the South Asian reality, security spirals leading to the inevitable 'security dilemma'. The peace process has not been able to nudge the two out of this spiral. To expect otherwise would be wishful thinking, despite the euphoria of the peace process.

SAARC and Regional Politics

Geopolitically, South Asia shows great peculiarities; geography and politics have resulted in a regional system in which six smaller South Asian states revolve round the Indian orbit. India dominates the region not politically, but geographically. India cannot but behave big, and the other states cannot but feel small! Most of the countries have or have had some kind of problem with India. India looms large in their foreign policy, if not the security considerations.

In extending hand of friendship to Pakistan, former Prime Minister Vajpayee said that we cannot change neighbours; this statement explains

South Asian geopolitics and attendant problems. Nepal nestles between two giants to the north; Pakistan and Bangladesh flank India to the west and east, as if balancing a geographic equation; Sri Lanka floats to the south; Bhutan and Maldives remain somewhat distant from the main theater.

What brings the seven South Asian nations together is SAARC. Just as during the Cold War, Europe became the main theater of US-Soviet rivalry, and a barometer of the state of East-West relations, South Asian stability is a function of Indo-Pakistan relations. Thus the region remains at the mercy of India-Pakistan relations; this fact explains the fate of SAARC.

Since its inception in 1985, SAARC has traversed an uneven path and generated skepticism as to its contribution, viability and future. True, compared to other regional arrangements it has not performed well. It has been hobbled by the rivalry of its two powerful members. SAARC has evolved under the cloud of Indo-Pakistan animosity, making modest effort to defuse crisis situations.

SAARC was created to find common ground among the states of the region. The example of EU and ASEAN were shining examples to follow. But as ensuing developments showed it did not fulfil the promise of close collaboration and integration. One problem was seen in India-Pakistan antagonism that would not go away. There were ups and downs in Indo-Pakistan relations during 1980s and 1990s, despite democratic governments in Islamabad. This coincided with the uprising in Kashmir that prevented any movement toward normalization. From the start India curtailed the organizations role in addressing political issues (while the smaller states would have welcomed that). The problem was thus both political and structural.

The smaller South Asian states saw/see SAARC as an opportunity to offset India's power and role and add to their regional role, whatever the size. For them this was an institutional check on India's power (projection). For them it was also a mechanism to balance India's power by a common policy or strategy. But this did not really work. India on the other hand, saw SAARC as an opportunity to further its regional role under a multilateral forum, particularly in the economic sphere. It also feared that SAARC would become a platform for the smaller states to gang up.

Looking deeply, SAARC lacked the factors that are behind the formation/success of most regional organizations:

> 'desire for integration (case of ASEAN);
> 'external threat (raison d' etre for NATO);
> 'role of external power (SEATO, CENTO).

In the case of South Asia, all three were lacking. Actually the threat was from within the region. In the eighties, Sri Lanka faced internal conflict in the form of the Tamil problem. As the problem deteriorated, India played a role after agreement with the Sri Lankan government by sending its peacekeeping troops to quell the uprising. This role and the mission did not achieve the desired results, and the force had to be withdrawn leaving a bitter taste for sometime. The problem continues today, exacting a heavy toll, but with no role for SAARC.

Cross border migrations between India and Bangladesh, between Bhutan and India and between Bhutan and Nepal have been additional sources of tension. These are due to economic and other reasons. Trade dispute, and water management issues have led to strains in Indo-Nepalese and Indo-Bangladesh relations respectively. In the case of India and Pakistan, such movements from the Pakistani to the Indian side of Kashmir have been seen as 'cross border terrorism', leading to a steady deterioration of relations before and after 9/11.

One serious shortcoming of SAARC has been its inability to spur regional economic integration. Intra-regional economic interaction is negligible, in contrast to the global system and other such regional groupings. Only in the case of Nepal, the percentage of imports and exports to the region is more than twenty per cent; in the case of all others, it is less than ten per cent, which seems rather appalling. For different reasons, India's neighbours are not keen to expand trade ties; one fear is dependence on India's more developed economy.[1] It can be pointed out that with India's economic boom and trade relations with countries like the US and China, regional trade is hardly a consideration for India. The low level of economic interaction poses a challenge for economic integration.

But one can see a silver lining, SAARC has some achievements to its credit – direct and indirect. During a tense interlude in India-Pakistan relations, SAARC summit at Kathmandu in 2002 brought together the two adversaries, affording an opportunity to President Musharraf to shake hands with Indian Prime Minister Vajpayee. It was during the 2004 summit at Islamabad that the two sides decided to start the peace process after a tense military standoff. Earlier, in 1988, on the sidelines of the Islamabad summit, Prime Minister Rajiv Gandhi and Benazir Bhutto signed an agreement "to refrain from undertaking ...any action aimed at causing the destruction of, or damage to, any nuclear installations or facility in the other country." This was a significant CBM.

SAARC has not been lagging in creating institutions. An agreement on SAARC Preferential Trading Arrangements (SAPTA) was signed during the seventh SAARC summit in Dhaka in 1993. SAARC Chamber of Commerce and Industry was established in 1994. Member countries have agreed to create a Free Trade Area, SAFTA, and plan a Customs Union by 2015 and Economic Union by 2020. Many of SAARC bodies are working well. Thus there is reason to be optimistic.

Post-9/11 South Asia

The 9/11 attacks changed not just the US and its approach toward the world, it brought about drastic changes in power settings and relationships in many parts of the world, particularly South Asia. The impact of 9/11 on South Asia has to be seen in three areas:

1. India-Pakistan relations;
2. US relations with South Asia;
3. India's changing world role.

The above three factors could be dealt with together. It the ensuing war against terrorism, the US looked for allies and enlisted both India and Pakistan, the traditional rivals. Interestingly, a few months later, India blamed Pakistan supported terrorists for attack on the Indian parliament, leading to a sharp downturn in relations. At the same time, the two remained coalition partners alongside the US. It was in the US interest that the two minimized their differences and conflict and engaged in handling their problems diplomatically. This initiative ushered in the peace process that the two sides undertook in 2004 following the SAARC summit in Islamabad.

Till this time, the US role in South Asia was limited to Cold War considerations and crisis management. This was probably the first time that Washington got involved in earnest in managing Indo-Pakistan disputes. The peace process received the blessing of the US, and it can be said that the US is watching progress with interest. Indo-Pakistan rapprochement and a movement toward resolution of Kashmir dispute would make the road ahead smooth for SAARC. While Pakistan still sees Kashmir as critical to normalization, "the conflict has become less and less relevant to India's relations with the great powers, which has meant a corresponding willingness on New Delhi's part to work toward a solution."[2] Pakistan and India would continue to see Kashmir and its 'resolution' differently.

While Pakistan became an ally in war against terrorism and is playing an active role in providing logistical and other support, the US has fundamentally redefined its relationship with India, in what could be seen as a conspicuous tilt. The new strategic partnership with India was cemented with the visit of President Bush to India in March 2006 and signing of a historic nuclear deal. This followed an agreement on a New Framework for the US –India Defense Relationship signed in 2005. The deal has been controversial in both Washington and New Delhi for different reasons. Pakistan's displeasure and reservations are understandable: it feels it has been bypassed and the deal comes at a cost to itself.

This leads us to India's new role; India has all the reason to be happy. A nuclear deal with the US, strategic partnership with the US, China and Japan; warming relations with China; a peace process going almost smoothly with Pakistan, and a booming economy. This is the new South Asian reality.

The new South Asian reality underlines some positive trends and developments. Indo-Pakistan rapprochement, the ongoing peace process, the US interest in the region that is based on an evenhanded approach toward India and Pakistan. This augurs well for SAARC. Ever since its inception, SAARC has been severely constrained by Indo-Pakistan rivalry. As two dominant powers they dominated the security agenda. In the changed post-9/11 environment this has changed.

While this phase is still evolving, SAARC no longer needs to be hobbled by the state of India-Pakistan relations. Easing of tension and desire to continue the peace process should infuse new life in SAARC. The smaller countries need to come forward to play an active role in making SAARC stronger and more meaningful. Along with the two bigger partners they should look for ways to enhance regional cooperation, especially economic. In 2004, the members took a number of steps to enhance cooperation in different fields; this needs to be extended to other fields, as in fighting terrorism.

India's new global role, both political and economic, calls for a more engaging and constructive relationship with the regional countries. True, in its (new) global strategy, South Asia figures lower in terms of priority, as in terms of trade. A stable South Asia environment facilitates India's global role. It has been observed that since 1991, New Delhi has consciously pursued a strategy of looking beyond South Asia to pursue the larger great power capabilities that eluded it throughout the Cold War.[3]

S D Muni identifies 'three fold challenges' confronting South Asia, "The challenge of unipolar world and globalization at the level of the world order; the challenge of upsurge in peoples aspirations and expectations from within the South Asian societies and the challenge of terrorism haunting most of the South Asian states."[4]

To these challenges can be added the conventional arms race between the two major powers. Most of these focus around Indo-Pakistan relations.

Both sides continue to augment their nuclear capability, strengthening deterrence posture by improving command and control apparatus. At the same time they continue to build up conventional arms capability. India is determined to enhance its military capability for reasons beyond the region. Pakistan is constrained to follow suit. This is a source of tension for the region and insecurity for the smaller states. The two have yet to address arms control. A symbolic reduction or limit on armament might sound idealistic, but can go a long way in building confidence bilaterally as well as multilaterally.

South Asia has been witnessing terrorism since 9/11, mostly in India and Pakistan. These are serious jolts for the peace process. It almost derailed it last year with Mumbai train attack killing hundreds of innocent commuters. The recent attack on Samjhota express can be seen as another attempt to derail the peace process. The two sides behaved rationally and continued with scheduled meetings. At a recent meeting the two sides agreed to share information on anti-terrorism mechanism. This mechanism needs to be extended to SAARC so that such incidents can be prevented in other states, and they can play an active role in this regard.

One challenge is to delink SAARC from the context of Indo-Pakistan relations. This does not seem to be easy and can be seen as a peculiarity of the South Asian system. The new South Asian reality, Indo-Pakistan peace process and India's new global role could do the delinking. This would free SAARC from the strains and pressures associated with India-Pakistan relationship. This would lead to greater cohesion, leading toward integration within the SAARC framework.

Conclusion

Today's South Asia can be viewed in two distinct perspectives, the past and the present; pre- and post-9/11. The political realities this paper has tried to address are post-9/11 'realignments', within the region and outside, and India's new role. Post-9/11 South Asia is being shaped and needs to be viewed in the light of these two developments. These have also impacted Indo-Pakistan relations in a significant way.

Post-world war II era saw a proliferation of regional organizations, some of which played a major role in regional defense or integration. South Asia was slow in taking such initiative and when it came it was halfhearted. Thus from the start SAARC bore the stigma of being a failure, though the actual problem lay with the regional dynamics, the compulsions and constraints of the members. An author has rightly commented that when SAARC is held responsible, the 'real culprit is South Asian political milieu.'[5]

An evaluation of the SAARC need to address the following:

1. SAARC needs to be delinked from the India-Pakistan equation.
2. SAARC needs to grow in terms of institutions and multilateralism.
3. SAARC needs to tune its institutions in order to face the challenges of globalization.
4. Ideas of a Customs Union and Economic Union need to be pushed.
5. India-Pakistan peace process can go a long way in facilitating smooth functioning of SAARC.
6. SAARC needs to address the peculiarities of the South Asian system and the power imbalance by a joint effort.
7. There is a need to downplay SAARC's shortcomings.

In terms of recommendations, two seem pertinent:

1. An Academic Forum, that should enhance academic exchanges among students, teachers, scholars at a regular and more frequent basis; right now it is limited to conferences. There is need to enhance short-term visits/exchanges between students.
2. SAARC should somehow bring itself around to address political issues; issues that need urgent attention, that threaten regional peace, like the India-Pakistan standoff. The Indian foreign secretary has recently expressed concern over the situation in Sri Lanka. This role could be mediatory than mandatory, and as facilitator of negotiations, so as to promote confidence building.

SAARC members need to learn from their experience and from the other regional organizations. They need to realize that the failure of SAARC is their failure. At the start of the twenty first century, and in the post-9/11 environment, SAARC is faced with new challenges. This calls for new thinking and initiatives on the part of member states if they wish to make SAARC a dynamic organization.

References

1. Rob A Johnson, *Region in Turmoil*, New Delhi: Viva Books, 2006, p. 86.
2. Raja Mohan, "India and the Balance of Power," *Foreign Affairs*, vol. 85, no. 4, 2006, p. 20.
3. Ashley Tellis, *Indias Emerging Nuclear Posture,* Santa Monica, CA: RAND, 2001, p. 728.
4. S.D. Muni, Urmila Phadnis, Kalim Bahadur, eds, *Dometic Conflicts in South Asia* (New Delhi: South Asia Books, 2003), p. 5.
5. Indra Mohan Jha, *SAARC: The Road Ahead,* New Delhi: National Book Organization, 2004.

5

Conflict Resolution in South Asia in an Age of Globalization

Rajpal Budania

The post-Cold War period and globalization dynamics have started to impact the conflict resolution thinking and strategies all over the world. Conflicts have been resolved through integrative or disintegrative approaches. On the negative side, new conflict formation has taken place after the end of the Cold War and intensification of the forces of globalization. New socio-economic and political conflicts are arising as a countermeasure to new world order and globalization. Migration, religious extremism and even terrorism are getting a boost from globalization. Already radical ideological formations are taking place against globalization, particularly in the traditional societies. Though most of these conflict formations are taking place within states, there is a danger of their spilling over across national borders and thus generating international conflict. South Asia has not remained unaffected from these developments.

South Asia has witnessed conflicts between states and within states. Most of these conflicts are still bothering the governments in the region. The task to deal with these conflicts involves prevention, management and resolution of conflicts. Most of the conflicts in South Asia, particularly those between India and Pakistan, are of protracted nature. Their speedy resolution has not been feasible. Therefore, prevention of conflict escalation and management of conflicts becomes important before a conflict can actually be resolved by addressing the root causes.

The focus of this paper is on the inter-state conflict between India and Pakistan. There are two main purposes of this paper: First, to understand the notion of inter-state conflict in South Asia and the post-Cold War and globalization dynamics, and second, to analyze the problem of Indo-Pakistani conflict and assess the prospects of conflict management and resolution after the intensification of globalization process in the region. The paper is centred round the argument that both national and transnational developments are shaping the prospects for conflict management and resolution between India and Pakistan. The paper seeks to build on the assumption that that the dynamics of globalization have by and large positively affected the domestic, regional and global variables for conflict resolution in South Asia, particularly between India and Pakistan.

The Notion of International Conflict in South Asia

There is no single universally acceptable theory of conflict in South Asia, particularly between India and Pakistan. There are several notions on the causes and resolution of conflicts in South Asia. It is often believed that conflict originates in human nature, which is aggressive and selfish or self-centred. Another view, which is less simplistic, holds that state is at the centre of causes and remedies of conflicts. According to this view, states compete for scarce resources and furthering vital national interests at the cost of others. Therefore, international conflict can be defined as a clash of interests and perceptions between states.

Kenneth N. Waltz's theories of military conflict are also useful in understanding the conflicts in South Asia.[1] He has located conflict at the level of human nature, and at the nature of international or state system (interaction of states in a particular system). It can be said that international system has also affected conflict at various levels such as formation, prevention, escalation, management or even resolution.

Sumit Ganguly has explained the underlying causes of conflict between India and Pakistan in terms of three structural factors: (a) the nature of British colonial and disengagement policy, (b) the persistence of rival ideological orientations and their implications for political action, and (c) the strength of the irredentist/anti-irredentist relationship between India and Pakistan.[2] These structural factors refer to certain profound social and historical forces that have shaped and continue to influence conflict resolution between India and Pakistan. Apart from this, lack of development, rise of radicalism, spread of advanced weapons and absence of democracy are identified as contributing to conflicts.

There is a notion of hegemony-inspired conflicts. The South Asian region has India-centric dynamics. India's policy and role for achieving hegemonic pursuits vis-à-vis the smaller states are believed to be a factor in conflict formation in South Asia.

States in South Asia have employed both military and political approaches to conflict resolution. The Cold War power politics generated new pressures and complexities on the ongoing conflict between India and Pakistan. The interests of extra-regional powers in the region were hardly conducive for developing alternative approaches to peace and conflict resolution. State-centric political realism has been at the centre of conflict resolution strategies. As a result, deterrence, arms race, aiding and abetting terrorism, proxy war and even military confrontation have had the primacy in conflict resolution.

Alternative or co-operative approaches such as peaceful co-existence, integration and interdependence, promoting democracy and development, practising bilateralism and pacific settlement of disputes, developing common security and world views and confidence-building measures (CBMs) can go a long way in effectively transforming and terminating a conflict by addressing the root causes of conflicts. Most of the conflicts in the region are of non-military nature and require non-military strategies of resolution.

There is a need to promote conflict resolution as an important national interest. States in the region must realize the prudence of conceiving and furthering this national interest through non-military co-operative strategies.

The Post-Cold War and Globalization Dynamics

Globalization in South Asia has coincided with the end of the Cold War. The South Asian regional conflicts, particularly the Indo-Pakistan conflict, have been associated with the Cold War geo-politics. Naturally, the end of the Cold War was believed to have a major impact on the existing conflicts. Also the end of the Cold War witnessed mutation of multi-ethnic societies and nation-states in Europe. Soviet Union, Czechoslovakia, Yugoslavia disintegrated. Canada has faced a serious problem of disintegration. It was believed that in the post-Cold War period there will be new conflict formation wherein multi-ethnic, plural societies might pose serious challenge to the unity of a state. South Asian states are highly multi-ethnic, and hence the fear of new conflict formation in this region became an area of academic and research interest.

During the Cold War period, the security structures and international institutions were not effective in preventing and resolving conflicts in South Asia. The end of the Cold War required overhauling of the existing security structures and institutions and initiatives of new approaches to preventing, managing and resolving conflicts. The UN Secretary General's report of 17 June 1992 to Security Council highlighted the importance of preventive diplomacy, peacemaking and peacekeeping for conflict prevention and resolution.[3] The Report of the Commission on Global Governance underlined the importance of a long term programme, partially to demilitarise security policies.[4] The new era called for the shaping of democratic institutions and civil societies, besides building political, military, humanitarian and economic structures for conflict prevention, management and resolution.

In the post-Cold War period, humanitarian intervention as a tool of resolving conflicts is being seriously debated. During the Cold War, humanitarian intervention was neither considered a legitimate method nor did the bipolarity allow its practice. But perceptions have changed in the twenty first century. Now the community of states is coming round to the perception that humanitarian intervention – forcible or non-forcible – must be tried as a legitimate method of resolving conflicts in the states where the state machinery has either failed to ensure safety and survival of people or the state itself is indulging in genocide or large scale human rights violation.

As we know, the traditional approach to humanitarian intervention puts primary focus on states and forcible intervention. Coercion and a breach of sovereignty are the main characteristics of intervention. It is also non-consensual. On the contrary, non-forcible humanitarian intervention is characterized by non-violent activities of states, international organizations and non-governmental organizations in humanitarian assistance. It promotes third party facilitating role in conflict resolution and reconstruction. It can be consensual or non-consensual. Both states and non-state actors are considered important actors in conflict management or resolution.

The Report of the High-level Panel on Threats, Challenges and Change (December 2004) spells out a new vision of collective security for the twenty first century. It says that the UN Security Council has the authority to act preventively and there is a need for it to be prepared to be more active in the future for conflict resolution through humanitarian intervention. The report underlines the responsibility of states to protect civilians from large scale violence. It outlines its strategy thus: "When a State fails to protect its civilians, the international community then has a further responsibility to act, through humanitarian operations, monitoring missions and diplomatic pressure – and with force if necessary, though only as a last resort. And in case of conflict or use of force, this also implies a clear international commitment to rebuilding shattered societies."[5] The report has also highlighted the need for new institutions to meet evolving threats and challenges. It has recommended the creation of a peace-building commission within the UN. This commission, working closely with regional organizations and international financial institutions, could fill a crucial gap by giving necessary attention to countries emerging from conflict.[6]

In South Asia we find states either failing or too weak to handle a conflict. There are serious human rights violations in almost all states, particularly in non-democratic states. Involvement of states in abetting transnational terrorism is a well-known fact. The issue of humanitarian intervention is very complex, involving the questions of legality and legitimacy of such an intervention. In the South Asian context, forcible intervention may generate further conflicts. Non-forcible intervention is more pragmatic, but for such intervention the criterion developed by the Panel or otherwise must be carefully considered.

The boundaries between external and internal security threats or conflicts are getting eroded. Most of conflicts in South Asian countries have both internal and external dimensions. If they have to be resolved or even managed then both the dimensions need to be addressed. The Kashmir conflict, the demand for a separate Tamil state in Sri Lanka, the Naxalite movement in India, the problem of extremism and terrorism reflect the scenario wherein the definitional boundaries of external and internal conflict or threat have got blurred and intertwined. The process of globalization has further helped this phenomenon. Globalization is having serious impact on the nature of conflicts. A social, ethnic, economic, political or even environmental crisis in a country can easily transform into an inter-state or a regional conflict due to the inter-connectedness and integrative processes unleashed by globalization.

The post-Cold War period has witnessed integration and disintegration as instruments of conflict management and resolution. The integrative approach has established peace in several parts of the world. States have reunited and inter-governmental organizations have stepped up regionalism and integration. Unification of Germany and emergence of European Union (EU) have gone a long way in conflict management and resolution. In contrast, in recent times disintegration has been employed more often to establish peace or resolve a conflict. Soviet Union, Yugoslavia and Czechoslovakia have disintegrated. The number of new states has steadily increased after the end of the Cold War.

Disintegration is seen as a lasting solution to the problems in Middle East, Iraq, Canada and elsewhere. In South Asia, disintegration was used as a method of resolving the communal conflict in the Indian sub-continent in 1947. In the same process, Bangladesh was created in 1972. At present, in India, Pakistan and Sri Lanka, the separatist movements seek disintegration as a solution to the ongoing conflicts. However, no state would like to disintegrate for resolving a conflict. As a result, conflict management or resolution has become a very difficult task to achieve. Policy-makers believe that conflicts need to be resolved without violating territorial integrity and sovereignty. The process of globalization has strengthened the belief that integration and interdependence as a result of increased functionalism will promote integrative approach for resolving or managing inter-state conflicts in the region. States of the region are trying to build institutional capabilities to manage conflicts.

Globalization furthers the values of democracy, pluralism and freedom. These values are not prevalent in all the South Asian states. The region has asymmetrical political systems. Most of the states are non-democratic and non-secular. In such states if democracy and secularism acquire roots then that will create political system symmetry. It is believed that if Pakistan adopts democratic system then many of the conflicts with India can be resolved or managed peacefully. However, the process of democratization is not free from challenges and new conflicts. Kumar Rupesinghe rightly observes: "Democratization itself will generate new conflicts, and the inability of fragile states to manage this will be a cause for concern. In the absence of an institutionalized capability to manage conflicts, it is likely that authoritarianism will reassert itself. Claims made upon the state on the basis of the right to self determination, territorial claims, minority assertions, and popular assertions for democracy are likely to lead to 'Lebanonization' and fragmentation of some societies."[7]

Globalization has increased the importance of the non-statist perspectives of conflict formation and conflict prevention, management and resolution. Non-state actors are influencing policy-makers to adopt people-centric and problem-solving approaches.

Regional Integration and Conflict Resolution

The world is dotted with transnational organizations. Most of these organizations have generated transnationalism and regional integration. Regional organizations, like the European Union (EU) and the Association of South East Asian Nations (ASEAN), have achieved success in transforming conflict behaviour into patterns of intensive and regularised cooperation and even integration. The EU is an example wherein cooperation in the economic field has led to the forces of integration in political, security and foreign spheres.

Functional theory or functionalism explains integration and interdependence achieved through the transnational organizations, such as the EU, ASEAN and SAARC (South Asian Association for Regional Cooperation). Functionalism emphasises creation of limited specialized technical agencies and organizations, such as in the field of mail or communications, across national orders. But the experience of the EU and the process of globalization have shown that there is a growth of supranational agencies that are not limited to specialized technical areas only. There is a development of more and more general and political organizations. For instance, the economic functions of the EU have led to the growth of other general bodies, such as the European parliament, common European foreign and security policies, common European constitution, etc. This phenomenon is known as neo-functionalism, in which economic integration leads to the growth of political integration and a security community or common security concepts.[8]

The growth of integration process all over the world has been uneven. Apart from the EU experience, supranationalism has not evolved that much in the case of other regions. South Asia represents the area where the growth of economic integration or supranationalism is least visible. The countries in South Asia are integrating with global economy, but they remain less integrated among themselves.[9] The intra-regional trade in the SAARC is a mere five per cent of total exports of the region. Intra-regional trade in the EU is fifty five per cent, in the North American Free Trade Association (NAFTA) is fifty two per cent and in the ASEAN it is 21.4 per cent.[10]

SAARC is an important step in the direction of development of supranational agency. It has taken decisions to step up economic cooperation among the member states. It is believed that the SAARC will witness economic integration and interdependence, which in turn will generate political dynamic that will transform the conflictual relations in the region, particularly between India and Pakistan. Regional organizations not only foster cooperation between states but also contribute to stability within states. They have provided opportunities and forum for conflict management and resolution. Regional cooperation and integration in South Asia is expected to achieve these goals.[11]

Regionalism in South Asia can be an instrument of peace and conflict resolution. SAARC constitutes a step in the direction of regional integration. It has the potential of helping a dynamic process of interaction for conflict resolution, and contribute to 'national' and 'regional' security simultaneously.[12] SAARC provides an informal mechanism – as contentious and bilateral issues have not been included in the SAARC charter – for conflict prevention and management. Moreover, regional cooperation can minimise the intrusive role of extra-regional powers and thus raise the level of national security of the countries of the region. SAARC can play a significant role in altering the prevailing competitive politics and security as existing between India and Pakistan.

SAARC has intensified its role in countering economic conflicts. It has also taken seriously the issue of containing terrorism. It has expanded its membership by including Afghanistan as the eighth member. As we know that Afghanistan has been an important factor in the South Asian security environment, its partnership with other SAARC members will help in tackling the conflict situations through better coordinative efforts.

Indian leadership has believed that the problems of the region can be transformed through integrative approach. Its idea of a South Asian confederation is part of that approach. Pakistan has been sceptical about India's concept of confederal solution. It has blamed India of wanting to dominate the SAARC for serving its economic, political and ideological ends. In fact, Pakistan's arguments are based on the neo-imperialist model of regional cooperation. The neo-imperialist model is based on the assumption that one state is dominant and uses its power to ensure that other states in the region are subservient to its national interests.[13] As a result we find that Pakistan has acted as a big constraint on the economic integration of the region. Pakistan is still adamant on not fully implementing the South Asian Free Trade Agreement (SAFTA) with India. Its negative role is hampering the prospects of SAARC as a forum for conflict prevention and management.

Reflections on Indo-Pakistan Conflict

Conflict over Kashmir and Cross-border Terrorism

The India-Pakistan conflict over the Kashmir issue remains one of the longest unresolved issues in international politics in the post-World War II period. The Kashmir conflict is an outgrowth of the complexities inherent in the notion of the nation-state. Pakistan's pursuit of 'two-nation' theory emphasises separate identities and interests for Hindus and Muslims. On the contrary, India has believed in one-nation based on psycho-cultural unity of all Indians, irrespective of their religion, language or region. Indian state is based on the principles of pluralism, synthesis and coexistence rather than religious homogeneity.

India and Pakistan have fought four wars over the Kashmir issue. Pakistan has unleashed proxy war or state-sponsored *jihadi* terrorism against India over the issue. Pakistan has succeeded in making Kashmir a core issue in its relations with India. Contrary to this, after 9/11 India has achieved significant success in making Pakistan sponsored terrorism a major stumbling block in the resolution of the issue. India has achieved success in addressing both the internal and external dimensions of the problem. However, the key factors responsible for the Kashmir issue are yet to be addressed. But certainly the Kashmir issue has become manageable, particularly after the tremendous international pressure on Pakistan to stop any kind of support to terrorist activities directed against India. Pakistan has consistently tried all means to internationalise the issue and win support for its policy on Kashmir. However, in recent years India's policy of settlement of Kashmir according to the Shimla agreement has won more and more support from key international powers.

It is believed that the Kashmir issue has become even more difficult to resolve due to the two new developments: One, the rise of religious radicalism in the domestic politics of both India and Pakistan, and two, acquisition of nuclear weapons capability by both India and Pakistan.[14] Religious radicalism in both India and Pakistan has witnessed alarming growth. Secularization of society and polity has faced reversal, particularly in Pakistan. Islamic radicalism has survived in Pakistan due to the support of the army. In fact, Islamic fundamentalism has been used by Pakistan against India. But after 9/11 events counter-India justification for Islamic fundamentalism has come under tremendous pressure and as a result the army is finding it hard to support religious extremism. In fact, recently Pakistan President Pervez Musharraf regime has faced a severe crisis over the issue of taming terrorism in Pakistan society and polity due to the international pressure, particularly from the US. Religious parties and groups have opposed Musharraf's moves to secularise Pakistan's political institutions and streamline educational system, particularly the *madrasa* system.

Rise of religious extremism either in Kashmir or the rest of India will obstruct the resolution of the conflict. Since the late 1980s the state has witnessed an alarming rise in the trend of communalization of the society. According to one argument, the Muslim communalism or separatism in the valley is fuelled by Hindu rivalism.[15] This has suited Pakistan's strategy of communalization of the Jammu and Kashmir (J&K) society and promoting *Jihadi* terrorism against India. Therefore, curbing communalization of society and polity within J&K and outside in the rest of India is fundamental to managing the Kashmir issue internally and externally as well.

There is some merit in the argument that the Indo-Pakistan conflict over Kashmir has acquired dangerous proportions after both the countries have declared themselves as nuclear weapon states. The Kargil conflict that took place just after nuclearization almost took both countries to a full-fledged war in the summer of 1999. The deterrence theory nullifying any war between two nuclear powers is questionable in the South Asian context. However, both the countries have made progress on nuclear risk reduction measures. In fact, the US believes that India is a responsible nuclear power and its nuclearization would promote stability in the region.

J&K is an important issue in the composite dialogue process initiated in 1997 between India and Pakistan. So far, several rounds of talks have been held under the composite dialogue process. Several CBMs have been taken to make the relations normal and the peace process more meaningful. Both the countries are trying to resolve the issue according to the principles of the UN Charter and the Shimla Accord. All the parties by now have realized the futility of UN Security Council resolutions passed on J&K under chapter vi of the UN Charter, which are non-binding. Even the UN Secretary General Kofi Annan, during his visit to India in March 2001, remarked that Kashmir can best be resolved bilaterally by India and Pakistan as it was a 'bilateral' issue in which the UN resolutions had become redundant. Both the countries have highlighted the need to promote a stable environment of peace and security. One issue that has hampered the peace process is related to the doubts over the Pakistan sincerity in controlling terrorism directed against India.

On the issue of Pakistan's support to terrorism, India believes that until Pakistan changes its policy the dialogue on the resolution of J&K will not bring concrete results. In this regard some progress has been made during the SAARC summit in January 2004 in Islamabad. The joint statement of 6 January 2004 by Indian Prime Minister Atal Behari Vajpayee and Pakistani President Pervez Musharraf highlighted that in order to take forward and sustain the dialogue process, violence, hostility and terrorism must be prevented.[16] Musharraf pledged that "he will not permit any territory under Pakistan's control to be used to support terrorism in any manner."[17]

During their meeting in Havana, Cuba, on 16 September 2006 during the Non-aligned Movement (NAM) summit, the Indian Prime Minister Manmohan Singh and Pakistani President Pervez Musharraf agreed upon the establishment of a joint India-Pakistan anti-terrorism mechanism.

During the first meeting of the anti-terrorism mechanism in Islamabad on 6 March 2007, it was agreed that specific information will be exchanged through the mechanism for (i) helping investigations on either side related to terrorist acts and (ii) prevention of violence and terrorist acts in the two countries.[18] The mechanism meets on the quarterly basis.

Infiltration of the militants in Kashmir from Pakistan side has come down considerably. But India still has maintained large levels of security forces in the state as Pakistan has not totally dismantled the terrorist network on its soil. India has fenced the line of control (LoC) and that has helped in bringing down the infiltration level.

India has made it clear to Pakistan and the international community that there is no territorial solution to the Kashmir problem and the borders between India and Pakistan cannot be redrawn.[19] Therefore, India believes that the Kashmir issue requires change of Pakistani policy of irredentism based on two-nation theory and completely stopping any kind of support to terrorism against India. India also believes in addressing the internal dimension of the problem in a more efficient manner. For this, India has adopted a multi-pronged approach, which includes consolidating democratic institutions and political process in the state, stepping up economic development and bring in a semblance of administrative efficiency and considering the state's demand for greater autonomy. India has engaged all the parties and groups of all shades of opinion in talks for a peaceful internal resolution of the issue.[20]

Pakistan has come up with several proposals on Kashmir. In December 2006, Musharraf made a statement to an Indian television channel that Pakistan would give up its claim on Kashmir if India showed similar flexibility.[21] Then came the statement from the Pakistan Foreign Ministry spokeswoman, Tasnim Aslam, that Pakistan had never claimed Kashmir as an integral part of its territory, that its legal position was based on the UN Security Council resolutions, and that it wanted a settlement that would be acceptable to itself, to India and to the people of Kashmir.[22]

President Musharraf made a four-point proposal for settling the Kashmir issue.[23] The four-point formula included: making borders irrelevant, demilitarization, self-governance and joint management. He also said that Pakistan would give up its claim on the state if India too did the same for resolving the issue.[24] India said that it was not ready to joint management of J&K as proposed by Pakistan.[25] It also did not agree to the Pakistani concept of self-governance in the state. India believes that the state already enjoys it by having a popular government. It is, however, supportive of the idea of softening of LoC, particularly to allow trade relations.

President Musharraf, while addressing the Foreign Affairs committee of the Spanish Congress in Madrid on 25 April 2007, observed that military solution was not an answer to resolve the Kashmir issue as the option of using force to settle bilateral disputes between India and Pakistan never worked in the past.[26] He rather optimistically said, "The world may see the resolution of the Kashmir dispute earlier than expected. A reasonable progress on this count (Kashmir issue) has already been achieved."[27]

Musharraf's proposal and pronouncements have been met with scepticism in Pakistan itself, in Kashmir and in India as well. Opposition parties in Pakistan, such as *Muttahida Majlis-e-Amal*, *Jamaat-e-Islami*, the Pakistan Muslim League (Nawaz), termed the proposals as a 'sell-out' on the Kashmir issue.[28] According to them the issue has to be resolved in accordance with the UN resolutions and the wishes of the Kashmiris. Pakistan based *United Jihad Council* – a coalition of terrorist groups – maintained that Musharraf's approach reflected unilateral concessions, but Kashmiris would not compromise on their right to self-determination.[29] *Jamaat-ud-Dawa*, which is considered as *Lashkar-e-Taiba* by a different name, has been opposed to the Indo-Pakistan peace process.

The government of India and parties in the state of J&K, particularly Peoples' Democratic Front, National Conference, Jammu and Kashmir Liberation Front, believe in being open to all new ideas on Kashmir. In that context, important ideas in Musharraf's proposals can be discussed. But India knows that most of Musharraf's pronouncements are aimed at his own political survival rather than resolution of the issue. The first task for Pakistan should be to help India in restoring peace and tranquillity in J&K. In this regard, his proposals will become meaningful only when Pakistan shows a change of policy and ability to end terror acts against India. Moreover, a resolution of the Kashmir issue has to be incremental. A hurried resolution is neither feasible nor practical.

Managing the Arms Race and the Nuclear Issue

Arms race has been an important factor in the origin and perpetuation of the Indo-Pakistani conflict. It has generated fears of military escalation, surprise attack, war and even a nuclear conflict. Defence expenditures have adversely affected developmental goals, which in turn have generated new conflicts. The worrisome trend is that arms race remains unabated. Nuclear weapons and the issues of command and control, and offensive-defensive nature of nuclear doctrines call for new CBMs. The issue of missile development does raise longer-term implications for South Asian stability and for the proliferation of missile and nuclear technology. Missile development competition has added a dangerous dimension to the region's strategic rivalry and arms race. Pakistan's missile development programme, in collaboration with China and North Korea, has provided a variable in India's threat perception and strategic environment. India-Pakistan strategic rivalry has operated on the pattern of action-reaction. The challenge for peace researchers is how to change the strategic rivalry and to ensure better management of the nuclear issue for the sake of peace-building in South Asia.

India, being a responsible and a rational democratic state, has a stake in enhancing long-term stability in the region through diplomacy and political means. For realising this objective, India must pursue three-pronged strategy based on: (a) bilaterally engaging Pakistan for confidence and security building measures, (b) motivating the United State and other friendly nations to engage Pakistan and China and put pressure on them against their proliferation activities, and (c) convincing other South Asian countries that India's nuclear capabilities will not be allowed to become a factor for deterioration of bilateral or the regional security environment.

Nuclearization of South Asia has imposed an obligation on both India and Pakistan to manage the disputes, crises, or issues through political means and initiatives. Understanding the diplomatic need and compulsions of the time, India took the initiative for concluding the Lahore declaration after the nuclear tests. Prime Minister Atal Behari Vajpayee visited Pakistan and signed on 21 February 1999 the Lahore declaration and the memorandum of understanding (MoU) with the Pakistani Prime Minister Nawaz Sharif. Both the documents bind India and Pakistan on the process of dialogue on a range of issues. These have been considered important steps towards initiating a political process for building peace by undertaking confidence and security building measures in conventional and nuclear fields.

The Lahore declaration and the MoU spell the framework in which the nuclear risk reduction measures can be undertaken and a peace process strengthened. The MoU says: "The two sides shall engage in bilateral consultations on security concepts and nuclear doctrines with a view to developing confidence-building measures in the nuclear and conventional fields, aimed at avoidance of conflict ... The two sides shall engage in bilateral consultations on security, disarmament and non-proliferation issues within the context of negotiations on these issues in multilateral fora."[30] The two sides decided to take measures and inform each other of any "accidental, unauthorised or unexplained incident" in the nuclear field.[31] Advance notification of ballistic missile tests by the two countries was also included in the MoU. Both the countries committed themselves to the objectives of nuclear disarmament and non-proliferation.[32] They have held several rounds of talks on nuclear CBMs. They have reaffirmed their commitment to unilateral moratorium on further nuclear testing. They have decided to upgrade the dedicated and secure hotline between the Director Generals of Military Operations. One more hotline would be established between the Foreign Secretaries for crisis avoidance.

Pakistan, along with the US and other Western countries, has often perceived South Asia a nuclear flashpoint in the context of the Kashmir issue. India has never accepted the nuclear situation as a flashpoint, particularly in the context of the Kashmir issue. Pakistan also seems to be gradually coming round to the Indian point of view. After the conclusion of the second round of the Expert Level talks on nuclear CBMs in Islamabad on 14-15 December 2004, the leader of the Pakistani delegation, Tariq Osman Hyder, conceded that South Asia was no longer a nuclear flashpoint.[33] It was for the first time since the 1998 nuclear tests that Pakistan had conceded that South Asia was no longer a nuclear flashpoint.

Contrary to the progress made on the nuclear CBMs and the change of the Pakistani perception on the situation of South Asia as a nuclear flashpoint, the two countries have hardly made any progress on the conventional military CBMs. India made nine military CBMs in June 2004. The proposals included an agreement on peace and tranquillity on the line of control, envisaging a series of measures: contact between Air Forces; contact between Navies; Sectoral/Core Commanders; face to face meeting between DGMOs; exchange of naval ships and interaction between the defence think-tanks.[34] Pakistan has ignored these proposals. Instead, Pakistan has mooted a concept of 'strategic restraint regime' envisaging conventional military balance by reducing force levels and freezing missile programmes. India has refused to accept these proposals as it believes its defence build-up is security-specific, that of Pakistan is India-centric.[35]

India has unilaterally decided to incorporate certain principles in its nuclear doctrine, which would help in providing stability to the nuclear issue. Just after acquiring nuclear weapons, Indian Prime Minister Atal Behari Vajpayee stated in the Lok Sabha on 27 May 1998: "We do not intend to use these weapons for aggression or for mounting threats against any country. These are weapons of self-defence, to ensure that India is not subjected to nuclear threats or coercion. We do not intend to engage in an arms race... Our policy has been marked by restraint and openness... Restraint, however, has to arise from strength...The action involved was balanced in that it was the minimum necessary to maintain what is an irreducible component of our national security calculus."[36]

The main features of India's nuclear doctrine, such as minimum deterrence, no-first-use, indicate the non-offensive purpose of India's nuclear weapons capability. India believes that even in the event of a limited conflict, like the Kargil in 1999, both India and Pakistan would behave rationally on the issue of actual use of nuclear capabilities. Political management of the Kargil conflict by India is a shining example of India's rational and responsible nuclear behaviour, as a result of which the crisis was not allowed to escalate into a full-fledged war. Indian External Affairs Minister K. Natwar Singh once remarked that there was a need for India, Pakistan and China to develop a common nuclear doctrine.[37] This indicates the sincerity and responsibility on the part of India to manage the nuclear issue in a manner which would promote nuclear stability in the region.

The best way to eliminate nuclear risks is to abolish all nuclear weapons, regionally and globally. India still believes in general and complete disarmament. It was in keeping with this objective that India moved a resolution in the October 1998 session of the UN General Assembly on nuclear risk reduction measures to be adopted by all nuclear weapon states. The resolution envisages de-targeting and de-alerting of all nuclear weapons as well as a no-first-use commitment. That is not likely to happen in foreseeable future. Analysts believe that even in a nuclearised South Asia some nuclear risk reduction measures can go a long way in averting a nuclear crisis or war. A primary risk reduction measure that has been suggested is that both India and Pakistan not deploy, as a matter of formal policy, nuclear armed missiles and aircraft.[38]

The prospects of nuclear stability in South Asia are challenged by the unchanged nature of strategic rivalry and competition between India and Pakistan. Both are deeply devoted to the superior technological developments, particularly in the field of missile development. Moreover, the domestic discourses in both India and Pakistan suggest the continuing hostility between the two countries and the need to upgrade their military, particularly nuclear, power. Within India the threats from the emerging nuclear order, both at the regional and the global levels, have influenced some strategic thinkers to advocate a more expansive or a maximalist nuclear strategy and force structure. It has been suggested that India should acquire high-value-high-yield nuclear forces. It is believed that the present Indian minimalist deterrence strategy is inadequate to defend the country's supreme strategic interests. Therefore, it is suggested that India should have a grand strategic vision and a thermonuclear force to realise that vision.[39]

Given the nature of radicalization of Pakistani society, polity and armed forces, analysts in India believe that success of CBMs in the nuclear or strategic field is highly doubtful. There are serious uncertainties over the issues of command and control of Pakistan's nuclear weapons. Pakistan's internal politics has become highly volatile. The fear of irrational and unauthorised use of nuclear capability cannot be brushed aside lightly. There is no hope that Pakistan will have a legitimate, democratic government on a sustained basis in near future. Moreover, Pakistan has not accepted India's key proposal of no-first-use policy. It has been suggested that India should move ahead on the strategic superiority logic. In other words, for stability and peace in South Asia, India needs to acquire overwhelming strategic superiority over Pakistan. So that India need not attack, and Pakistan dare not attack.

Interests of Extra-regional Powers

Almost all major powers have welcomed the peace process between India and Pakistan. Most of them have appreciated India's perception of the conflict, based on bilateralism and peaceful resolution of contentious issues, and stopping all kinds of support to terrorism. In fact, the US considers that both India and the US can work together in promoting peace and democracy in the region. Both believe that evolution of Pakistan as a moderate Islamic state will help in maintaining peace and stability in the region. Both of them have achieved some success in bringing peace and democracy in Nepal.

The US is considered as the most important extra-regional player in the South Asian international politics. It has shown interest in the resolution of the Kashmir issue, mostly according to the wishes of the Pakistani leadership. After nuclearization of South Asia, the US has made several overtures for managing the nuclear issue. The Afghanistan situation has added another dimension to the US interests in the region. A recent work on the US interests in South Asia has observed: "Having accepted the sub-continent's nuclearization, US interests in South Asia are likely to remain in the background, preserving the status quo and preventing the spread of nuclear arms race between India and Pakistan and its spread via Pakistan to North Korea and possibly elsewhere... Its independent interest in solving the Kashmir problem remains, despite India's appeals for US pressure on Pakistan to reduce its support for insurgents in Kashmir and despite Pakistan's appeals for US involvement in obtaining proper status in the region."[40]

There has been a view in India that the US policy of regional balance or equating India with Pakistan has emboldened Pakistan to be aggressive against India and create an atmosphere of hostility in the region. India has believed that the US arms to Pakistan have encouraged it to resolve disputes with India through military approach. The peace process between India and Pakistan can also be adversely affected by any arms supplies to Pakistan. The US arms package worth $1.2 billion for Pakistan, including eight P-3C surveillance aircraft, did not go down well with India. However, in recent years the Indo-US strategic partnership is indicative of the US willingness to no more treat India and Pakistan on parity. Both India and the US are engaged in the Next Steps in Strategic Partnership (NSSP) and the US has offered India its latest weaponry. Both have entered a historic phase in their relationship after the conclusion of the Indo-US nuclear deal in the civilian field. Now the US considers India as a responsible nuclear power, which has a significant role in the US goal of nuclear non- proliferation. The US has not granted the same status to Pakistan.

Russia has welcomed the peace process between India and Pakistan. The Russian President Validimir Putin welcomed the peace process and believed that it would add to the development of the region and resolution of the bilateral problems.[41] Russia has been supportive of India's stand on Kashmir and its resolution according to the Shimla Agreement. Russia considers India as an important player for promoting Asian security. Both India and Russia have similarity of perceptions on transnational security threats like international terrorism and religious extremism. Apart from Russia, the US, China and other countries are also concerned on these issues, and hence they have mutuality of interests. The convergence of interests between India and other major powers on these issues will put pressure on Pakistan for mending its policies on Kashmir and transnational terrorism.

China's role in promoting peace and stability in South Asia is constrained by both India and China having a competing perception of their geo-political role in South Asia and Asia simultaneously. Analysts believe that the relations between the two will become more competitive in the time to come.[42] China's growing strategic relationship with Pakistan puts a severe constraint on China's claims of promoting peace and stability in South Asia. Lasting peace in South Asia is possible only when China resolves its problems with India and does not cooperate with Pakistan on anti- or counter-India basis. China needs to rethink its strategy of aiding Pakistan to tie down India in the South Asian wrangle. The forces of globalization have compelled China to develop new understanding with India in the economic field and also take joint measures against terrorism, increase bilateral military cooperation and take new CBMs for resolving the border dispute. China is all set to emerge as India's largest trading partner. In such a situation, China's national interests would dictate normal relations with India. Indian Defence Minister Pranab Mukherjee, after his visit to China in June 2006, stated that India and China did not perceive each other as a threat.[43] Similarly, the Indian Prime Minister Manmohan Singh recently remarked that India wanted "the strongest relationship with China. China is our greatest neighbour, and it has been the constant endeavour of my Government to do everything in our power to cement this relationship."[44]

China has supported the resolution of bilateral disputes between India and Pakistan through negotiations. It has adopted a careful stand on the Kashmir issue. When the Chinese President Jiang Zemin paid a state visit to India in 1996, he suggested that both India and Pakistan put the Kashmir issue on the backburner and devote more time to cooperating in other areas.[45] China is also against any third-party mediation in the conflict, fearing that such mediation would allow the US even more leeway in the region.[46]

It is believed that India and China together can sustain peace and stability in the region. Both India and China share the perception that "there could be no Asia-Pacific century or Asian century without India and China forming crucial elements of such architecture."[47] Both share the perception that terrorism is a threat to both of them, and they need to have a regular dialogue and develop anti-terror mechanism. China is facing separatist threat in its Xinjiang province from the Uighur militants, who have close connections with the Al Qaeda and the Taliban terrorist outfits.

In an era of globalization and post-Cold War the nature of interests of major powers vis-à-vis South Asia is not the same as it was during the Cold War. The change in the major powers' economic and geo-political considerations towards the region will certainly have an impact on the management and resolution of conflicts in the region. Kashmir and the issue of arms race and nuclearization have already witnessed more appreciation of India's approach and policies for resolving these issues.

Conclusion

In the South Asian context, nationalism and supranationalism are still contradictory forces. The state sovereignty is still sacrosanct. The region is yet to develop supranational structures capable of transforming or actually resolving conflicts. Transnational actors are yet to bridge national borders and create a structure of interdependence among the states of the region. Things are changing but slowly. The process of globalization is making its impact. The effects of information technology are already being felt. Now there is greater transparency and openness in all aspects of life, particularly in governance and decision-making apparatus.

Globalization is both a part of the problem as well as a part of the solution. It has led to counter-reaction, particularly in non-democratic, conservative societies. As a result, culture has become a source of conflict. The problems of migration, religious extremism and even terrorism have led to new conflict formations. Globalization has helped terrorism through networking and easy access to technology and material.

The positive side of globalization is reflected in the growth of integration and interdependence at the regional and global levels. If South Asia achieves a reasonable level of economic integration and interdependence, that will make borders irrelevant. In such an atmosphere an irredentist issue like Kashmir can see resolution through transformation of hostility between India and Pakistan. Globalization has put pressure on South Asian states to develop institutions to deal with social, economic and political challenges and conflicts. South Asian states seek to merge with global economies. In this pursuit of integration at the global level, these countries are bound to make integrative efforts at the regional level as well. There is a likelihood that this will lead to a common market civilization, which will be a good countermeasure to the fear of clash of civilization.

India is better qualified and equipped to follow and take advantage of the globalization dynamics. Globalization has been a helpful factor for India to emerge as one of the largest economies of the world and a centre of great power. It will have a positive impact on recasting of its relations with Pakistan and other extra-regional powers. It will also positively mould the Indian Union's relations with the state of J&K. A prosperous, secular and democratic India, compared to a failing state of Pakistan, will certainly make the secessionists in Kashmir or elsewhere in India to rethink their strategy of self-determination or disintegration from India.

Both domestic and international developments have shaped the prospects for conflict resolution. The international environment is becoming more suitable for conflict management and resolution in the region. The domestic factors which have thwarted the efforts for conflict resolution have remained largely unchanged or even worsened, particularly in the case of Pakistan. There are serious problems within Pakistan. The rise of religious extremism there is a worrisome factor. In the absence of a secular society and polity, without a legitimate elected government and serious law and order problems, Pakistan is being described as a failed state. It is doubtful whether a weak Pakistan will be ready for a reasonable settlement of the Kashmir issue without redrawing borders. Resolution of the Kashmir issue is possible only through long-term transformation of internal variables in Kashmir, India and Pakistan. In this process of transformation, Pakistan needs to democratise and secularise its India and Kashmir policies that are yet based on religious fundamentalism and terrorism.

In the present circumstances, conflict resolution of the Kashmir issue is remote in the sense of everlasting termination of conflict by addressing the root causes. Settlement is possible on minor and less contentious issues such as the Siachen and Sir Creek. But these issues might recur in the absence of an early solution to the Kashmir issue. Non-state third party mediation has played a constructive role in settling disputes, as in the case of the Indus Water Treaty and more recently in the Baghlihar power project. So far the bilateral mechanism has been constrained, mainly due to Pakistani attitudes, in resolving the main contention over the fate of Kashmir. The bilateral initiatives are more likely to lead to the peaceful management of the issues rather than actually resolving them according to the wishes of both India and Pakistan.

Some progress has been made on political management of nuclearization by undertaking nuclear risk reduction measures. But the edifice of the strategic rivalry is still intact. Both countries are involved in technological developments for strategic superiority. Internal political dynamics in Pakistan have worsened. This puts a serious question over the safety of Pakistan's nuclear arsenal.

There is an increasing convergence of perceptions and interests between India and the major powers of the world on issues like religious extremism and terrorism. India's role as a responsible nuclear power and a democratic stabilizer in Asia is becoming a key factor in India's bilateral relations with the great powers. There is a greater appreciation of India's non-military approach to resolving the Indo-Pakistan conflict. Consequently, Pakistan is under pressure to mend its strategies on terrorism and Kashmir.

References

1. Kenneth N. Waltz, *Man, the State and War*, New York: Columbia University Press, 1959.
2. Sumit Ganguly, *The Origins of War in South Asia: Indo-Pakistani Conflict Since 1947*, Boulder and London: West-view Press, 1986, 1994.
3. Boutros Boutros-Ghali, *An Agenda for Peace*, New York: United Nations, 1995.

4. The Report of the Commission on Global Governance, *Our Global Neighbourhood*, New York: Oxford University Press, 1995.
5. Report of the High-level Panel on Threats, Challenges and Change (December 2004), *Strategic Digest*, vol. 35, no. 1, January 2005, p. 18.
6. *Ibid*, p. 19.
7. Kumar Rupesinghe, "The Disappearing Boundaries Between Internal and External Conflicts," in Elise Boulding (ed), *New Agendas for Peace Research: Conflict and Security Re-examined*, Boulder and London: Lynne Rienner Publishers, 1992, p. 44.
8. For details see, Emanuel Adler and Michael Barnett (eds), *Security Communities*, Cambridge: Cambridge University Press, 1998.
9. "Economic Cooperation in SAARC: SAFTA and Beyond," *Strategic Digest*, vol. 37, no. 4, April 2007, pp. 450-451.
10. *Ibid*, p. 451.
11. Rajpal Budania, "South Asian Association for Regional Cooperation: Issue of Cooperation and Security," in B.C. Upreti, (ed.) *SAARC: Dynamics of Regional Cooperation in South Asia, Nature, Scope and Perceptions*, vol.1, New Delhi: Kalinga Publications, 2000, p. 91.
12. *Ibid*, p. 93.
13. Hamid H. Kizilbash, "SAARC: Security Concerns and Regional Cooperation," in Zillur R. Khan (ed), *SAARC and the Super Powers*, Dhaka: University Press Limited, 1991, pp.119-121.
14. For details see, Rafiq Dossani and Henry S. Rower (eds), *Prospects for Peace in South Asia*, Hyderabad: Orient Longman, 2006.
15. Ajit Bhattacharjea, *Kashmir: The Wounded Valley*, New Delhi: UBSPD, 1994, p. 85.
16. "Joint Press Statement on PM's Visit to Pakistan (January 2004)," *Strategic Digest*, vol. 34, no. 2, February 2004, pp. 113-114.
17. *Ibid*, p. 114.
18. "On the first meeting of the India-Pakistan Anti-Terrorism Mechanism," *Strategic Digest*, vol.37, no. 3, March 2007, p. 337.
19. "No redrawing of boundaries: Manmohan," *The Hindu*, 22 December 2004.
20. Till April 2007 three Jammu and Kashmir Roundtable Conferences have been held to put together all shades of opinion. One recommendation that has emerged out of these conferences is aimed at enhancing cross-border linkages.
21. "Pakistan says it never claimed Kashmir as its territory," *Hindustan Times*, 12 December 2006.
22. *Ibid*.

23. "Musharraf faces criticism for Kashmir proposal," *The Hindu*, 7 December 2006.
24. *Ibid.*
25. "India not ready for joint management of Kashmir," *Hindustan Times*, 12 January 2007.
26. "Kashmir issue will be resolved soon: Pervez," *Hindustan Times*, 27April 2007.
27. *Ibid.*
28. "Musharraf faces criticism for Kashmir proposal," *The Hindu*, 7 December 2006.
29. "Jihad Council attacks Musharraf offer," *The Hindu*, 7 December 2006.
30. Amit Baruah, "Bus to Pakistan," *Frontline*, vol.16, no.5, 27 February-12 March 1999, p. 5.
31. "View from Lahore," *Hindustan Times*, 23 February 1999.
32. "India, Pak to reduce risk of nuclear strikes," *The Times of India*, 22 February 1999.
33. "South Asia no longer a nuclear flashpoint: Pakistan," *The Hindu*, 16 December 2004.
34. *Ibid.*
35. *Ibid.*
36. "Evolution of India's Nuclear Policy," a paper submitted by the Indian Prime Minister to the Lok Sabha on 27 May 1998. See "Text of PM's statement in Lok Sabha," *Hindustan Times*, 28 May 1998.
37. "Common N-doctrine needed," *Hindustan Times* (Lucknow), 2 June 2004.
38. R. Rajaraman, MV Ramana, Zia Mia, "Possession and Deployment of Nuclear Weapons in South Asia: An Assessment of Some Risks," *Economic and Political Weekly*, vol. 37, no. 25, 22 June 2002, p. 2465.
39. For details see, Bharat Karnad, *Nuclear Weapons and Indian Security: The Realist Foundations of Strategy*, New Delhi: Macmillan India Ltd., 2002.
40. Rafiq Dossani and Henry S. Rower, "Introduction," in R. Dossani and H.S. Rower (eds), n.14, p. 16.
41. "Dangers to construct world on unipolar principles: Putin," *The Hindu*, 4 December 2006.
42. For details see, Jown W. Garver, *Protracted Contest: Sino-Indian Rivalry in the Twentieth Century*, Seattle: University of Washington Press, 2001; Francine R. Frankel and Harry Harding (eds), *The India-China Relationship: What the United States Needs to Know*, New York: Columbia University Press, 2004.
43. "India, China do not consider each other a threat: Pranab," *The Hindu*, 14 June 2006.

44. "China our greatest neighbour: Manmohan," *The Hindu*, 18 June 2007.
45. John Cherian, "Zhu Rongji in India," *Frontline*, 15 February 2002, pp. 122-123.
46. *Ibid*, p. 123.
47. "India is a core state for Asian security: Pranab Mukherjee," *The Hindu*, 4 June 2006.

PART II

HUMAN SECURITY

6

Human Security in South Asia: The Varied Dimensions

T. Nirmala Devi

As per the Mehbub Ul Haq's report, the conceptuliazation of human security would mean inclusion of income, employment, food, health, education and environment to human development. It emphasizes human security in the form of well-being and dignity of the people, rather than on the protection of national borders. However, a region like South Asia which is characterized by large scale human deprivation and visualized by high incidence of poverty, malnutrition, illiteracy, etc. does not ensure human security in the appropriate way. The colonial rule for almost a century has had a great impact on the socio-economic fabric of South Asian countries. The nearly sixty years of self-governance has not improved the quality of life significantly in these countries. Even though the governments introduced several programmes in the past for removing income inequalities and raising the welfare levels of the people, they could not be implemented properly in most of the countries and economic vulnerability remained the same. This poor display reflects the ineffective governance and lack of firm commitment on the part of policymakers. The South Asian economies are basically characterized as agricultural and the majority of people lives in rural areas in the region. Hence, the declining priority of agriculture sector in South Asia from the early 1990s further deteriorated the levels of standard of living of the rural masses. The neglect of social sector in most of these countries also indicates the increased allocation of funds to the defence sector. The region is confronted with territorial conflicts and nuclear arms race, in contrast to the global trend in which the other regional groupings are shifting their focus from military to human security. Thus, the paper focuses on the increase of funds on social services, which in turn, largely ensures human security. The paper attempts to examine the status of human security in South Asia and to analyze the reasons behind the low levels of human security in majority of the countries in the region. Further, it stresses on the need to cut down the unproductive spending on defence and to divert the funding to the social infrastructure. Thus, it emphasizes the greater role of the governments to ensure proper implementation of various programmes for raising the existing standards of living of the people.

The structure of the paper is as follows. The paper begins with section 1 which provides the backdrop of the weak social fabric of South Asia, in terms of human deprivation and poverty. Section 2 presents the vital aspects of human security, viz. health, education, and employment. Gender disparity in the region is also dealt with in this section. In section 3, the paper examines the priorities in public spending in the region and highlights the need to increase public expenditure on social sector. India's role in the economic security of South Asia is discussed in section 4. Finally, concluding observations are presented in section 5.

Introduction

The social challenge in South Asia remains quite acute and the progress in eliminating poverty is found to be difficult in most of the cases. The asymmetry in socio-economic indicators is significantly visible in the SAARC countries. The size of 1,095 million population of India in 2005 outweighed the population of the rest of SAARC countries, as the former accounted for more than three times of the latter. The South Asian region, with the exception of Bhutan, registered a considerable decline in the growth rate of population from the period 1980-90 to 2000-05, particularly in Sri Lanka and Pakistan. The size of less than one per cent in Sri Lanka was impressive in the context of reducing overhead costs on the existing population. Both India and Bhutan showed a tremendous increase in per capita income in PPP terms in a decade, owing to the consistent GDP growth rate and the impact of Chukha power project respectively. Notwithstanding the considerable levels of per capita income, Bhutan witnessed a decline in the growth rate of GDP per capita in recent years, in contrast to India. Over the years, Sri Lanka has been consistently experiencing an increase in the per capita income in the region. While Pakistan, of late, registered an impressive growth in its GDP per capita.

1) Human Deprivation

The low quality of life in most of the countries reflects not only the burden of human deprivation – denying access to basic needs and services – but

Table –1
Human Deprivation in SAARC

Country	*Population without access to safe water (as % of total popn.)*	*Population without access to sanitation (as % of total popn.)*	*Illiterate adults (as % of total adult popn.)*	*Illiterate female adults (as% of total adult female popn.)*	*Child malnutrition (weight for age)*	*Under-5 mortality rate (per 1000 live births)*	*People living with HIV/AIDS Adults (% age 15-49)*
	2002	2002	2003	2003	1995-2003	2003	2003
Bangladesh	25.0	52.0	58.9	68.6	48	69	<0.20
Bhutan	38.0	30.0	53.0	66.0	19	85	...
India	14.0	70.0	39.0	52.2	47	87	0.9
Maldives	16.0	42.0	2.8	2.8	30	72	...
Nepal	16.0	73.0	51.4	65.1	48	82	0.3
Pakistan	10.0	46.0	51.3	64.8	38	103	0.1
Sri Lanka	22.0	9.0	9.6	11.4	29	15	<0.10
South Asia	14.8	64.8	42.1	54.8	46	86	...

Source: MHHDC, *Human Development in South Asia*, New York: Oxford University Press, 2005.

also the difficulty in eliminating the poverty. Table 1 shows that human deprivation is strikingly visible in most of the SAARC countries, as majority of people is deprived of the basic necessities. A considerable section, i.e. nearly fifteen per cent of people did not have access to safe water in the region, while more than three–fifths were denied access to sanitation facilities. A relatively better picture was seen in Pakistan for safe water and in Sri Lanka for sanitation. The percentage of illiteracy was still alarming in adults, particularly among female adults in the region with the exception of Sri Lanka and Maldives. The health crises were also palpable in the region – Bangladesh, Nepal, India and Pakistan had high levels of child malnutrition; Pakistan followed by India, Bangladesh and Maldives recorded high under-five mortality rate and India revealed high incidence of HIV in adults.

2) Poverty

The incidence of poverty has spread unevenly among the regions of the world and is deeply rooted in the South Asian region, despite the continued efforts of the governments. In South Asia, forty per cent of population lives below the poverty line, in which more than two-thirds reside below the poverty line of two dollar a day. This type of condition not only forced the people to settle for lower quality of food, clothing and shelter and spend less on their children's education and health; but also limit their current ability to perform.[1] The SAARC region, with the exception of Sri Lanka and Maldives, is still suffering from significant incidence of poverty.

Table-2
Human and Income Poverty in SAARC

Country	*Population below Income Poverty Line (%)*			*Human Poverty Index*	
	$1 a day 1990-2004	*$2 a day* 1990-2004	*National Poverty Line* 1990-2003	*Rank*	*Value (%)*
Bangladesh	36.0	82.8	49.8	85	44.2
Bhutan	..	..	..	71	39.0
India	34.7	79.9	28.6	55	31.3
Maldives	..	..	..	36	16.9
Nepal	24.1	68.5	30.9	68	38.1
Pakistan	17.0	73.6	32.6	65	36.3

Source: UNDP, *Human Development Report*, New York: Oxford University Press, 2006.

Table 2 presents the percentage of population below income poverty line and the levels of human poverty. Basing on the estimate of one dollar a day, the incidence of income poverty was more than one-third in Bangladesh and India and nearly one-fourth in Nepal during 1990-2004. If measured in two dollar a day, the extent of poverty was strikingly visible in almost all countries of the region, with a lesser extent in Sri Lanka. The national poverty line estimate also showed a little lower size of poverty in Sri Lanka, while the variation of poverty among the rest of countries was between twenty nine to forty per cent. The human poverty index also confirmed the better status of Sri Lanka and Maldives, whereas human poverty was high in Bangladesh, Bhutan, Nepal and Pakistan in terms of both rank and value.

Environment insecurity is another problem in South Asia. Though protection of environment is a prerequisite to sustain human security levels, the region continues to suffer from extreme deforestation, scarcity of water, emission of carbon dioxide, wastage of heavy industrial material, pollution and other environmental problems. Environmental degradation affects health status through undermining the natural support systems of human activity.

Social Infrastructure in South Asia

1) Health Security

The improvement in health status in South Asian countries is seen in the decline of crude death rate through the control of communicable diseases. However, mortality rates among infants, children and mothers did not show considerable decline, indicating the inadequate health services available to the people of the region. Though an overwhelming proportion of people lives in rural areas, health care is mostly inaccessible to the rural residents. South Asia, by and large, has always lacked a proper health care system which ensures human security. Moreover, the health status in the region is not able to provide the same quality of services to all. Those deprived from the health facilities include the poor, rural population and the less educated women and children in this region. These people are ignored by the healthcare system due to the absence of adequate infrastructure in the public health centres and non-availability of services in the rural sector.

Table 3 reveals that Sri Lanka, notwithstanding the moderate record of malnourished people, is the better performer in health status in the region by having high longevity of life; lowest infant and maternal mortality rates and higher number of deliveries carried out by the skilled

Table-3
Status of Health in SAARC

Country	*Life expectancy at birth (years)*		*Infant mortality rate (per thousand live births)*		*Probability at birth of surviving to age 65 (% of cohort)*		*Maternal mortality ratio (per one lac live births)*		*Population under-nourished (%of total)*		*Births attended by health personnel (%)*	*Physicians (per one lac people)*
	1990	*2004*	*1970*	*2004*	*Female 2000-2005*	*Male 2000-2005*	*Reported 1990-2004*	*Adjusted 2000*	*1990/92*	*2001/03*	*1996-2004*	*1990-2004*
Bangladesh	52.0	63.3	145	56	63.7	53.3	380	380	35	30	13	26
Bhutan	49.0	63.4	156	67	65.3	60.2	260	420	...	...	37	5
India	59.0	63.6	127	62	67.4	59.2	540	540	25	20	43	60
Maldives	62.1	67.0	157	35	67.5	67.8	140	110	17	11	70	92
Nepal	52.0	62.1	165	59	61.0	57.9	540	740	20	17	15	21
Pakistan	56.0	63.4	120	80	65.6	62.7	530	500	24	23	...	74
Sri Lanka	71.0	74.3	65	12	85.6	76.1	92	92	28	22	96	55

Source: World Bank, *World Development Report*, New York: Oxford University Press, 1992 & 2007; UNDP, *Human Development Report*, New York: Oxford University Press, 2006.

health personnel. Maldives too projected a good picture with a reasonably high life expectancy at birth, low infant and maternal mortality rates, higher number of physicians available and more importantly with the low levels of malnutrition among its people. In contrast, a majority of the countries, viz. Pakistan with high infant mortality; Nepal with lower life expectancy at birth and highest maternal mortality; Bhutan with lowest number of physicians; Bangladesh with low probability of birth, high malnutrition and lowest number of births recorded in hospitals could not safeguard health security. India neither revealed a good show nor projected a dismal picture in the health scenario. This country has to perform better in time to come to attain reasonable health standards.

2) Education Security

During the nearly six decades of independence in these countries, the efforts of the governments could not wipe out illiteracy completely. The existing literacy levels continue to impede the development process by affecting the general quality of life in the region. With the exception of Sri Lanka and Maldives, the region still constitutes a majority of illiterates.

The total adult literacy rate increased from thirty two per cent in 1970 to fifty eight per cent in 2003 in the South Asian region, out of which Maldives and Sri Lanka registered above ninety per cent in the latter year. In general, the increase was more conspicuous in adult literacy rate of the females in the region. Gross primary enrolment in South Asian region, with the exception of Pakistan, increased from sixty eight per cent in 1970 to ninety six per cent in 2002-03. Gross secondary enrolment of the region increased from twenty five per cent in 1970 to forty seven per cent in 2002-03. Again, Sri Lanka followed by Nepal performed better in the region.[2]

The adult literacy rate as well as youth literacy rate was more striking in Maldives and Sri Lanka, while the progress from 1990 to 2004 was sizeable in Nepal, followed by Pakistan (Table 4). Besides the above countries, the net enrolment ratio at primary level was significant in Bangladesh and India. Bhutan registered a higher number of children reaching fifth grade and completing ninth grade. Available information suggested that above one-fifth of tertiary level students in India were in science and technical disciplines, suggesting an inclination towards them.

3) Employment Security

It is a known fact that a lion's share of the region's labour is in the informal sector, viz. agriculture and allied activities and small and medium

Table-4
Literacy and Enrolment in SAARC

Country	*Adult literacy rate (% ages 15 and older)*		*Youth literacy rate (% ages 15-19)*		*Net primary enrolmt ratio (%)*	*Net secondry enrolmt ratio (%)*	*Children reaching grade 5*	*Grade 9 completion rate*		*Tertiary students* (% of tertiary students)*
	1990	2004	1990	2004	2004	2004	2004	M	F	1999-2004
Bangladesh	34.2	..	42.0	…	94	48	65	38a	41a	13
Bhutan	38.0	..	…	…	…		91	53b	40b	…
India	49.3	61.0	64.3	76.4	90	…	79	…	…	22
Maldives	94.8	96.3	98.1	98.2	90	51	…	43c	45c	
Nepal	30.4	48.6	46.6	70.1	78		67	0d	0d	
Pakistan	35.4	49.9	47.4	65.5	66		70	30e	18e	
Sri Lanka	88.7	90.7	95.1	95.6	97	…	…	…	…	…

Source: World Bank, *World Development Report*, New York: Oxford University Press, 1992 & 2007; UNDP, *Human Development Report*, New York: Oxford University Press, 2006.

Note: a =2000; b=2003; c=1998; d=1995; e=2001

*= science, engineering, manufacturing & construction

enterprises. There is no security for the labour in this sector, as this sector is not effectively protected. Moreover, the raising level of inequalities in income and wealth during the process of globalization has aggravated the insecurity of labour in the unorganized sector. In the South Asian context, the labour market is characterized by pervasive unemployment and under employment. The declining share of agriculture in total employment is largely seen in the region, particularly in India, which registered a decline from 61.67 per cent in 1993-94 to 58.54 per cent in 1999-2000 and further to 54.19 per cent in 2004-05. Thus, the scope for absorbing substantial additional labour force in agriculture appears limited.[3] The same situation applies more or less to the other countries in the region.

Table 5 provides the employment by three sectors and its growth in the SAARC countries. In agriculture, females constituted a well above three-fourths, a less than three-fourths and nearly one-half shares of economic activity in Bangladesh, Pakistan and Sri Lanka respectively, against the share of well above one-half in Bangladesh, a well above two- fifths in Pakistan and a less than two- fifths in Sri Lanka recorded by males. The share of males absorbed by the industry sector was well above one-fifth in Sri Lanka and one-fifth in Pakistan, less than one-sixth in Maldives and more than one-tenth in Bangladesh. The share of females employed in industry was considerable in Maldives and Sri Lanka due to the engagement of a sizeable section of female workforce in boat construction activities and in textiles industry respectively. Higher share of employment in services sector by both males and females was also clearly visible in Maldives, owing to the vital role of tourism in the economy. Sri Lanka and Pakistan too registered a considerable share of employment by males in the services sector. The growth in employment during 1995-2001 was higher in small countries, viz. Nepal and Maldives, than in India and Pakistan. In contribution of family workers, the general trend – the higher share of females than that of males – was seen in Sri Lanka, Bangladesh and Maldives, in contrast to Pakistan which showed a reverse trend of higher share of males over females.

In India, the result of NSSO's 61st Round large-scale survey during 2004-05 showed that the annual growth rate of employment went up to 2.5 per cent during 1999-2005, after registering a decline of 1.6 per cent during 1993-2000. However, the rate of unemployment also went up marginally from 2.8 per cent to 3.1 per cent during 1999-2000 to 2004-05.[4] This situation, indicated a weak employment security in this country. The unemployment levels were also high in Pakistan and Sri Lanka.

Table-5
Employment and Growth in SAARC

Country	*Employment by economic activity in 1995-2003 (%)*						*Employment growth (%)*	*Contributing family workers in 1995-2004 (%)*	
	Agriculture		*Industry*		*Services*				
	Women	*Men*	*Women*	*Men*	*Women*	*Men*	*1995-2001*	*Women*	*Men*
Bangladesh	77	53	9	11	12	30	1.6	58	42
Bhutan							..		
India	..	..	..	..	..	..	1.0	..	..
Maldives	5	18	24	16	39	55	4.2	57	43
Nepal	..	..	..	...	..	...	5.9	..	..
Pakistan	73	44	9	20	18	36	3.2	33	67
Sri Lanka	49	38	22	23	27	37	2.4	70	30

Source: UNDP, *Human Development Report*, New York: Oxford University Press, 2006;
MHHDC, *Human Development in South Asia*, New York: Oxford University Press, 2003.

4) Food Security

Human security involves the food security which denotes mainly the purchasing power of the people to acquire the requisite amount of food items. In South Asia, food security is not guaranteed in most of the cases, due to the prevalence of large scale unemployment and the absence of social safety nets. The governments were unable to ensure employment opportunities and welfare programmes to the majority of the people. Food security can be attained when there is an increased agricultural production and an enhanced productivity per worker. Agriculture has lost priority, relative to industry and services sectors for the past two decades. As poverty is largely concentrated in rural provinces of South Asia and majority of people lives in the rural areas, the livelihood of the masses has further deteriorated. In this scenario, the only alternative available to achieve food security is to increase the agricultural production. Food security in terms of food production net per capita in 2004 (1999-2001=100) was 98.5 for the SAARC region,[5] in which Maldives, Nepal and Pakistan were impressive with 102.1; 101.1; and 100.3 respectively, while Bhutan followed by Sri Lanka registered lower per capita than the region's average.

5) Gender Justice

Gender inequity is among the sharpest social disparities in many developing countries, despite the growing concern for its reduction all over the world. It is not a single homogeneous phenomenon, but a collection of disparate and interlinked problems.[6] Though women do not enjoy the same opportunities as men, women's reduced access to health care, education and other basic needs in South Asian countries is a reflection of their worse off conditions than men. Evidence shows that the level of gender disparity in health and education is greater in South Asia than in any other region in the world.[7] Empirical studies[8] have clearly established that women in South Asia are much poorer and deprived than men. The gender gap which is largely attributed to low socio-economic status and deep-rooted patriarchal values is quite strong and conspicuous in vital areas like health, literacy, labour participation and political representation. The disparity in some of the above areas is comparable with that of sub Saharan Africa.

Table 6 projects the picture of gender disparity in the SAARC region. In societies where females are treated more equally, there are 106 women for 100 men. This pattern is not true in South Asia, in which female proportion to total population is significantly low. The shortfall was more

Table 6
Gender Disparity in SAARC
(Females as per cent of Males)

Country	*Female popn.*	*Adult female literacy*	*Female primary school gross enrolmt*	*Female 1st, 2nd & 3rd level school gross enrolmt. ratio*	*Female life expectancy at birth*	*Female economic activity rate*	*Female professional &technical workers*	*Seats in Parliament held*
	2003	2003	1998-2002	2003	1995-2003	2002/3	2003	2004
Bangladesh	96	62	101	104	101	76	25	2.0
Bhutan	97	...	76	88	104	65		8.7
India	95	65	84	88	102	50	...	9.3
Maldives	94	100	99	101	99	80	40	4.8
Nepal	102	56	87	83	99	67	...	6.4
Pakistan	94	57	74	72	100	44	26	20.6
Sri Lanka	97	96	99	102	108	56	46	4.9
South Asia	95	64	85	88	102	52	27	9.7

Source: MHHDC, *Human Development in South Asia*, New York: Oxford University Press, 2005.

pronounced in Pakistan and Maldives, reaffirming the deficit of women in their societies. The sex ratio was favourable only in Nepal, notwithstanding the gender gap in literacy, health and economic activity rates. Sri Lanka, Bhutan and Bangladesh also showed female deficit, reflecting the strong prevalence of patriarchal values. The gender disparity was significantly seen in adult literacy rate in Nepal, Pakistan, Bangladesh and India; in primary level net enrolment rates in Pakistan and Bhutan; in gross enrolment at three levels of education in Pakistan and Nepal; in life expectancy at birth in Nepal and Maldives, against the biological tendency of longevity of females over males; in female workforce in professional and technical fields in Pakistan and Bangladesh; and in the number of parliament seats held by women in Bangladesh, Maldives and Sri Lanka. Thus, even in the present years of globalization, women in the region remain far behind men in enjoying basic human rights, let alone participating on equal footing with men. However, statistics reveal that Sri Lanka and Maldives possess better education and health status of women in the region.

Priorities in Public expenditure

Today, South Asia is considered as one of the most militarized regions in the world. India and Pakistan have been suffering from historical animosity, stemmed from the violent partition of the subcontinent. These countries engaged in a number of large scale wars, smaller conflicts and unresolved disputes.[9] The other member countries also have mistrust and apprehension about each other and India is the centre for all disputes due to spill over effect from the borders, as it touches the borders of all South Asian countries. Besides, there are inter-state conflicts and internal political instabilities in majority of these countries. There is practically no South Asian country which is not disturbed by some kind of terrorism, militancy or disorder. All these conditions culminated in the escalation of military expenditure, mostly at the cost of social services.

Table 7 shows the priorities of public spending in the SAARC region. Over the decades, social spending has been neglected in South Asia, resulting in today's poor social infrastructure. Public expenditure on education as a percentage of GDP was not significant in the region as a whole, barring Bhutan and India. The increase over the years was appreciable in Nepal followed by Bangladesh. India registered only marginal increase, whereas Sri Lanka experienced a decline, owing to the corresponding increase of military expenditure. In health sector also, public expenditure as a percentage of GDP was unimpressive in South

Table 7
Priorities in Public Spending in SAARC

Country	*Public expenditure on Education (as % of GDP)*		*Public expenditure on Health (as % of GDP)*		*Defence expenditure (as % of GDP)*		*Defence expenditure (as % of central govt. expenditure)*		*Defence expenditure per capita (U S $1999 prices)*	
	1990*	2000-02	1990	2002	1985*	2003	1980	2003	1985	2003
Bangladesh	1.5	2.4	0.8	0.8	1.3	1.2	9.4	12.8	3.1	4.4
Bhutan	...	5.2	...	4.1	...	...	...	...	...	...
India	3.9	4.1	0.2	1.3	2.5	2.3	19.8	14.2	9.4	11.7
Maldives	...	3.9	...	5.1	...	...	...	...	...	...
Nepal	2.0	3.4	0.8	1.4	0.7	1.5	6.7	8.6	1.3	3.4
Pakistan	2.7	1.8	0.8	1.1	5.1	4.1	30.6	23.9	22.0	22.1
Sri Lanka	2.7	1.3	1.7	1.8	2.6	2.5	1.7	13.6	14.0	27.9
South Asia	...	3.6	...	1.0	3.0	2.4	21.3	15.0	9.9	12.2

Source: MHHDC, *Human Development in South Asia*, New York: Oxford University Press, 2005; World Bank, *World Development Report*, New York: Oxford University Press, 2000/01.

Note: * = as a % of GNP

Asian countries, with the exception of smaller countries like Maldives and Bhutan. The military spending in South Asia escalated from $ 9,839 million in 1985 to $17,190 million in 2003. The increase in annual expenditure on defence from 1985 to 2002 is surprisingly more in smaller countries, viz. Nepal and Sri Lanka, attributing to Maoist movement and the continuous ethnic struggle respectively. As per cent of GDP, the defence expenditure in 2003 is 2.4 per cent for the total region, in which Pakistan recorded the highest of 4.1 per cent. The defence expenditure of the region in 2003 as per cent of central government expenditure was fifteen. Notwithstanding the higher share in the latter year, Pakistan recorded a decline from 1980 along with India. In contrast, Sri Lanka followed by Bangladesh and Nepal witnessed a rise in the share. Defence expenditure per capita has increased in the region in general from 1985 to 2003. Sri Lanka followed by Pakistan registered the highest per capita in the region and it was doubled in the case of the former country during the above period.

India's role in Economic Security of South Asia

India, with its recent economic clout, capacity building measures and IT prowess, together with the gradual shift in the foreign policy regime to suit to the rapid changes in the global issues, deserves a special status in the SAARC region. India will continue to benefit from the demographic dividend until 2045 and will provide a huge market for the global consumer products. India is one of the fastest emerging global powers and is both a factor for peace and stability, as well as a dynamic economic player in the region, despite its relatively lower human development index (HDI) than the smaller neighbours. Since one and a half decades, Sri Lanka and Maldives have been registering a medium human development (as per the HDI, estimated by the UNDP). The rest of SAARC countries were under the category of low human development till recently. Of late, these countries have also joined the former group with improved performance, despite the wide disparity in HDI values. India's latest efforts at improving social infrastructure assumed significance, in view of its low HDI ranks in the recent years.

The central government expenditure of the country on social sector and rural development have gone up consistently over the years. However, there has been insignificant growth in the social indicators. This again is pointing out to the ineffective governance in implementing various programmes, besides the limited increase in its funding.

Table 8
India's Position on Human and Gender Development in South and Southeast Asia

Country	*Human development index (HDI)*		*HDI Rank*		*Gender development index (GDI)*		*GDI Rank*	
	2000	*2004*	*2000*	*2004*	*2000*	*2004*	*2000*	*2004*
Singapore	0.885	0.916	25	25	0.880	...	24	...
Korea, Rep. of	0.882	0.912	27	26	0.875	0.905	29	25
Malaysia	0.782	0.805	59	61	0.776	0.795	54	51
Thailand	0.762	0.784	70	74	0.760	0.781	60	58
China	0.730	0.768	96	81	0.699	0.765	77	64
Philippines	0.754	0.763	77	84	0.751	0.761	63	66
Sri Lanka	0.747	0.755	89	93	0.737	0.749	70	68
Maldives	0.743	0.739	84	98	0.739	...	68	...
Indonesia	0.682	0.711	110	108	0.678	0.704	91	81
India	0.577	0.611	124	126	0.560	0.591	105	96
Pakistan	0.511	0.539	138	134	0.468	0.513	120	105
Bangladesh	0.510	0.530	145	137	0.468	0.524	121	102
Nepal	0.500	0.527	142	138	0.470	0.513	119	106

Source: UNDP, *Human Development Report*, New York: Oxford University Press, 2002 & 2006.

As in Table 8, India's HDI in terms of value and rank is much lower not only than that of major Southeast and East Asian countries, but also of the South Asian countries, Sri Lanka and Maldives, reflecting the absence of improvement in its social fabric from 2000 to 2004 and more so, it shows a marginal fall from the former year. Philippines in the Southeast Asian region also recorded a decline in the ranks of HDI and gender-related development index (GDI). Aside from the considerable drop in HDI in Maldives, the countries showing a moderate decline were Thailand, Sri Lanka and Malaysia, against China with a record of appreciable rise during the above period. The GDI rank of India in the latter year showed a considerable improvement from the former.

Being the lead country in the grouping, India draws attention in the SAARC framework. The other South Asian countries try to emulate India's growth pattern in their own ways. India, recognizing the vital importance of the agriculture sector in maintaining human security in various forms, has turned back its focus on its once primary sector. Though

India has not attained social security, it can ensure economic security to some extent by enlarging its economic space and opening its doors to the member countries. Thus, with redefining priority on agriculture, India could pave the way for the enhancement of economic growth of the neighbouring countries, because most of these countries were agro-based till recently and majority of the people eked out their livelihood from agriculture sector.

Conclusion

South Asia is now being projected as one of the important regions unlike earlier, as the global players have shown keen interest to join the SAARC as observers. Though the governments of the South Asian states have realized that it is high time to shift their focus from the security of the borders to human security along with regional cooperation, much action is not taken in this direction, perhaps due to the mindset about the territorial security and national sovereignty.

The low levels of human security in South Asia is revealed by the high incidence of poverty, the poor show by the education and health sectors and the lack of employment potential, which also indicates the food insecurity to the rural masses. The role of the government is vital in ensuring job opportunities to the raw and unskilled labour through strengthening the existing training programmes, besides setting up new ones. A faster growth in employment is greatly needed not only to wipe out the unemployment rate of the additional labour force, but also to be in tune with the on going demographic changes. Firm commitment is required on the part of the governments to transform the physical labour into human resources through raising the expenditure on social infrastructure. Implementation of welfare programmes and provision of social safety nets are required in the region to improve the standard of living of the deprived sections. Needless to say, committed governance will deliver the goods. The gender gap in the social indicators also emphasizes the urgency of greater participation of women in development programmes to mitigate the influence of patriarchy, besides underscoring the need for devising affirmative action plans to ensure a fair deal for women.

The performance of some of the South Asian countries on the human security count is impressive. The region has varied experiences in poverty reduction and social development. Hence, it is important for policy makers to draw up on success stories within their own countries, apart from the neighbouring countries in the Southeast Asian countries. The success stories of Sri Lanka, Maldives and Kerala in India, which achieved progress in expanding basic human capabilities, in terms of education, health care, welfare measures, community and state participation and implementation of effective poverty alleviation programmes, etc, serve as a paragon in the region. Notwithstanding the income levels, these states proved that the reasonable quality of living can be attained with strong will.

The rising spending on military expenditure in South Asia has a negative impact on access to education, health care and other welfare measures. This kind of non-productive investment undermines the living standards of the people, whose standards are already under the normal standards. The higher percentage of GDP on military implies the lower share on social services. Hence, there is a greater need to divert the scarce resources from the defence to the welfare of the people, which in turn requires higher degree of peace process and regional cooperation among the countries. These low income countries will have to raise the human security levels, otherwise they will suffer further by lagging behind the rest of the world.

References

1. Mehbub Ul Haq Human Development Centre, *Human Development in South Asia*, New York: Oxford University Press, 2005, p. 12.
2. *Ibid.*
3. Government of India, Ministry of Finance, *Economic Survey*, 2006-07, p. 211
4. *Ibid.*
5. See n.1.
6. Amartya Sen, "Many Faces of Gender Inequality", *Frontline*, 9 November 2001, pp.4-9.
7. Deon Filmer, Elizabeth King and Lant Pritchett, 'Gender Disparity in South Asia: Comparisons between and within Countries', Mimeo, January, World Bank, Washington D.C., 1998.
8. Ponna Wignaraja, *Women, Poverty and Resources*, New Delhi: Sage Publications, 1990, pp. 18-20.
9. Haq, n. 1.

7

Peace, Neighbourly Diplomacy and Poverty Reduction for Building a New South Asia

Som P Pudasaini

The South Asian region is confronted with varieties of conflicts. Insurgencies have been matters of concerns to India in the North East and the Maoists problem in over 130 districts in a dozen states, to Bhutan in areas adjoining NE India and Bangladesh in the Hill Tracts. The Maoists insurgency has seriously affected Nepal for over a decade and Sri Lankan ethnic conflict that started in 1983 has already cost over 65,000 lives and tremendous drag to its progress. Afghanistan is troubled with conflicts for a long time. The tensions between India and Pakistan have been going on for over five decades. Pakistan's North West Frontier Province, Karachi and some other parts of the country have also been troubled with ethnic conflicts. South Asia also suffers from significant and mundane diplomatic irritants. Pakistan-India tensions and a small nation Indian mindset in dealing with its smaller neighbours in spite of its overwhelming size and military strength have been serious impediments to good neighbourly diplomacy and regionalism for years. Over 437 million people of South Asia, which accounts for thirty one per cent of its population, suffer from extreme poverty and survive on less than one dollar a day. South Asia is surpassed only by Sub-Saharan Africa in terms of severity of poverty problem. In short, South Asia is a broad conglomeration of eight big and small nations with over twenty two per cent of the global population and less than five per cent of the physical area. Poverty eradication, lasting peace and good neighbourly diplomacy is indispensable to build a prosperous South Asia based on shared wisdom, destiny and comparative advantages.

South Asia includes the seven original members-Bangladesh, Bhutan, India, Maldives, Nepal, Pakistan and Sri Lanka of the South Asian

Association for Regional Association (SAARC) plus a new entrant Afghanistan. It represents a broad conglomeration of eight big and small nations of South Asia region with varying levels of conflict, poverty, population, economic growth and political stability (Tables 1-3). Three members – Afghanistan, Bhutan and Nepal – are landlocked. Two members – Maldives and Sri Lanka – are sea locked. The remaining three – Bangladesh, India and Pakistan – are linked to both sea and landmass. India with a population of about 1.1 billion people is the largest while the Maldives with about 300,000 people is the smallest. Broadly speaking, India represents almost seventy per cent of the population, economy, and geographic area of SAARC and is the only member state that shares boarders with all the seven.

SAARC with over twenty two per cent (1.45 billion) of the global population (6.37 billion, 2004) and less than five per cent of the physical area is one of the most densely populated regions of the world with a huge mass of poor, illiterate and deprived peoples. The global population (7.57 billion) share of South Asia is projected to rise to over 24.4 per cent (1.84 billion) by 2020 (Table 1). India is galloping with annual economic growth rate of seven to nine per cent while the others have also registered impressive economic growth rates. Four of the key SAARC nations – Bangladesh, India, Pakistan, Sri Lanka – registered GDP growth rate of over six per cent in 2005 and expected to do as well in the future, including 2008 (Table 3). Nepal going through turbulent economic and political times resulting from the Maoist conflict registered economic growth rate of 2.5 per cent in 2005 and is expected to register 4.5 per cent in 2008.

Afghanistan with population of 22.2 million in 2003 was reported to have attained GDP growth of five per cent in 2003.[1] However, Afghan politics, security and economy have been shaky and are likely to continue to be so in the near future. Bhutan's economy seems to be doing well, largely due to its ability to harness hydro-electricity and sell it to India with a massive financial and technical assistance from the latter. The Maldivian economy generally doing well is overly dependent on tourism and needs to diversify to ward off unduly adverse consequences in the periods of tourist slump resulting from internal or external or both factors. Two nations – India and Pakistan – are now nuclear powers. Most nations suffer from various degrees and types of illegal boarder activities, cross-boarder terrorism, internal insurgencies and conflicts, socio-economic inequalities and poverty. Minor and major irritants exist among a number of South Asian neighbours.

Table 1: Population, Per Capita Income, Poverty and Human Development Index

Country/ Region	*Pop. Below 1 $ a day (%)*	*Population (millions)*		*%population Growth Rate in 2004*	*HDI*	*$ Per capita GNI 2004*
		2004	*2020*			
Bangladesh	36	139	181	1.7	139	404
Bhutan	–	0.9	–	2.7	134	–
India	35	1080	1332	1.5	127	620
Maldives	–	0.3	–	2.2	96	–
Nepal	39	27	36	2.2	136	260
Pakistan	17	152	212	2.5	135	600
Sri Lanka	6	19	23	1.3	93	1010

Sources : *World Development Indicators 2006*; *World Development Report 2006*

Most of the nations of the SAARC have been linked with history, geography, culture, economy and people-to-people contacts. Diplomatic, economic and political relations between member states can and must be sorted out by removing any prevailing irritants to attain prosperity, build regional amity and peace, and eradicate poverty. This paper aims to briefly deal with the situation and importance of building peace, friendly diplomatic relations and poverty reduction for the wellbeing of the peoples of the South Asia and promotion of regionalism.

Conflict Resolution and Peace Building

The South Asian region is confronted with varieties of conflicts, insurgencies and terrorism that affect nations internally, bilaterally or the region collectively. Some have been around for decades. Others have cropped up in not so distant past. However, all of them must be managed or resolved to an acceptable level through national, bilateral and collective efforts to build peace, stability and harmony so vital for the progress and prosperity of the peoples of South Asia. Insurgencies have been matters of concern to India in the North East and to Bhutan in areas adjoining Northeast India.

The Maoists insurgency in India that started in Naxalbari of West Bengal over four decades ago has left its seed in many states, including Andhra Pradesh and Bihar, and is now believed to be a serious and rising threat in over 130 districts scattered over almost a dozen states.

Bangladesh has faced insurgency in the Hill Tracts. The Maoists insurgency in Nepal has seriously affected political stability and socio-economic progress for over a decade now.

It is believed that the Maoists insurgencies in Nepal and India are reported to be linked to some extent and such insurgencies cropping up in other countries may be fed by the Maoist insurgencies in Nepal and India. Sri Lankan ethnic conflict that started in 1983 has already cost over 65,000 lives and tremendous loss of economic progress for the Island state. It has socio-economic and strategic implications to India, particularly to the state of Tamil Nadu. Afghanistan is troubled with long lasting internal conflict. Its internal and tribal conflicts have been influenced by external forces. It is now one of the most unstable nations in the South Asia region and attempting hard to ensure peace and stability. The presence of external army consisting of various nationalities, including the US and EU, and the threat of Al-Qaeda and Taliban is a matter of serious concerns for security and peace of Afghanistan and the region, particularly to that of Pakistan. Similarly, the Taliban and Al-Qaeda fighters and sympathizers hiding in the Pakistani territories bordering Afghanistan are reported to be problematic to the security and stability of the latter.

The tensions between India and Pakistan, including over the Kashmir issue, has been going on for over five decades seriously dampening their bilateral relations. The conflict has affected political, economic, trade and security strengthening initiatives in the SAARC. Pakistan's North West Frontier Province, Karachi and some other parts of the country have also suffered or are continuing to be troubled with ethnic conflicts and insurgencies. Bangladesh and India have encountered tensions related to water sharing arrangements and at times clashes in their border. For SAARC to prosper as a region and for its members as individual nations the prevailing internal as well as bilateral conflicts must be managed better or resolved with internal as well as collective efforts. Since the domestic as well as bilateral tensions or conflicts are unlikely to have military solution they must be addressed through dialogues.

Success of negotiations or dialogues depends on five Cs: clarity, confidence, compromise, continuity and commitment. The five Cs may have relevance to both the internal and intra-country conflicts. First of all, successful negotiations demand a minimum clarity on negotiating position or 'bottom-line.' Secondly, adequate confidence between the negotiating parties and amicable chemistry between negotiating teams are essential to sustain talks to logical conclusion in the face of many unexpected roadblocks. Thirdly, compromise or flexibility to adjust expectations, egos and positions as per the unfolding reality remains at the heart of sound negotiations. Fourthly, continuity must be maintained in talks or dialogues regardless of setbacks in the processes. Fifthly, without a rock-solid commitment nothing succeeds. Last but not least, the sooner the remedies for root causes of the conflict – strategic, political, economic, territorial, ideological, ethnic, linguistic, inequalities – are addressed the better will be the prospects for a lasting peace. Over forty per cent of internal conflicts are reported to return within five years and fifty per cent within ten years if the root-causes are not handled adequately as a part of a post-conflict development.[2]

Promoting non-violence and building peace within a nation and between nations has never been more important than it is now as the contemporary world is being inflicted by varieties of conflicts, religious fundamentalism, ethnic tensions and terrorism. The Gandhian philosophy of peaceful coexistence, non-violence and respect for human dignity was against the medieval doctrine of the 'Might is Right.' At the heart of his model of non-violence exists religious tolerance, ethnic harmony and secularism. Justice, equality, non-interference and democracy are integral part of building peace and promoting non-violence. Gandhi was for stemming the tide of too materialistic civilization based on competitive greed and exploitation of man by man. Since man can not live by 'bread alone' his crusades placed due focus on spiritualism and human values. Gautam Buddha, the son of this region born in Lumbini in Nepal and achieved Nirvan under a bodhi tree in India, has been inspiring and guiding generations for the past 2700 years, including Gandhi, to follow the path of non-violence and peace. Nevertheless, our own generation and region has failed to adequately benefit from his wisdom and teachings in building peace within nations of the SAARC and in the South Asian region.

Norwegian experience of supporting peace initiatives across the continents, including Palestine and Sri Lanka, demonstrates that today's conflicts around the globe and within the South Asian region are overwhelmingly asymmetrical and the internal armed rebellions or insurgencies that are unlikely to be settled militarily. The purpose of peace dialogue is to transform violent conflict into a problem-solving partnership concerning political power, access to resources and imbalanced development.[3] Peace process needs to address immediate issues related to violence cessation as well as the longer term root causes of the conflict such as inequality, poverty, gender discrimination. While peace processes vary from one conflict to the other, it is invariably essential to have commitment of the parties to negotiate and reach a political resolution for any talks to succeed.

A pragmatic peace process follows a gradual approach dealing with confidence building measures and urgent issues related to violence in the beginning and more contentious issues in the later part of negotiations. Non-territorial conflicts need to deal with disarmament, demobilization and reintegration of the combatants but should also handle root-causes in the long term. Involvement of non-armed groups and civil society in the peace process is crucial for lasting peace as the whole society is affected or involved in the conflict. External actors can contribute to peace process provided that all the parties in conflict agree and the external actors have influence and genuine commitments to the welfare of the concerned people. However, the parties in the conflict must take a lead and resolve their own problems. Others, if at all, can help at the most.

In terms of internal conflicts, all the nations of the South Asian region are making efforts to find solution internally or with some external support. The Maoist insurgency in Nepal that started in 1996 and cost over 13,000 lives is being settled through a dialogue between the Maoists- Communist Party of Nepal CPN (Maoist) and the Seven Party Alliance (SPA). The United Nations is involved in supervising and monitoring arms management with the formal consent of the Maoists and the government of Nepal. The UN involvement in Nepal has a tacit support from global and regional powers; including India and US. The resolution of Sri Lankan ethnic conflict has been facilitated by the Norwegians. After some impressive negotiation between the LTTE and the Sri Lankan government in February 2002 ceasefire, the Sri Lankan conflict has faced serious setbacks in the past years as over 4,000 deaths are reported to have occurred since 2005 as a result of violent encounters between the LTTE and the government forces. The internal insurgencies and conflicts in India, Pakistan and Bangladesh are being tackled internally with a combination of dialogue and military force. Bhutan insurgency suppression is aided by the Indian security forces in northeast India.

It is recently reported that the Bhutanese refugees (over 40,000) "languishing in north Bengal, Sikkim and Assam, which boarder with Bhutan" have formed the Bhutanese Communist Party-Maoists (BCP-M)" as they are frustrated with the 'debhutanization' undertaken by Bhutan during the early 1990s that "rendered over 150,000 Bhutanese citizens stateless."[4] Almost 108,000 of the Bhutanese refugees are also languishing in several refugee camps in eastern Nepal over the past sixteen years and a group of the refugees "seems to have lent support to BCP-M for raising armed-struggle in Bhutan.....The delay and subsequent denial of repatriation have forced the refugees to opt for a radical solution to the problem." In addition to the Bhutanese refugees, the South Asian region is also yet to handle the problems of Afghan, Bangladeshi, Tamil, Tibetan, Chakmas refugees properly. The frustration that brews among refugees living under almost inhumane conditions with no hope of return to their rightful places and better outlet in the foreseeable future turns out to be a breeding ground for insurgencies and socially unwanted activities.

Countries of the SAARC have adopted various strategies to resolve their internal conflicts and bilateral tensions with some success and some failures. Based on the past experiences, the strategies may have to be carefully analyzed to come up with useful lessons learned to introduce more effective corrective strategies. For instance, in many internal conflicts it may be more effective to support dialogues on sound socio-economic and political packages that address the root-causes of the conflicts than the current practices of greater focus on the use of force. Similarly, the key political actors within every country and important powers in the South Asian region may have to play a more harmonious and active role if the external interferences, such as in Afghanistan, are to be minimized. Being two most powerful countries of the region, the resolution of Pakistan-India tensions will have an overwhelming bearing on the resolution of socio-economic and political tensions and their constructive role will have a very beneficial effect on the resolution of conflicts in the region.

Good Neighbourly Diplomacy

The nations of the South Asian region suffer from significant and mundane economic, political and diplomatic irritants. Three dominant problems may need prompt and adequate attention.

First, Pakistan-India tensions are the biggest bottleneck for the promotion of SAARC regionalism and functioning of the region and hurdle for the promotion of peaceful neighbourhood and neighbourly diplomacy. Secondly, a small nation Indian mindset in dealing with its smaller neighbours in spite of its overwhelming size, population, economy and military strength has been an impediment to good neighbourly diplomatic and economic relations in the region. The Cold War politics and India's sluggish economy may have played a role in setting the mindset. Thirdly, the smaller nations' inadequate confidence and inability to handle their own economic, social and political issues internally may also have apportioned a share of the blame larger than deserved by India.

However, there are signs of positive changes in all the three fronts in the recent years and months. Pakistan-India relations are beginning to take positive momentum unseen in the past five decades. India is now a dynamic nation seeking to rub its shoulder with the global powers and seems to be increasingly interested to have its regional turf in harmony and peace to be trusted as a power to recon with by others. With Indian attitude, particularly its foreign policy establishment sounding much more pragmatic and friendly, 'peace periphery' and peaceful neighbourhood and much more friendly diplomacy conducive to regionalism appears to be in the offing.

India is reported to be planning to announce a special package to facilitate market access to the four least developed SAARC member states – Bangladesh, Bhutan, Maldives and Nepal – to expedite its commitments in line with the South Asian Free Trade Agreement (SAFTA). This is an encouraging move if it happens in both principle and practice. India's commitment to regionalism would be reassuring to the smaller member states as they have been insisting on SAARC regionalism from the beginning of its establishment for over two decades while India has been perceived to have taken the SAARC as a mechanism to gang up against it by the smaller neighbours initially.

Almost 1,08,000 Bhutanese refugees are languishing in temporary camps in Nepal for sixteen years and there is no sign of the resolution of the problem. India has a big role to play in the resolution of the problem as the refugees came to Nepal through Indian territories and India has significant leverage in its relations with both the countries. The Kathmandu Post in its editorial entitled "who is responsible?" dated 21 March 2007 states that both India and Bhutan are responsible for the potential insurgency by CPB (Maoist) as they "denied the refugees right to return to Bhutan, despite Nepal's persistent repatriation effort. The recent deployment of three battalions of paramilitary forces along the Indo-Bhutan border also indicates that India is well aware of possible flare up of an armed insurgency." The issues related to Bangladeshi and Afghani refugees largely concentrated in India and Pakistan may have to be dealt properly. Tamil, Chakmas and host of other refugees are languishing in the region. The right to return to their country of origin is an inviolable right of the refugees under international law and has assumed the status of a 'Peremptory norm' under such law. However, under many circumstances the refugees are not allowed to return by their own country rulers as a matter of political vendetta, ethnic cleansing or other reasons. Local assimilation and/or the third country resettlement then become alternative options. SAARC may have to consider a regional mechanism and procedures to resolve refugee issues based on bilateral and regional arrangements

The foremost need is to build a good neighbourly foreign policy among SAARC nations by resolving irritants through dialogue. Poverty reduction, security, water resources, river-linking, energy, border demarcation, terrorism, trade and regulating illegal activities at the international borders demand greater commitment and understanding. Proper review of past treaties and conventions, including the 1950 India-Nepal treaty, may have to be undertaken and more equitable agreements in the future must be assured. Consistent and clear positions must be initiated to deal with the refugee problem. Millennium development goals, environment, girl trafficking and gender are serious matters. Rights based approaches are at the heart of contemporary developmental and diplomatic debates. Human rights standard is now important issue to be addressed properly. The pressures, benefits and risks from globalization and other regional blocks must constitute a priority for both regional and national economic diplomacy as business and diplomacy are quite inter-linked in the contemporary world.

Intellectuals, diplomats and media personalities in the SAARC appear optimistic in their debates on the need and prospect for regionalism in South Asia. Kanak Dixit[5] from Nepal observes that "India has been the late comer to South Asia" in spite of its size and long history and has been "locked up for too long in a small country mindset." India has now realized that it needs a 'tidy home turf' with commitment to South Asian regionalism if it is to find a proper place among the global powers. While the Indian foreign policy establishment was believed to have taken SAARC as the small neighbours 'ganging up' against it initially, its changed economic, political and strategic interests as a fast expanding economy and military power are significantly enhancing its commitment to regionalism and SAARC. Obviously, the South Asian regionalism contains strong potential for social and economic progress across the SAARC countries through peace dividend, commerce and comparative advantage.

C. Raja Mohan[6] from India believes that India's new regionalism commits to "creating long-term economic interdependence" and has a strong will to move the South Asian region to 'shared prosperity.' He finds New Delhi's foreign policy establishment's emphasis on a 'peace periphery' and resolutions of disputes in the neighbourhood are unprecedented. Negotiations with Pakistan have picked up sincere momentum and both the nations are believed to be much more serious not to let the initiatives to reduce tensions and resolve long standing bilateral problems, including the Kashmir issue, be sidelined by any minor events as in the past.

M. Yusuf[7] from Pakistan emphasizes that India-Pakistan relations largely determine the peace and prosperity of the South Asian region "given the over-bearing size of the two economies and their military strength." Peace and harmony between India and Pakistan will energize the SAARC region. Yusuf emphasizes that balancing 'disparities' in military strengths and India's strong 'market leverage' will be crucial for regional peace and progress. Imtiaz Ahmed[8] from Bangladesh believes that "putting the Indo-Bangladesh relationship on stable foundations requires looking beyond Dhaka-New Delhi bilateralism to SAARC regionalism or multilateralism."

India's acceptance of UN arms monitoring mission in Nepal designed to facilitate peace process to mainstream the Maoists insurgents waging a violent conflict since 1996 and its revision of Bhutan Treaty in February 2007 to release it from foreign policy and security clutch existing for over five decades bodes well to promotion of regionalism. While India has a major responsibility to promote and strengthen South Asian regionalism all the other nations will have to politically, economically, diplomatically and strategically do their shares to expedite the process faster.

Poverty Reduction

Reduction of poverty and hunger constitutes an important objective under the millennium development goals (MDG). The SAARC also aims to alleviate poverty and has been working on poverty reduction strategies for a long time.

Table 2
People Living on Less than $1 per Day

Region	*1981*		*2002*	
	per cent	*No (millions)*	*per cent*	*No (millions)*
East Asia and Pacific	58	796	12	214
Europe and Central Asia	0.7	3	2	10
Latin America and Caribbean	10	36	9	47
Middle East & North Africa	5	9	2	5
South Asia	52	475	31	437
Sub-Saharan Africa	42	164	44	303
Total	40	1482	19	1015

Source: World Development Indicators 2006

Regardless of the global and regional strategies and goals, over one billion people of the world, which account for about nineteen per cent of the global population, suffer from extreme poverty and survive on less than one dollar a day (Table 2). The problem of poverty is even worse in South Asia as thirty one per cent of its population live on one dollar a day.

While the proportion of the people living below absolute poverty line has been reduced from fifty two per cent in 1981 to thirty one per cent in 2004, the number of poor in the SAARC nations has been only marginally reduced from 475 million to 437 million during the period. South Asia is surpassed only by Sub-Saharan Africa in terms of severity of poverty menace. A significant reduction in poverty is indispensable to build a humane, fair and prosperous South Asia. While progress is being made in poverty reduction in the region and the fifty per cent poverty reduction target set under the MDG is likely to be achieved by 2015, a concerted and significant effort will be necessary to reduce poverty to a desired level if it can not be eradicated completely in the near future.

Poverty reduction efforts will have to have a greater rural focus as the level and proportion of the poverty is much higher in the rural areas relative to urban areas. For instance, the proportion of people below poverty line declined in Nepal from forty two per cent in 1995-96 to thirty one per cent in 2002-03.[9] However, the proportion of rural poverty (34.6 per cent) is significantly higher than that in urban areas (9.6). Illiteracy, poor or no skills, malnutrition and poor health, and lack of productive resources, including landlessness, are among the key factors to be considered in poverty reduction.[10] The experiences of SAARC countries so far is that either the increase in labour force has exceeded employment generation or employment increases have occurred in low productivity areas, including self employment.

Effective and pragmatic poverty reduction approaches demand that women and youth receive due focus. Significant increase in gainful employment, particularly for youth and rural sector, is obviously crucial. The global youth population (12-24 years) is over 1.5 billion of which over 1.3 billion are in the developing nations; quite a few being in South Asia. Youth unemployment is one of the biggest sources of social discontent and root-cause for insurgencies and tensions in many developing countries.

Health, education and gainful employment are among the most critical areas for poverty reduction. The three leading factors for disease, disability or death are poor nutrition, unsafe sex; unsafe water and poor sanitation. HIV/AIDS are becoming serious menace in the SAARC region, particularly India and Nepal. They must be addressed in the context of poverty reduction. Poor living conditions and the pandemic clearly thrive on poverty and accelerate poverty as demonstrated by experiences in Asia, Africa and beyond. SAARC has taken some initiatives to develop poverty reduction strategies and establish poverty reduction fund but has not made much headway. The region has expertise and can mobilize internal and external resources to tackle the poverty menace provided political commitment and pragmatic roadmap is assured.

Many countries of the region are registering impressive economic growth (6-9 per cent per year) and India is likely to do even better in the future. However, the benefits of growth and development has failed to adequately reach the most needy people and disadvantaged regions, particularly the urban poor, disadvantaged in the villages and far flung peripheries. One can not totally rely on the 'trickle down effect' of growth. Consequently, poverty reduction strategies must be given adequate emphasis while promoting a faster economic growth.

Table 3: GDP Growth in per cent

Country/Region	*1990-2000*	*2000-2004*	*2005*	*2008*
Bangladesh	4.8	5.2	6.2	6.5
India	6.0	6.2	8.5	7,2
Nepal	4.9	2.5	2.7	4.5
Pakistan	3.8	4.1	7.8	6.5
Sri Lanka	5.3	3.7	6.0	6.0
South Asia	5.6	5.8	– –	– –
East Asia and Pacific	8.5	8.1	– –	– –

Source: *World Bank, 2006, 2007*

The average per capita gross national income in the region is very low, about $300 in Nepal to slightly over $1000 in Sri Lanka. The Human Development Index (HDI) is also not impressive. The best HDI is ninety three for Sri Lanka and the worst is 139 for Bangladesh, the rest being in between. Consequently, efforts to enhance overall economic status must be combined with poverty reduction strategies, including better and reasonable distributive approach. Poverty reduction is recognized as an important issue in the region and there are desires for shared prosperity, particularly among common folks. Agreeing on policies for poverty reduction may be easier but prompt and proper implementation is likely to be much harder. However, the people of

SAARC are envisioning a New South Asia free from abject poverty and leaders must not fail the people.

Poverty and inequality are considered to be among the key causes of conflicts and human miseries in the developing world. Both poverty and socio-economic inequalities are endemic in the region. For instance, the income of ten per cent richest in the region is 6.8 to 9.3 times higher relative to the ten per cent poorest in the region – for Bangladesh, India, Pakistan, Sri Lanka and Nepal – the figures being 6.8, 7.3, 7.6, 8.1 and 9.3 times respectively. "By placing equity and fairness as central elements of an efficient development strategy, developing countries will be better able to reach sustainable growth – equitable growth paths are likely to lead to faster reductions in the many dimensions of poverty, the central objective of development everywhere."[11]

Conclusion

India-Pakistan dialogues are taking unprecedented momentum. The Maoists insurgency in Nepal is being gradually tackled through peace talks and efforts are underway to mainstream the Maoists. There is agreement to settle contentious socio-economic and political issues through the Constituent Assembly elections scheduled for mid June 2007 (postponed and likely to be in 2008) followed by a new democratic and inclusive constitution. Bhutan is in the process of moving towards more democratic governance with elections planned for 2008. Sri Lanka's peace initiatives have been facing some setbacks after making significant headways after the ceasefire agreement was signed between LTTE and the government in February 2002. The elections planned for January 2007 have been postponed in Bangladesh and political disturbances seem to be developing. Afghanistan will probably take time to stabilize its economy and security. India's foreign policy is now friendlier towards the promotion of regionalism and is emphasizing the development of peaceful neighbourhood. Poverty reduction is recognized as an important issue in the region and there is a desire for shared prosperity. The counties of the SAARC, particularly India, are growing much faster economically.

The resolution of Pakistan-India tensions will have an overwhelming bearing on the resolution of socio-economic and political tensions as they are the two most important economic and military powers within the South Asian region. SAARC may also benefit if some appropriate mechanism is established to facilitate conflict resolution and refugee repatriation in the best interest of its member nations and the region. Peace building and good neighbourly relations are crucial to strengthen regionalism and enhance shared prosperity in the SAARC.[12]

Agreeing on policies and plans for regionalism, poverty reduction, good neighbourly diplomacy and peace building is one thing but prompt and proper implementation is likely to be much harder. A thousand miles journey always starts with the first step. SAARC has now willingness, rising commitment and favourable environment to move together. It is important that the leaders of the SAARC and the people of the region build on this foundation and enhance it in every opportunity. India, as the biggest and most powerful member nation of the SAARC has a big responsibility to steer the region forward with a magnanimous heart.

The other nations, particularly Pakistan as the second most powerful country in long conflict and competition with India, will have to genuinely contribute their share. India is reported to have already pledged $100 million to a SAARC Fund to be used for poverty reduction and development activities. Establishment of a South Asian University in India and Agricultural Fund to deal with regional food security is being considered during the meeting. The US, EU, China and South Korea would be participating as observers. Iran is interested to acquire an observer status. Obviously, the interest of key players seems to be increasing towards the Association.

While two decades have been lost with only limited progress it is hoped that SAARC leaders are ready to truly commit to the South Asian regionalism. Can the SAARC leaders now rise above petty national interests and ego to commit to the South Asian regionalism to build a prosperous region through shared wisdom and resources based on equality, friendship, understanding and comparative advantages? The people of SAARC are envisioning a new South Asia free from violent conflicts and poverty. They wish to have a dynamic region where peace, good neighbourly relations, poverty eradication and shared prosperity represent a collective dream.[13]

References

1. World Bank, *Afghanistan- State Building, Sustaining Growth and Reducing Poverty*, February 2005.
2. Som P. Pudasaini, "Peace Talks and Post-Conflict Roadmap", *The Kathmandu Post*, 5 July 2006.
3. Som P. Pudasaini, "An Overview of the Norwegian Experiences", A Report of the Seminar on *Sharing Norwegian Experiences in Conflict Resolution and Mediation*, Nepal Council of World Affairs, Kathmandu, 5 March 2006.

4. Editorial, "Who's responsible?", *The Kathmandu Post*, 21 March 2007.
5. Kanak Mani Dixit, "India Realizing Southasia", *Himal South Asia*, vol.20, no. 3, March 2007.
6. C.Raja Mohan, "India's New Regionalism", *ibid.*
7. Moeed Yusuf, "India-Pakistan Roadblock to Regional Peace", *ibid.*
8. Ahmed Imtiaz, "The Indo-Bangla SAARC Puzzle", *ibid.*
9. National Planning Commission, *Poverty Trends in Nepal*, NPC Secretariat, Central Bureau of Statistics, Kathmandu, September 2005
10. SAARC Secretariat, *SAARC Regional Poverty Profile 2005: Poverty Reduction in South Asia through Productive Employment*, Kathmandu, August 2006
11. World Bank, *World Development Report 2006.*
12. Som P. Pudasaini, "SAARC, Conflict Resolution and Peace Building", nepalnews.com, http://www.nepalnews.com.np/archive/2007/others/guestcolumn/mar/guest columns 12php, 26 March 2007
13. Som P. Pudasaini, "SAARC and Poverty Reduction Commitment", *The Kathmandu Post*, 26 March 2007.

8

Human Security in South Asia: Some Observations

Adluri Subramanyam Raju

The term security is often regarded securing the state and protecting its borders from external threats. Since the Westphalia, the states have become the building blocks of the international system. Thereafter, the military security acquired special attention and thereby the states started allocating more budget for defence related activities. Security is constructed in military terms and against the external threats. Thus, all nations showed a tendency to protect their national interests.

In the post Cold War period, there are rapid changes on many fronts – economic, social, political, environmental and human. These changes provided not only opportunities but also challenges to the security of people. As a result the focus has been shifted from the protection of borders to security of people. The factors for the paradigm shift from traditional to non-traditional security could be as follows:

- Globalization,
- Rise of civil movements and questioning the authority,
- Collapse of effective governance,
- Penetrating new technology,
- States inability to tackle issues,
- Increasing conflicts within national borders (intra-state conflicts) than external aggression,
- Old threats are being intensified and new threats to human security are emerging.

In the contemporary times, the non-military threats are gaining importance. There is a sharp increase in drug trafficking, massive spread of AIDS, environmental degradation, unemployment, poverty, starvation, epidemics, ethnic conflicts[1], religious animosities and civil wars etc. All of these issues are posing a far more serious and immediate challenge to the security of human beings than the military threats. People are suffering more within the states than from external aggressions. Many people have died or suffered from internal conflicts within countries than in wars between countries in the past two decades. In the 1990s 3.6 million people lost their lives in intra-state conflicts, whereas 2,20,000 have died from inter-state wars. About six million people were forced to leave their homes by the end of 2000.[2] People should lead a normal life without facing any threat.

Human security is concerned for people – how they live, how they exercise their choices and whether they live in conflict or in peace. Mahbub Ul Haq in the UNDP's Human Development Report of 1994 observed that "Human security is a child who did not die, a disease that did not spread, a job that was not cut, an ethnic tension that did not explode in violence, a dissident who was not silenced. Human security is not a concern with weapons – it is a concern with human life and dignity.... It is concerned with how people live and breathe in a society, how freely they exercise their many choices, how much access they have to market and social opportunities – and whether they live in conflict or in peace."[3] Hence, there is a pressing need to focus on the humanistic aspect of the security debate.

The concept of security is extended from military to political, economic, environment or human security. In other words, human security does not mean that issues related to military can be ignored. They are equally important to protect people from violence and restore democracy. For instance, the state has to protect its people from terrorist activities. The fight against terrorism will reinforce a focus on state security and defense of borders and thus one cannot ignore the military preparedness against the non-state belligerents. The state is expected to maintain the security of its borders as well as the security of the individuals. It is state's obligation, apart from protecting the people from external conflicts, to ensure that its people enjoy their rights and are able to live with a sense of dignity without any fear. Thus, the state has to reorient its policies to address the problems of human beings. The threats to human security are far more numerous and complex than the threats to state security. Thus, the absence of bi-polar world order and the quest for a new international system initiated a debate on alternative approach to security, i.e. comprehensive security, combining traditional and non-traditional dimensions. Human and state security should be treated on par since both are equally important. Both are interlinked and cannot be separated. The UNDP has called for "a transition from the narrow concept of national security to the 'all-encompassing concept of human security."[4] There are two approaches to human security, i.e. UNDP and Canadian approaches. Both approaches oppose traditional instruments of security – force, deterrence and balance of power.[5] The UNDP's emphasis is on economic development, whereas Canadian's focus is on political development.[6] Khosla maintains that "at a deeper level, both are in fairly strong disagreement."[7] The UNDP approach is that freedom from want is essential where as Canadian approach argues for freedom from fear. Both are equally important for ensuring the security of human beings. Freedom from fear would be meaningful only when freedom from want is ensured and freedom from want is possible only when freedom from fear is achieved.[8]

In the past six decades, the scholars and policy-making community in South Asia constructed and debated the issue of security from military point of view. As a result, threat is perceived from neighbours and advocated military preparedness to face the challenge. The South Asian states have focused more on defence related issues than on human related issues. As a result, for majority of people food is not affordable resulting in hunger and starvation, inadequate water, primary health care, deprivation of basic needs, increasing poverty, unemployment, violation of human rights by the individuals, organizations and state. The governments of respective countries in South Asia are not concerned with these issues and they are not in a position to address them adequately due to various reasons, i.e. political differences; animosity and misunderstanding between/among the states which are still persistent. In this paper, an attempt is made to analyze three issues, i.e. problems of fishermen who fish in neighbouring borders, terrorist activities and energy security in South Asia.

Fishermen Insecurity in South Asia

As fishing is the only source of livelihood, the fishermen go in search of fish wherever they are available. In their pursuit, they hardly respect the maritime boundaries. This is the case everywhere and the South Asian fishermen are no exception. For instance, the Indian fishermen are crossing maritime boundary and entering into the Pakistani, the Sri Lankan and the Bangladeshi waters. Similarly, Sri Lankan fishermen are entering into the Indian and the Maldivian waters and the Pakistani fishermen entering into the Indian waters. The increasing depletion of fish in the traditional catchment zones further contributes to the fishermen crossing the neighbours' waters. Sometimes, the fishermen unwillingly and unknowingly cross into other's territorial waters owing to engine failures, non clear demarcation, tidal currents, cyclones and lack of navigational aids.

As crossing international maritime boundary is an offence, the fishermen are arrested/punished by authorities of the other side. In the process, human rights are being violated when the trespassers undergo trial. Worse still, the treatment given to them is justified in the name of nationalism. Any action against the so-called 'poaching' is a gross violation of all human rights. This section discusses the case of the fishermen, who fish in Indo-Sri Lankan and Indo-Pakistani waters and does not focus on fishermen who fish in Indo-Bangladeshi waters because clashes between them are very minimal.

Indian and Sri Lankan Fishermen Problems: The short distance of 12 km between Rameswaram (India) and Talaimannar (Sri Lanka) makes it difficult to restrict the fishermen crossing neighbours waters. In spite of the restrictions imposed by the Indian navy, the Indian fishermen enter into the Sri Lankan waters for fishing, as it is the only source of livelihood.

During the civil war, the Sri Lankan navy was not able to distinguish between the fishing boats and the boats involved in the nefarious activities. The navy, instead of identifying the boats engaged in illegal activities, treated all boats' activities as threat to its security. The navy personnel used to fire at boats killing innocent fishermen. They have followed a policy of shoot first and question later. They argue that they suspect the sailors as LTTE forces and they couldn't come closer to them for identification because the LTTE cadres may attack them. The number of incidents has decreased since 1998. However, when the Sri Lankan government lifted the ban on its fishermen fishing in their waters in 2002, it was reported that the LTTE and the Sri Lankan fishermen began attacking the Indian fishermen who are crossing their waters. It is to be noted that a few Indian Tamils particularly fishermen are believed to be the sympathizers of the LTTE. However, when Sri Lankan naval authorities were arresting, prosecuting and sometimes shooting the fishermen from Tamil Nadu, there was never any record of the LTTE showing any sympathy towards them. The fishermen of different places in Ramnathpuram district told the author that the punishment of the LTTE is more severe than that of the Sri Lankan navy.[9]

On the Indian side, the authorities are also arresting the Sri Lankan fishermen, who are entering into the Indian waters. Once the fishermen are caught and brought before the authority it is a long procedure to release them. Both central and state governments are to be involved in decision-making process. Unlike in Sri Lanka, the prosecution procedure in India takes longer. Under the Indian law, punishment is more severe than in Sri Lanka.

This is against the United Nations Convention on Law of Sea (UNCLOS)-III Article-73, which forbids the imprisonment of fishermen who are found 'poaching'.

Fishermen Problems in Indo-Pakistani Waters: The Indian and the Pakistani fishermen are being arrested/ killed by authorities of the other side. The Indian fishermen are suspected collaborating with the Research & Analysis Wing, while the Pakistani fishermen are suspected to be the agents of the Inter-Service Intelligence. The fishermen of both the countries are often arrested for crossing borders and they are becoming victims of undefined boundaries. Worse still, they are being treated as prisoners of war.

Till date the fishermen of each nation have not been arrested on the grounds that they were carrying arms and ammunitions on board. There is no clear policy regarding the release of the arrested fishermen. There are incidents where the fishermen were arrested and kept in jails for years together on both sides. Often the fishermen are released in equal numbers on both sides. The arrested fishermen on both sides suffer during their stay in jail. There are no proper sanitation facilities; lack of privacy and many of them are kept in a crowded place. Their release always depends on the state of relations between the two countries. Though India and Sri Lanka demarcated their maritime boundary, the Sri Lankan government understood the problem of Indian fishermen, who are 'poaching' in its waters and its naval authority started handing over the fishermen to the Indian navy.

Though India and Pakistan are yet to demarcate their maritime boundary, the two governments must adopt a humanistic and sympathetic approach towards the fishermen who are crossing each other's waters. Fortunately a breakthrough has been made by India and Pakistan to agree on a bilateral code of conduct minimizing the inter boundary cross over by the fishermen. Over the last five years, as part of the on going peace process the maritime dispute mechanism has been consciously incorporated into the negotiation agenda. There is evidence of both the countries adopting a benign and human approach in treating the maritime trespassers. Both the countries are in favour of creating a buffer zone, extending five nautical miles into each other's maritime boundary. They are also in favour of setting up a hotline between the two sides. If a buffer zone is set up and hotline installed, the problems of the fishermen, who cross neighbour's waters would be reduced.

Nevertheless, positive bilateral initiatives need to be concretized into long term plans to put an end to the arrest of the fishermen, who cross into each other's waters.

For fishermen, survival is important and they do not believe in borders. For them, Ocean is their work place. They cross maritime boundary and enter into the neighbours' waters. It is important that the governments of coastal states should consider that the fishermen problems are to be understood on humanitarian grounds. They have to address the problems being faced by them by sharing their experiences, collaborative analyses of the current situation and assessing future scenarios and prospects for human development. They have to think in terms of encoding a common maritime conduct and regional maritime law. So that most of the problems of the fishermen can be addressed without much delay in case they enter into each other's waters.

Terrorism in South Asia

Terrorism is a global phenomenon, whose tentacles have spread to all aspects of human life. Barely a day passes without its violence. Resistance to terrorism is difficult to organize as its strategies are unpredictable and targets are skewed. In the post-Cold War period it is increasingly assuming transnational dimension making difficult for states to curb this menace. Since no single state is capable of tackling it effectively, collective strategies at regional and global level are imperative.

South Asia is scene to terrorist violence over the few decades. Since all the countries in the region are contiguous and close, there is a need for them to work collectively in tackling terrorism. Otherwise, the terrorist activities in one country are impacting on the other with terrorist groups of several hues are spreading their networking operations across the intra-regional boundaries. Unemployed young people are being attracted by religious groups for propagating their programmes. For instance, there are reports which reveal that young unemployed people are ready to work for the terrorist activities, who in return get Rs.100 per day.

South Asia is experiencing terrorist activities. Hundreds of people are becoming victims in the region. Before the 11 September 2001 attacks on the World Trade Centre, there were many terrorist attacks which made South Asian countries more vulnerable to the terrorist activities. The phenomenon of terrorism, thus, demands urgent response and hence a collective effort by the South Asian states against terrorism is the need of the hour.

South Asia is the region where some of the states either directly or indirectly support terrorism. For instance, Pakistan governments' involvement and collusion with terrorists in Kashmir cannot be denied. Bangladesh is providing shelter to many groups from northeast India is a known fact. Thus, terrorism in a way is a state-supported and sponsored activity in South Asia. For one man's terrorist is another person's freedom fighter. For India, militant activities in Kashmir are terrorist activities, whereas for Pakistan they are freedom fighters. The South Asian states are unable to have a commonly agreed regional definition of terrorism.

Since the central obligation of the state is to protect its citizens, policies must aim at preventing terrorism. The states and the policymakers have to take up the issue seriously. The legal response to this challenge is very much needed. Since terrorism has both national and trans-national causes and targets, it requires policy responses to coordinate at national, regional and global levels. It requires substantial improvements in multilateral legal tools and framework to tackle terrorism.

South Asian countries, individually far more vulnerable to cross-border militant activity, have introduced statutory measures at both national and regional level. They have agreed to have cooperation at regional level among themselves to prevent and eliminate terrorism from the region. There are a number of regional conventions held at SAARC meetings on suppression of terrorism. The SAARC Regional Convention on Suppression of Terrorism of 1987 was passed and the member states agreed 'to take effective measures to ensure that perpetrators of terroristic acts do not escape prosecution and punishment by providing for their extradition'. Recently at the SAARC meeting, the member states have agreed to fight against terrorism collectively. However, they are yet to make serious efforts in combating terrorism.

Energy Security in South Asia

Many people in South Asia still lack access to electricity in meeting their basic needs. The South Asian countries are largely dependent on energy imports. Though these countries have natural resources in abundance, they are yet to be tapped and exploited. South Asia is important to world energy market because it contains 1.3 billion people. It consumes about 5.9% of world commercial energy.[10] The energy needs would continue to increase with the ongoing liberalization programmes in South Asia.

Hence, regional cooperation in the energy sector among these countries is most desirable.

South Asian countries' consumption in coal by 2020 would be increased by more than double the coal consumed in 1997 (233 million metric ton (MMT) to 516 MMT). In oil consumption, it would be three times more than what these countries consumed in 1997 (111 MMT to 304 MMT), whereas in gas consumption in 2020, it would increase more than four times of gas consumption in 1990 (33 billion cubic meters (BCM) to 147 BCM).

South Asia depends on coal (47%), petroleum (33%), Natural gas (12%), hydropower (7%) and nuclear power (1%).[11] There is a significant variation in energy mix in the South Asian region. For instance, Bangladesh depends 69 per cent on natural gas, India on coal by 55 per cent, Sri Lanka and Maldives use 76 per cent and 100 per cent of petroleum respectively, Pakistan depends 43 per cent and 38 per cent on oil and natural gas respectively, Nepal and Bhutan consume 90 per cent of petroleum and hydropower.[12]

In most of the rural areas of South Asia, people use non-commercial energy for their consumption. Though it causes air pollution leading to respiratory, heart and lung problems[13], it is reducing import of oil and gas. In India, the largest country in South Asia, there are 80,000 villages, which are yet to be electrified. Out of these 18,000 villages can be electrified by using renewable resources. Apart from the inability of the government, rural people are often not in a position to pay electricity bills and instead they use sources like firewood, cow dung, agricultural residue and kerosene.

At present, every country's approach towards power planning and development is carried out from its domestic point of view. As a result all the countries are overlooking the opportunities in their neighbourhood.

To have energy security as a collective task in the region, a South Asian forum on energy can be established to reduce the costs of research to improve energy efficiency and to promote energy cooperation among the countries of the region. This, in return, will improve relations among the countries of region on win-win situation. While India can benefit from electricity and gas imports from neighbouring countries in achieving faster economic development, Bangladesh, Nepal and Bhutan too can get economic benefits from the export of hydroelectric power and natural gas to India. Pakistan's economy too can benefit from exporting electricity to India. Through mutual help and cooperation, all of them can reduce their dependence on energy imports. This in return can help in improving their political relationships. The South Asian states must make greater efforts to have regional cooperation through action rather than rhetoric. We can reconstruct South Asia through human development and we can have South Asian Union in future, provided there is a political will among the South Asian leaders.

Conclusion

In South Asia, traditional security issues still dominate in the respective states' foreign policy. The disputes and conflicts converted the region backward and worse and the South Asian countries have to realize that cooperation and mutual benefits are the only alternatives left to them. The South Asian countries have to keep the political differences aside and to work for mutual benefits, economic prosperity and regional cooperation. They have to focus on removal of poverty, control of population growth, empowering women, promoting human rights and developing human resources.

The South Asian countries have to realize that they have to shift from the security of the borders to the security of the people. A future South Asia can be seen only when we work towards human development.

References

1. For instance, the conflict between the state and Tamils and between Sinhalese and Tamils has been continuing for the last two decades. The main factors that have led to the conflict are: (1) the declaration of Sinhala as the sole official language replacing English in 1956, which led to a serious reduction of opportunities for Tamils in the state services; (2) the enactment of the 1972 Constitution removed minority safeguards and gave Buddhism foremost place; (3) state-aided settlement schemes in Tamil regions changed demographic patterns.

   The Tamils protested against discrimination and demanded some degree of regional autonomy and power sharing but were ignored by the Sinhalese and the government. As a result, the Tamil United Liberation Front (TULF) and the LTTE emerged as the dominant militant groups and fought for a separate state for the Tamils. Later, the LTTE became the most powerful organization and spread from the northern and eastern provinces to other parts of the country through sporadic attacks against military establishments and the Sinhalese. The Tamil youth began to fight for their rights. They trained people, procured weapons, established an army and procured their rights. Women were also actively involved in the LTTE's activities. Slowly, by 1986, they were able to control most of the areas of northern Jaffna peninsula. They demanded that the government make the Northern and Eastern Provinces of Sri Lanka an independent Tamil State.

The ethnic conflict was intensified by the anti-Tamil riots in 1977, 1981, and 1983. Of these, the 1983 riots were unforgettable because the government troops and police supported the Sinhalese who attacked Tamils. After the riots, the fights between the government and the Tamils intensified. In order to compete with the government forces, the Tamils started procuring arms from outside the country, particularly from Western countries. As the Tamil armed group became more powerful, the Sri Lankan forces took a harder line against it.

2. Cited in Sakiko Fukuda-Parr, "New Threats to Human Security in the Era of Globalization", in Lincoln Chen, Sakiko Fukuda-Parr & Ellen Seidensticker (ed.), *Human Insecurity in a Global World*, New Delhi: Viva Books Pvt. Ltd, 2005, p.11.
3. *Human Development Report, 1994*, New York: Oxford University Press, 1994, p.22.

Some of the definitions for human security are:

Kofi Annan describes human security: Human Security in its broadest sense embraces far more than the absence of violent conflict. It encompasses human rights, good governance, access to education and health care and ensuring that each individual has opportunities and choices to fulfill his or her own potential. Every step in this direction is also a step towards reducing poverty, achieving economic growth and preventing conflict. Freedom from want, freedom from fear and the freedom of future generations to inherit a healthy natural environment – these are the interrelated building blocks of human and therefore national security. See Kofi Annan, 'Secretary-General Salutes International Workshops on Human Security in Mongolia', Ulaanbaator, May 8-10, 2000. Press Release SG/SM/7382, see http://www.Un.org/News/Press/docs/2000/2000508.sgsm7382.doc.html.

Amartya Sen and Sadako Ogare defined human security as: Human Security means protecting fundamental freedoms – freedoms that are the essence of life. It means protecting people from critical (severe) and pervasive (widespread) threats and situations. It means using processes that build on people's strengths and aspirations. It means creating political, social, environmental, economic, military, and cultural systems that together give people the building blocks of survival, livelihood, and dignity.

The vital core of life is a set of elementary rights and freedoms people enjoy. What people consider to be 'vital' – what they consider to be 'of the essence of life' and 'crucially important' – varies across individuals and societies. That is why any concept of human security must be dynamic. And that is why we refrain from proposing an itemized list of what makes up human rights. Cited in Sabina Alkire, "Concepts of Human Security", in Chen, Fukuda-Parr & Seidensticker (ed), n. 2, p. 32.

4. *Human Development Report,* n. 3, p. 24.

5. I.P. Khosla, "Evolving a Theoretical Perspective on Human Security", in P.R. Chari and Sonika Gupta (ed), *Human Security in South Asia*, New Delhi: Social Science Press, 2003, p. 24.
6. See Kanti Bajpai, *Human Security: Concept and Measurement*, Kroc Institute Occasional Paper, no. 19, August 2000, p. 35.
7. Khosla, n. 5.
8. A.K.M. Abdus Sabur, "Evolving a Theoretical Perspective in Human Security: The South Asian Context", in Chari & Gupta, n. 5, p. 44.
9. Author's Interview with the fishermen in December 2003.

   The Sethusamudram Ship Canal Project too has been equally serious threat to the fishermen of Tamil Nadu. They opposed the project, as it would deny their traditional fishing rights. The livelihood of five lakh fishermen in 138 fishing stations along the five coastal districts will be severely affected. The gravity of the situation seems to have had no impact on the government. Nor has the concern over the impact of the project on the environment. It involves extensive dredging of the Pamban channel where coral reef is available in abundance. The dredging will lead the depletion of the fish and the destruction of the marine ecology. Besides, once the construction of the canal is completed, it would break the continuous limestone formation which would cause sudden tilting drift and gravitational pull setting in motion various other violent processes. It seems that the Indian government has taken only the economic benefits into consideration, while ignoring the ramifications, consequences and calamities which follow the dredging of the sea.
10. It excludes the non-commercial energy sources – wood, animal waste and other biomass, which account for more than half of the region's total energy consumption.
11. Shanker K. Malla, "Energy Cooperation in South Asia", see http://www.cpd-bangladesh.org/saceps/ energy. PDF
12. *Ibid.*
13. For instance, an Indian government report estimated that 0.59 million Indians die each year due to polluting traditional fuel.

9

Human Security: An Indian Perspective

Nalini Kant Jha

Attaining peace has been one of the most important concerns of Indian thinkers and statesmen since even the Vedic era. Even a cursory look at some of famous Vedic verses shows that the desire for maintaining peace and security through ensuring welfare of all living creatures was the dearest desire of ancient Indian thinkers. This was reflected in works of the post Vedic scholars also. In fact, the Indian theorists have delved much deeper into this problem and their thinking has a great relevance for addressing contemporary issues concerning both national and international peace and security. Surprisingly, however, contemporary discourse on peace and human welfare hardly takes into account the thoughts of ancient Indian thinkers in this debate. The paper, therefore, examines the relevance of traditional Indian wisdom for securing peace and security at national as well as international levels. Before throwing light on ancient Indian view, it is, however, useful to briefly discuss the contemporary debate about national security.

The Post-Cold War Discourse on National Security

Contemporary debate about national security often focuses on transformation of the concept of national security from a narrow prism of territorial security to a wider canvas of human security. It is argued that while scholars during the Cold War perceived the state as an actor in international politics with a distinct territorial base and sovereign authority without giving much attention to the peoples residing within a state; the end of the Cold War over a decade ago heralded a seminal change about the concept of national security. Many scholars began to move away from the state-centric realist approach to liberal view of international relations that stresses on imperatives and possibility of international and regional cooperation. A unilateralist notion of security must give way, in this view, to *cooperative security.* As threat to national security can come not only from other state(s), but also from non-state actors and natural calamities, a much wider notion of security, which broadens the nature and sources of threat and which may be called *composite* or *comprehensive security,* got currency after the Cold War.

Certain critiques of the classical Western notion of security went further to suggest that security cannot be restricted to the well-being of the state, but it must aim at protection and well-being of individuals and citizens residing in a state. This concept of security, which is centred above all on the sanctity of the individual, is known as *human security.* The concept of human security or the security of the individual and humane governance, therefore, gained wide currency, as poverty and deprivation enlarged the problem of human security in the developing world.

Ensuring Peace and National Security: Ancient Indian Perspective

While the above-discussed transformation of the concept of national security may indeed be revolutionary in the West, as far as India is concerned, the primary strategic objective of security policy has had been, and will remain, the socio-economic development of its people. This has its roots in ancient political tradition, where the ruler's primary duty *(Dharma)* was perceived to be the prosperity and happiness of his people. In fact, kings were expected to nourish their subjects as a father nourishes his offspring.

This is how *Srimadbhagvatam* describes the rule of king Ram: "*Jugop pitravad Ramo manire pitra ch tam*" (King Ram used to protect his subjects like a father and they too treated him as their father). According to the *Valmiki Ramayan*, common people declared during King Ram's rule that the territory beyond Ram's kingdom will be a forest, but if he would reside in a forest that too would be converted into a sovereign nation. This popular faith in King Ram emanated from his scrupulous observance of his promise given to people at the time of his coronation, namely, that he would not at all hesitate in scarifying his affection, kindness and personal pleasures including his most beloved wife, Janaki. Not surprisingly, the ancient Indian literature describes *Ramrajya* (the rule of Lord Ram) as full of happiness, where no woman became widow, no one got incurable disease or snake bite. There was no question of any theft, robbery or untimely death. Every one followed principles of *dharm* (righteousness) and lived happily.

While one may regard this merely an imagination of poets, these descriptions, suggest that foundations of political order or state lie, according to Indian theorists, in people's consent obtained by a king through ensuring their welfare. *The Mahabharat* describes the origin of state and bases of political obligation thus, "Harassed by those who have force, the helpless and the hurt have only the king as their refuge, and their protector." "When a king wipes the tears of the poor, the dispossessed and the old, and thereby creates happiness among the people, that behaviour is called the king's *dharma*." The *Mahabharat,* thus, prescribes that by its very justification, the state, if it is to be itself and not something else, must be an instrument for the protection of people, for protection from violence. And since caring is the essence of protection, the state in all its acts must be caring, as only in a caring nation-state wishes expressed in the *Yujurved* can be realized.

It was this philosophy and practice of human welfare that influenced modern Indian political thinkers like Gandhi, Nehru and others, who stood for a people-centred organization of society, economics and politics. The Directive Principles of state policy enshrined in Part IV of the Indian Constitution, which prescribe popular welfare as prime duty of the Indian state, reflect this traditional thinking in India. Though it is not mandatory for the Indian state to implement these Directives, successive governments have taken several steps to realize these popular welfare goals of the Constitution. Indian Judiciary too have joined in implementing this vision of the founding fathers of our Constitution by enlarging, through judicial interpretations, the meaning and ambit of fundamental rights of freedom, life and liberty guaranteed to the people by Articles 19 and 21 of the Constitution.

Maintaining International Peace and Security: Traditional Indian Thinking

Indian thinking concerning popular welfare has also guided its post-independent perspective of peace and security at the international level. A look at the ancient Indian literature shows that Indian sages held the view that international peace is not possible without well being of individuals in the society. They emphasized that without popular welfare and equitable distribution of resources peace cannot be achieved and without peace both national and international security would remain a wishful thinking. They, therefore, prayed the God saying, "O God, kindly take away from us all sorts of elements or harmful thoughts, which are the sources of all kinds of sufferings. And please give us the things favourable to our well-being – mental, physical and social."

The above-mentioned Vedic prayer indicates that since the roots of conflict lies in negative thoughts such as hatred and jealousy, peace is not possible without promoting positive and friendly attitude towards all living creatures of the world among all individuals that can form a solid bedrock for global peace and security. To put it differently, international peace and security is closely related with peaceful state of individual and society. If individuals can develop positive thoughts and enjoy healthy state of mind and body through feeling of oneness or unity among individuals, this can promote national and international peace and friendship. This in turn will create a sense of security among individuals, within a nation and among nations.

As Indian thinkers were also aware with the fact that a sense of peace and security cannot be developed without eradicating felling of enmity towards others, they devoted considerable attention to techniques of developing a sense of non-enmity. Sage Patanjali, for instance, prescribes guiding principles for developing a sense of non-enmity and thereby enjoying mental bliss (*chitta prasadam*). He suggests that any aspirant should maintain bliss and peace by awakening and applying appropriate attitudes like friendship, kindness, happiness and avoidance in dealing with persons surrounding him or her. Similarly, the *Yajurved* advises to human beings to pay respect and look each other with a friendly outlook.

Indian theorists were, however, aware with the fact that a friendly vision towards other will not be possible without developing a sense of equality. While they agreed that complete equality in practice is neither possible nor desirable, as equality is feasible and desirable only among equals and inequality among non-equals, they believed that avoidable or undesirable inequality can be avoided or minimised by developing a sense of empathy towards others and regarding them as diverse manifestations of the same soul which is the driving force of living creatures of the universe, will strike at the roots of avoidable and undesirable inequality and thereby pave the way for peace and security every where in the world. Lord Krishna, therefore, declares in *Shrimad Bhagvadgeeta*, "He whose mind is restrained by Yoga beholds his own self-dwelling within all beings and all beings dwelling within his own self, he sees the same self everywhere with an even eye."

The above-verse of the *Shrimad Bhagvadgeeta* shows how human unity can be achieved despite diversity of religion, sex, caste, creed, belief, race and nationality, etc. Since all human beings are the manifestation of the same God, every one must cherish a sense of empathy and oneness towards others. This alone can make possible peace and security at all levels, namely, individual, family, society, nation, and the world.

The Contemporary Vision of Peace and Security

The above-mentioned thinking of ancient Indian theorists has a profound impact on the contemporary Indian vision of peace and security. Echoing ancient Indian emphasis on need of developing a sense of non-enmity and peace, Jawaharlal Nehru, India's first Prime Minster, declared in a broadcast from London on 12 January 1951:

> What we need is a passion for peace and for civilized behaviour in international affairs. It is the temper of peace and not the temper of war that we want, even though peace is sometimes casually mentioned....If we desire peace, we must develop the temper of peace and try to win even those who may be suspicious of us or who think they are against us. We have to try to understand others; just as we expect them to understand us; we cannot seek peace in the language of war or of threats.[1]

The above-mentioned temper of peace approach had two aspects, negative and positive. On the negative side, this approach reflected India's rejection of the Western power politics approach with its concomitants, the reliance on armaments, war, spheres of influence, alliance and balance of power. Nehru was aware that the balance of power approach to international relations that prevailed during the nineteenth century might have been able to preserve a precarious peace, when there were a number of states, more or less equal in power, and there was a moral consensus that prevented blatant use of power. But the bi-polar rivalry and discovery of nuclear weapons in the post 1945 period changed the situation, which led Nehru to believe that power politics with an uneasy balance of power in its wake cannot guarantee peace but only lead, sooner or later, to war, which in the nuclear age may lead to destruction beyond imagination.

On the positive side, India's approach to peace in an atomic age has had two elements: (a) tackling the roots of conflict (socio-economic and political); and (b) attempting to resolve a given conflict without recourse to violence to reduce international tensions arising from that conflict if it was not possible to resolve the main conflict. India, therefore, led struggle for end of colonialism and racialism, the raising of the living standard of peoples in developing countries, and promotion of temper of peace through disarmament and respect for sovereignty and integrity of other countries and through following the principles of co-existence. This positive aspect of Indian approach was symbolised in its five principles of *Panchsheel*.

India's policy of non-alignment, on the other hand, symbolised both the negative and positive aspects of Indian approach to peace. While the negative aspect of non-alignment found expression in its rejection of the Cold War politics of military alliance, its positive aspects could be seen in its emphasis on five 'Ds,' that is decolonization, disarmament, democratization of international relations, development of underdeveloped countries, and discrimination, i.e. taking stand on any issue on the basis of merit of the case and national interest.

Significantly, Nehru envisaged this approach not as an alternative to the Western approach to peace based on power, but as a supplementary to the one based on power, though supplementary with a difference. He knew that merely temper of peace cannot prevent conflicts as paper statements are not always kept and *Panchsheel* may be broken as he realized most clearly in the case of Hungary in 1956 and China's encroachment on Indian territory during 1959-62. He, however, believed that a peaceful approach to conflict resolution must be given priority before using force.

Nehru, thus, stressed that even though mere peaceful approach cannot guarantee peace, it should be tried as discussion, negotiation and accommodation are the best ways left for settlement of differences. Of course, reliance on peaceful negotiation is not by any means India's monopoly; every nation resorts to negotiation to disputes settled or to get satisfactory solutions to international problems from the point of view of its own interests. In a Cold War environment, however, when the world was divided into military blocs, a non-aligned nation like India was in an advantageous position to explore more fully than others the possibilities of negotiations as India demonstrated through the use (also limitations) of this technique in trying to resolve tensions in Korea and Vietnam during 1950-54.

India applied this approach to negotiation for dealing with India's bilateral disputes as well. This was illustrated by India's offer of a no-war pact to Pakistan in 1949 and its repeated renewal of the offer in the subsequent years, its willingness to accept division of Kashmir on the basis of the ceasefire line in the interest of Indo-Pakistani peace, its *Panchsheel* agreement with China in 1954, the premium it put on diplomatic negotiation for a settlement of the border dispute with China event after the situation worsened in 1959, and, finally, its acceptance of the Colombo proposal formulated by certain friendly countries after the Sino-Indian conflict of 1962 as the basis of a resolution of the Sino-Indian border dispute. In recent years, India's repeated attempts to bring peace with Pakistan through Prime Minister, Atal Bihari Vajpayee's bus journey to Lahore in 1999, his Ramzan peace initiative in Kashmir at the end of 2000, Agra summit talks with Pakistan in 2001, and the continuance of the latest peace initiative (April 2003) despite provocative violence by Pakistan sponsored terrorists in Kashmir too illustrate India's emphasis on a peaceful settlement of disputes.

In the process of reconciliation and negotiation, however, India neglected its own defence preparedness, especially during the Nehru era. This contributed to India's defeat at the hands of China in 1962. Shocked Nehru ruefully admitted: "We were getting out of touch with reality in the modern world and we were living in an artificial atmosphere of our own creation."[2] Not surprisingly, the Indian government paid more attention to defence preparedness after 1962 and conducted nuclear experiments in 1974 and 1998 defying international opinion. This increasing attention paid to defence preparedness enabled India to inflict cursing defeat on Pakistan in 1971 and also in 1999. This ample evidence of the realization that an adequate foreign and defence policy must be based on greater military power than government of India originally thought it necessary.

Striking a Balance between Idealism and Realism

India's defence preparedness after India-China war of 1964 should not, however, be regarded as contrary to India's traditional love for peace and harmony After all ideal Indian rulers had tried to strike a balance between idealism and realism or between non-violence and violence as evident in Shri Ram's declaration of "*Agratah sakalam shastram, pristah ssharam dhanuh*" (Wisdom must be backed by power of armaments).

However, Indian thinkers have prescribed violence only as a last resort. On the contrary, from the time immemorial the mainstream school of Indian thought has advocated that penance, self-abnegation and non-injury are the means to get rid of sin and securing salvation. The *Upnishads*, for instance, give us the basis of the theory of non-violence. There is one undivided and indivisible spirit – above and below, without and within, without beginning and end – which may be called God or truth. The universe is an expression of it, and all beings form part of it. Since perfection consists in realizing this truth any kind of violence would be repudiation of this truth. Even the *Bhagvadgeeta*, which is apparently a plea to engage in war, in fact, recommends non-violence as a way of life and prescribes war only as a last resort.

Needless to add, this Indian emphasis on peace has more relevance today than any time in the past, as there is an overwhelming evidence to show that any kind of nuclear war would not only shatter human civilization as we know it, it would also poison the air and the oceans and render earth virtually uninhabitable, a charred and ravaged planet, incapable of supporting more than extremely primitive life-forms. Whether this happens through political foolishness, or an accident, a flight of geese or a malfunctioning computer chip, matters little. With all our tremendous knowledge, man has finally come to a single three-letter *mantra* – MAD – Mutually Assured Destruction. Thousands of years ago, at the dawn of human civilization, the Vedic seers had also discovered a three-letter *mantra* – AUM – as the symbol of the divinity that pervades the universe. Perhaps the time has come when we should revert from MAD to AUM, so that this greatest of all transitions, the transition to the global consciousness, can be safely completed and the earth becomes a crucible for the next major step in evolution.

It is in this chilling context that the necessity for an alternative approach to both national and international peace and security becomes so imperative. Based upon the collective wisdom of generations of seers and sages, the traditional Indian thinking provides insights, which can be of crucial value not only for the survival of the human race in this nuclear age, but also for their development and happiness within and bound national boundaries.

References

1. Jawaharlal Nehru, *India's Foreign Policy: Selected Speeches, September 1946-April 1961*, New Delhi, 1961, pp. 184-185.
2. *Indian Information*, New Delhi, vol. 6, 1962, p. 712.

PART III

Non-Traditional Security and Other Core Issues

10

From Traditional to Non-traditional Security
Building Constituencies for Change in South Asia

M.J. Vinod

The post-Cold War times have opened out a new debate in the security discourse. The traditional concept of national security that evolved during the Cold War perceived security in terms of a successful pursuit of interstate power. However in the post-Cold War world, threats to security emanate less from military considerations. These have often been described as non-traditional security issues. The term security encompasses a broad spectrum of issues. Security issues are getting both 'personalised' and 'globalized'. With the end of the Cold War, and the reduced salience of conflicts among the major powers, focus has increasingly shifted to civil wars, ethnic strife, domestic social conflict and the various types of humanitarian disasters. South Asia faces a complicated security environment. Through the non-traditional security prism, one could broaden and deepen one's understanding of security.

The late Mahbub-ul-Haq broke new theoretical ground by projecting the yardsticks of human security, designated as 'Human Development Index'. To him human security represents the 'bedrock' for security. Human security is inextricably linked to human rights and the state should be vitally concerned with human security to ensure its own security. Hence the first step to harness national security is to pursue the path of human development. In the present context the non-military sources of security has acquired a new salience. Threats to human security can be placed under seven categories: economic security, food security, health security, environmental security, personal security, community security and political security. Over-stretching the concept of human security can also be problematical. Hence there is the need for delimiting the concept.[1]

Traditional understanding of security revolved essentially around the security of the state. The new thinking on security suggests that the concept is neither fixed nor permanent. Neither is it a doctrine nor a dogma. It is now being perceived as being part of an ongoing discourse and dialogue. In the traditional sense protecting a country's security meant nothing more than military security, and the defense of a country's sovereignty and integrity. New forces and factors are now very much part of the security debate. It needs to be realized that national security is the product of various factors, which includes the social, economic, political, technological and military dimensions. What is required is an integrated and holistic view of the relationship between security and development. The focus of the paper is on the non-military challenges to security in South Asia. The paper intends to present a wider agenda than the conventional state-centric and defense-oriented perspective. An attempt is made to show how non-traditional issues affect relations between communities, peoples and states in South Asia. This could perhaps provide a better understanding of the problems afflicting the region, and could help promote collective consideration of alternative visions, options and approaches to the resolution of conflicts.

Non-traditional issues are now a part of security studies to the extent that they affect the security, stability and the capability of the states in South Asia. The emergent dimensions of security are the micro-issues that are essentially non-military in nature. Moreover, South Asian security cannot be studied in isolation from the international context. Hence the future agenda of security studies should include the impact of globalization, neo-liberalism and the movement towards a free market system. Certain types of challenges facing South Asia that have not been much emphasized as part of traditional security perceptions and calculations deserve to be mentioned :

- Internal conflicts associated with the process of nation-building and national integration. In this context the ethnic, religious and cultural factors very much fall into place;
- Domestic and cross-border conflicts arising from the movement of population related with natural disasters, environmental degradation and economic factors;
- Issues of political violence and social instability;
- Sharing and management of resources and environment;
- Economic transformation, globalization and external economic relations;
- Intra and inter-state conflicts related to ethnicity; migration and population displacement;
- Spread and trafficking of small arms, explosives and drugs; and

- Challenges of good governance, particularly the growing incidence of the nexus between the political world, the lumpen elements that manifest themselves in various forms.

The non-traditional security issues in South Asia can be discussed under the following sub-themes

Ethnic, Linguistic and Religious Pluralism and Security

Managing ethnic, linguistic and religious pluralism is a common challenge facing all the South Asian states. In certain cases it has generated the possibility of both intra-state and inter-state tensions. The spillover of ethnic, linguistic and religious groups across borders has at times added to friction among the states in the region.

In the context of the social and cultural threats to security the following issues may be noted:

- State, identity and ethnicity;
- Issues of 'majorities' and 'minorities';
- Insurgencies and its varied responses and strategies;
- Linkage of factors like land, language and culture; and
- Religious and sectarian politics and militancy.

Migrations (external and internal), the problem of Displaced Persons, Refugee flows and security

Migrations into areas of distinct ethnic, religious or national identities can be a source of instability, violence and social tension. The outcome can be a restructuring of societies and redistribution of political power.[2] Migrations - external and internal - are a growing security concern. The asymmetry in economic conditions in South Asia has led to large scale migrations in search of economic opportunities. In addition, discriminatory state policies have led to migrations across borders in the region. Such large scale migrations not only result in economic, social and political problems, but could also result in the possibility for inter-state tensions. Nepal, for example, is experiencing a two-way migration, straining its ties with most of its neighbours. The diaspora of a variety of Nepalese from Bangladesh, Myanmar and northeastern parts of India is in the range of ten to fifteen million. This has raised fundamental questions of citizenship. The influx of Bhutanese refugees into the tarai has further complicted the situation.

The second dimension of migrations is the problem of internal migrations and displacement and their effect on state security. Migrations to urban areas has led to big slums, pollution and sanitation problems; epidemics of various types; and drugs, crime and violence. It is believed that today the world has some fifty million people who are victims of forced displacement. The World Bank estimates that these numbers can be as high as ten million per annum. It is estimated that between 150 and 300 million people will be displaced primarily for 'environmental' reasons by the year 2050.

The following issues assume relevance in the context of migrations in South Asia:

- Economic, social and political consequences of migration;
- Displacement and migration as an outcome of uneven development; and
- Migration and the potential for conflict.

The refugee phenomenon is today a truly global issue. Last century had witnessed the institutionalization of refugees as a matter of global concern. The existence of refugees poses a complex and challenging agenda, and has emerged as major area of academic inquiry and research. The refugee phenomenon is today truly a global issue. Refugees are the result of a variety of factors. The area is highly inter-disciplinary, and requires a coherent and integrated outlook. They are largely created as a result of war, by economic deprivation, class conflicts and by external interventions. It is estimated that since 1947, between 35-40 million people have crossed the borders of Afghanistan, India, Bhutan, Myanmar. Pakistan, Sri Lanka, Bangladesh and Sri Lanka. It may be recalled that military atrocities in Bangladesh in 1971 generated about ten million refugees who sought refuge in India. Today, there are an estimated 2.5 million Afghan refugees in Pakistan. Perhaps an equal number of refugees are in Iran.

The phenomenon of refugees and the tensions and conflicts associated with it have been the product of war, violence, politics, extreme ideological proclivities and government policies. Refugees also represent a human rights issue. The issue of forced migration is particularly linked up to human rights. The question here is whether refugees are created as a product of human decisions?

Environment and Security

Environmental problems arising out of rapid social and economic change and flawed state policies are a major non-traditional security concern. The environmental security rubric encompasses several related sub-areas. The environment-security linkage has recently generated much interest at the academic and policy making levels. The environmental realities transcend political boundaries, and require collaborative and concerted policy interventions, without being blind to the regional and local dimensions.

Seven major areas comprising the environmental security agenda are: efforts to redefine security; theories about environmental factors in violent conflict; the environmental security of the nation; the linkages between the military and environmental issues; the ecological security agenda; the environmental security of people; and issues of securitization. What is required is a 'human-centered' account of environmental security. Environmental security may be defined as 'the process of peacefully reducing human vulnerability to human-induced environmental degradation by addressing the root causes of environmental degradation and human insecurity'. Environmental security as an absolute condition is arguably impossible, not least because security is a highly relative concept.[3]

As population of the region approaches the one-and-a-half billion mark, the strain on the basic resources of air, water and land is expected to reach intolerable limits. Environmental related threats to security in South Asia can be classified into two broad categories:

- Those arising as negative effects of the very process of development; and
- Those arising from conditions of poverty and underdevelopment. This has to do with the very health and integrity of the natural resources – land, water, soil, resources, forests, wildlife – as a result of poverty and the inadequate availability of the basic human needs. Besides population which is an important resource for development can also be a major source of environmental degradation when it exceeds the threshold limits of the support systems.

It needs to be stressed that both these two problems are interrelated. The causes and effects of environmental degradation and its impact on security are interwoven in complex webs of social, economic, political, technological and environmental factors. Development in South Asia needs to proceed along rational and sustainable lines. In short development has to be sustainable and all round.

Energy and Security

Energy security may be perceived as a major security concern in the twenty first century. The growing competition for access to energy resources holds out the possibility for conflict. Energy is yet another important security issue for the present and the future. Needless to say there are possibilities for cooperative endeavours too, such as oil and gas-pipelines. Energy is amongst the most important motifs of environmental quality as well as human security. The shortage of energy resources and the consequent competition for access to these resources holds out the potential for conflict in South Asia. The issue also presents itself with opportunities for cooperation with the possibility of installing oil and gas pipelines. The Iran-India gas pipeline project has often run into snags due to the hostile regional environment. There are other projects like the Pakistan-Iran $ 1.1 billion refinery, the proposed gas supply from Iran's Pars offshore gas field to Pakistan. Yet another gas import plan of Indian interest is the proposed $ 3 billion Pakistan-Qatar gas pipeline project, which if implemented would be a 1000 km long pipeline to be laid under the Arabian sea. When completed it could help Islamabad import 1.5 billion cubic feet gas per day. The possibility of gas import from Qatar to India also through Pakistan can be viewed as another gas pipeline dream in South Asia. In the whole process, by extending transit facilities to neighbouring countries, Pakistan could even earn substantial revenues.

India-Pakistan negotiations on energy have been proceeding at a slow pace. A South Asian power grid could help for sharing of power among India, Pakistan, Bangladesh and Nepal.

Water and Security

South Asia is blessed with rich water resources being gifted with three major river basins – the Indus, the Ganges and the Brahmaputra. However, rising population has put pressure on water resources for drinking, irrigation, industries and human habitation. Water as a security issue assumes various dimensions in South Asia. These include the problem of silt, floods, water pollution, industrial waste, untreated water, chemical waste, sewage.

The construction of the Katpai reservoir on Karnaphuli in 1963 in the then East Pakistan led to the movement of the non-Muslim tribal population in the Chittagong Hill tracts by the resettlement of Muslims in the region. Besides, it led to the displacement of 1,00,000 tribals, which was one of the reasons for the migration of tribals to Tripura and Meghalaya, giving birth to a major irritant in India-Bangladesh relations – the Chakma refugees.

Because of political differences, South Asia has not been able to fully exploit the abundant water resources to the advantage of the region. For example the hydroelectric power potential of Nepal is estimated to be 83,000 MW, while the actual production is only 240 MW. In the case of India and Bangladesh (then East Pakistan) the water dispute began in 1951 when it was decided to build the Farakka barrage in order to divert water from Ganga to the Bhagirathi-Hooghly to make Calcutta port navigable throughout the year. The barrage is 17 Km away from the India-Bangladesh border. Since then, the issue has surfaced from time-to time as a potential irritant in relations between New Delhi and Dhaka.

The World Bank brokered the Indus Water Treaty on 19 September 1960 signed between Jawaharlal Nehru and Ayub Khan solved the water problem between India and Pakistan. The agreement has been respected to date. Presently, differences persist on the Wular barrage issue, following the construction of the Tulbul Navigation project on the Wular lake on the Jhelum river in 1984 by India.

Water has become a key security issue in South Asia. The Tata Energy Research Institute has estimated that the demand for water will double from 564 billion cubic metres (bcum) in 1997 to 1,048 bcum in 2047. Moreover, the growing demand for power forces governments to exploit hydro- potential. Besides, in the case of international rivers, demand for a greater share, has often led to regional altercations.

One may identify four varieties of conflicts over water resources in South Asia. These can be divided into four genres:

1. Firstly conflicts within a state: Such intra-state water conflicts can be further categorized into three broad categories:
    - Conflict between two or three constituent states/provincial governments like the Cauvery waters dispute;
    - Conflict between the provincial and the Union government like the dispute over the Kalabagh dam project in Pakistan; and
    - Clash between civil society and the respective governments like the dispute over the Katpai in Bangladesh or the Tehri and Narmada in India.
2. Conflicts in South Asia at a bilateral level between two states in the region like the Farakka waters dispute between India and Bangladesh.
3. Conflict regarding the sources of funding at the bilateral and international levels. Projects like that of Kosi and Gandak built under the Indian aid projects and the Arun III projects which were supposed to be built with the World Bank aid come in this category.

4. Conflict with private investors : This involves the independent power producers and the government. The Enron case is a good example of a conflict between Enron and a provincial government, in this case the state of Maharashtra.

Narcotics and Arms Peddling Networks and Security

Narcotics trafficking and its associated criminal activities are a major security concern in South and Southeast Asia. The problem of porous borders and the lack of a regional consensus has led to the spread of the drug and arms peddlers in the region. The three largest opium producers in Asia are Afghanistan, Myanmar and Pakistan. They provide the raw materials for much of the world's heroin. This constitutes a major security threat to the region. The link between 'drug trafficking' and 'drug related violence' has been fairly well established. The links between sub-national forces and these transnational networks have further complicated the situation. The dependence of some of these groups for external support of various kinds has taken the shape of low intensity conflicts in the region. Terrorism and militancy across borders have only abetted these low intensity conflicts.

Corruption and violence resulting from such activities have had its impact on the process of governance. Small arms trafficking, which to some extent are related to narcotics trafficking along with the criminal activities, are increasingly emerging as a major security concern. One is witnessing the increasing 'militarization of societies.' Studies go to show, for example, that during the last fifty years over one hundred million Kalashnikovs and over 115 million mines have been planted the world over. A UN Task Force in 1994 had estimated that narcotics trade generated about five per cent of Pakistan's Gross Domestic Product.

The spread of small arms has heightened tensions and conflicts in domestic societies, with cross-border implications in some cases. Hence low intensity conflicts continue. The induction of weapons into any situation of conflict- be it ethnic, religious or political – can only escalate the situation. Afghanistan is one country with the largest quantities of weapons that are not produced within. Demand is sustained because of many 'hot spots' in Central Asia, Southern Asia and South East Asia. One can see the 'transnational' basis of these conflict ridden regions – the money, the weapons, the men in liaison with the world of 'organized crime.' One also cannot ignore the impact of radical religious ideologies that fuels the situation in most of these regions. Hence, 'organized crime' in terms of its various nefarious activities has serious immediate and longer term implications for the security and stability of states in South Asia. India finds itself sandwiched between the two major narcotic growing centres of Asia – the Golden Crescent (Pakistan-Afghanistan border) and the Golden Triangle (the Myanmar-Thailand border).

Impact of Globalization on Security

Globalization as a concept refers both to the 'compression of the world' and the 'extension of transactions' beyond national borders. It is, perhaps, the most debated concept in recent times. We are increasingly seeing the 'internationalization' and 'deterritorialization' of the state in response to the diverse modalities of globalization. The emergence of the global civil society has been an uneven and uncertain process so far. The world is witnessing an increasingly level of interdependence between the 'national systems by way of trade, domination and cultural imperialism'. Globalization is being motorized in a variety of ways and the tightening web of global interdependence presents both opportunity and danger. The global agenda has shifted to new issues and problems. Globalization is taking place at the level of ideas, beliefs, perceptions and tastes through the 'process of global homogenization.' This has been made easier and faster by the revolution in technology, especially information technology. The following implications of globalization need to be noted particularly in the context of South Asia :

- Tension is mounting between the fixed geography of nation-states and the non-territorial nature of global problems and their solutions, and its impact on a region like South Asia.
- Traditional security threats are being influenced by non-traditional threats like organized crime, drug trafficking, arms peddling, cross border terrorism, etc.
- New technologies are making the world increasingly inter-dependent. South Asia is no exception. These technologies are accelerating the movement of goods, services, ideas and capital across national boundaries.

Globalization has affected the capacity of states in South Asia to perform their traditional security functions. The state itself is undergoing change in terms of sovereignty. Even if one focuses on state security, the ability of the state to act cohesively and strongly has been substantially weakened. Concerns about globalization in South Asia is not only limited to its economic dimension, but also underlines the importance of the political, cultural, technological globalizing forces and factors, and its potential implications for national security.

Governance and Security

Though the state is still the major actor, it would be useful to examine the reasons for tensions in state-civil society relations. It is necessary to take into account the non-military newer threats to security that pass under review concepts like human security and human governance to appreciate their implications for national security. It is also necessary to discern the systemic challenge to the governance process and establish the linkage between 'misgovernance' and 'insecurity' in various states in South Asia.[4] Good governance is required for countries at all stages of development. This adds to the security of the state. As part of the kit of governance, the following characteristics can be particularly emphasized: accountability, transparency, rule of law, greater efficiency, equity, social justice, participation, decentralization and devolution. It requires 'effective goal setting' and 'effective public accountability' leading to effective governmental performance.

The crisis of governance in South Asia is much more a 'crisis of values'. Unfortunately in many states the present system of governance and the present set of values seem to reinforce each other. The symptoms of the crisis are manifold. In this context civil society mechanisms for conflict-resolution and consensus building could also play a vital role along with the state structures.

Conclusion

The challenges that confront South Asia represent a combination of political, economic and security issues. South Asia presents a variety of conundrums – these include among others population growth, economic deprivation, environment and resources, ethno-nationalism, armed insurgency, the problem of 'regime interests' versus 'national interests', terrorism, fundamentalism and the strategic security environment in South Asia. Regional security derives as much from the internal security dimension of states, as it does from regional and global dynamics. These new security threats derive not from state strength, geopolitical ambition or military strength, but from:

- The weakness of states, and often due to the absence of political legitimacy.
- The failure of states to provide minimum conditions of public order within their borders, given the way domestic instability and conflicts, spill over into neighbouring states.
- Inequality (understood in terms of aggregate levels of deprivation) decisively enters into the new agenda on security studies in South

> Asia. The link between inequality and the growth of social violence, ethnic conflict and civil wars is important. Poverty, over-population, resource scarcity and environmental degradation can foster social conflict in the region.

It is hoped that the wide array of non-traditional security threats would highlight the potential for more meaningful regional cooperation in South Asia. There is a widely shared view that these non-traditional security issues need to be tackled within the context of economic development, rather than via the traditional security instruments.

Issues like international terrorism, drug trafficking, organized crime, environmental degradation, ethnic strife, food and energy scarcities, unchecked population growth, uncontrolled migration, these can hardly be considered as new problems. However, the explicit characterization and treatment of these as 'security issues' and 'security challenges' is a relatively recent development. Whether such problems are appropriate subjects for security policy, and what priority they should be afforded relative to traditional military-related concerns are questions that have generated an intense debate in South Asia.

It is not the intention of the paper to denigrate the importance of state security. However, over-emphasis on state security can endanger human security. Today the state-centric world is being supplemented by a multi-centric world. This is reflected in a situation where national economies have become increasingly intertwined, borders more porous and societies more amenable to external influence. The state, market and civil society are all important for any meaningful discussion on security in an increasingly inter-dependent world. Studies have shown that both security-related factors and the economic factors influence patterns of trade and war.

In the context of globalization, a more broadly defined concept of national security seems to correspond to a more narrowly defined concept of national sovereignty. Information, institutions and culture seems to matter more than the mere use of the state's traditional capabilities. One is clearly seeing the emergence of new forms of power as embedded in advanced technology and other networks of interaction, signaling the importance of the linkage between economics and security.

Reconciling economic development with environmental security has become an unavoidable necessity. In the recent years environmental issues have resulted in environmental conflicts. These conflicts have resulted in certain political movements based on ecological concerns about the quality of man's habitat. These are also linked to the regional and global implications of the environmental movement. It is important to ensure that in the process of development, the threshold limits of human sustenance are not crossed. No nation can claim to be secure without adequate development. Without development, there can be no security. Security is not merely to do with military hardware, though it may include it. Security is not merely military force, though it may encompass it.

Maintaining a balance between the traditional and non-traditional security issues is the greatest challenge. The new security agenda goes to show the changing perceptions and attitudes that could help develop a 'comprehensive' understanding of security. The time has come for greater collaboration, understanding and networking between institutions, individuals and groups working in the field of security studies. South Asia is a region where the linkage between development, environment and security is intrinsic. The emerging dimensions of security are essentially the 'micro' issues that basically go beyond the military dimensions of security. The non-military dimensions of security can no longer be neglected.

References

1. P.R. Chari and Sonika Gupta, *Human Security in South Asia: Gender, Energy, Migration and Globalization*, New Delhi: Social Science Press, 2003.
2. Charles B. Keeley, "Demographic Developments and Security", in Michael E. Brown (ed), *Grave New World: Security Challenges in the 21st Century*, Washington D.C: Georgetown University Press, 2003.
3. Jon Barnett, *The Meaning of Environmental Security: Ecological Politics and Policy in the New Security Era*, London: Zed Books, 2001.
4. P.R. Chari (ed), *Security and Governance in South Asia*, New Delhi: Manohar Publishers, 2001.

11

Regional Integration in South Asia: From Discord to Free Trade

J. Laxmi Narasimha Rao

Regionalism in international relations is based upon the notion that relations among states in a particular geographical region are germane or distinctive. It is only in the last quarter of the twentieth century that the idea received attention and started being systematically studied and analyzed. It is also assumed that relationships that exist among a group of nations in a region are often more important than their relationships with states outside the region. Moreover these relationships are to be more dynamic and often in a state of change promoting greater and greater understanding and integration economically, politically and finally leading to realization of a security community.

The concept of regionalism has gained acceptance among scholars as well as policy makers and statesmen. Integration among states in a region is a widespread phenomenon that transpires in almost every part of the world. The multiplicity of regional organizations brings home the idea that states are interdependent and cooperative. The end of the Cold War has been traversing regionalism from a limited positive interaction to unlimited explorative cooperation among states to derive political, economic and security benefits. Globalization is adding an impetus to regional integration.

At present all the major regions of the world formed regional groupings. It is estimated that nearly 134 members of the WTO have entered into regional groupings. In the period between 1948 and 1994, GATT contacting parties notified 118 Regional Trading Arrangements (RTAs) relating to trade in goods. Since the creation of the WTO, ninety additional arrangements have been made notified covering trade in goods and services.[1] Currently, almost every member of the WTO is a member of at least one regional organization. In the last few years regionalism/

regional integration has transformed into a movement with proliferation of regional groupings and increased diversification of membership.

In the early phase integration process took place in the Western Europe among the developed countries. During this phase regional organizations mostly acted as security groupings. Later on European regionalism was motivated in part by a desire for economic and political integration through developing institutions of transnational governance. To study the integration process many approaches were developed. In the European context scholars such as Ernst Haas, Joseph Nye, Karl Deutsch and David Mitrany contributed a lot to the integration theory in the form of functionalism, neo-functionalism and communication approaches. Further, Jacob Viner and Bela Balassa provided economic theory of regional integration.

The economic integration was developed as an offshoot of new-classical welfare economics. The underlying principle of this theory is comparative advantage and the attainment of increased welfare through the freeing of trade. Elimination of trade barriers among participating countries will create a large market which stimulates investment accelerating economic growth thus contributing welfare.[2] Theoretically economic integration is conceived as tariff arrangement in the form of free trade area, customs union, common market, economic union and complete economic integration showing various degrees of integration.[3] To Balassa, economic integration is (a means) resolving conflict between national sovereignty and economic self interest through political will and political interest. Thus regional integration is part of a political process and the final outcome is essentially determined by political factors.

In the 1960s regional integration emerged among the developing countries with different levels of economic development. The European experience inspired these nations to follow in their footsteps. However, they faced various difficulties due to variation in political structures, low level of economic development and security perceptions. In the case of Southeast Asia, the ASEAN integration process was successful as the nations were facing communist threat internally and externally. Since after the threat receded regional integration in the region has been slow. In Latin America, integration though started in 1950s, could not take off. In South America a Common Market – MERCOSUR – was established in 1991 by Argentina, Brazil, Paraguay and Uruguay.

In the 1980s, attempts were made in the direction of regional integration. The scope of activity largely was limited to trade and investment in the form of preferential trade arrangement or free trade area. Much of the emphasis aimed at economic integration because countries tried to seek security from the vagaries of the international markets and attempted to pool their resources together to become players in a globalized economy.

In the contemporary period regionalism is a strong force in the world. Regional integration is no longer an option but a necessity thrust upon countries. It has been expanding the economic orbit of the nation-states. Never before domestic reforms have been taken up and linked so closely to regional integration.

II

Emerging global scenario and the increasing problems in the region influenced the South Asian countries to move towards regional integration. But South Asia is a late starter in regionalism. One of the smaller countries took the initiative followed by several rounds of talks among the countries of South Asia which resulted in institutionalizing the regional organization – South Asian Association for the Regional Cooperation – in the region in the mid-1980s.

Prior to the establishment of the SAARC, all the South Asian countries faced economic difficulties within the region and discrimination in the global economic system. Trade with the West resulted in balance of payment crisis and increasing debt year after year. Their unsuccessful effort in addressing the trade related problems through the UNCTAD, failure of the North-South dialogue and the South-South cooperation deepened the crisis on the economic front. The rise of conservative leadership in the West in the form of Ronald Reagan and Margaret Thatcher and their advocacy of supremacy of market forces in the economy and emphasis on economic efficiency, fiscal discipline and cuts in social security and in subsidy programmes, denationalization, reducing the interventionist and regulatory role of state[4] further worsened the asymmetric relationship between the developed and developing countries. The then President of the United States, Ronald Reagan, laid the conditions for the US participation in a global dialogue saying that the developing countries should liberalize trade and improve investment climate, recognize the competence of international financial agencies including private institutions and aim at achieving greater economic growth that benefits all.[5] Subsequently free trade, removal of trade barriers, opening the economies for foreign investment have become dominant themes in the WTO negotiations, the IMF and the World Bank policies. They have become the dominant themes in regional integration processes throughout the world.

The global changes have far reaching effect on the South Asian countries. In the 1980s and early 1990s the countries of the region started liberalizing their economies by opening them for competition and removing restrictions on market forces under structural adjustment programmes.

The region, South Asia, is defined differently by various agencies. The World Bank includes SAARC countries and the newly joined Afghanistan. The UNDP includes Iran in South Asia. In this paper, South Asia means the founding members of the SAARC as cooperation has been going on for more than two decades from which Afghanistan was kept away due to domestic turmoil.

The countries of South Asia are divergent significantly in terms of population, geographical size and level of development. Population in 1998 ranged from 0.3 million (Maldives) to 983 million (India), while land area for countries other than Bhutan and Maldives, ranged from 66,000 sq.kms. (Sri Lanka) to 3,288,000 sq.kms.(India). The per capita GNP in the same year ranged from $210 (Nepal) to $1130 (Maldives) and in PPP terms, from $1090 (Nepal) to $4083 (Maldives).[6] There are variations in political institutions ranging from monarchy to military dictatorships to democracy. India is the only country which shares common borders with the rest. There is also a huge gap in threat perceptions. Most of the countries in the region view India with suspicion and perceive threat from it. Probably South Asia may be the only region where member countries' try to intervene clandestinely by extending support to groups that destabilize political regimes.

A comparison of South Asia with other regions in terms of economic indicators, infrastructure facilities and social indicators shows that the region remains one of the world's underdeveloped regions. Even at the end of the 1990s after a decade of reforms, it remained one of the poorest in terms of per capita in spite of one of the fastest growing regions in the world. Though the region witness fastest growth in export of goods and services, its reliance on external trade, a measure of the degree of integration with the global economy, continues to be the least.[7] Furthermore, it significantly lay behind in the fields of social provisions, information flow and performance of public institutions. Similar is the situation in literacy, education and health reflecting the enormity of challenges ahead for the region to catch up with other regions.

III

The South Asian countries, despite their asymmetries, political rivalries, suspicion and border disputes came together and formed the SAARC organization to deal with emerging challenges and to promote cooperation and integration at the regional level.

The SAARC charter contains peace, freedom, social justice and economic prosperity as objectives to be achieved by the member states through mutual understanding, good neighbourly relations and meaningful cooperation. It provides a framework within the spirit of friendship, trust and understanding. The Charter also aims at welfare of people of the region through economic growth but there are no clear indications how that can be attained. In the initial years, the member countries of the SAARC have agreed and adopted the Integrated Programme of Action in the areas of agriculture, rural development, telecommunications, meteorology, health and population control, science and technology, postal services and sports and culture.[8] The leaders expressed the confidence that regional cooperation in these areas make optimum use of their capacities for the benefit of the people of the region, accelerate the pace of economic development. It is viewed that such a cooperation is to complement and not to substitute bilateral or multilateral cooperation. Further, it is agreed that decisions would be taken unanimously and bilateral and contentions issues are barred from deliberations.

During the first decade of SAARC's existence, main objective was to promote cooperation in the agreed non-controversial areas among the member countries. Hardly any steps were initiated to integrate the region economically. During this period a number of technical committees were formed to look into different aspects of issues in the agreed area. The committees related to the field of science and technology were to promote exchanging and sharing of data and information to promote agricultural activities, eradication of poverty, promotion of literacy, rural development, etc. This was followed by SAARC treaties, conventions and agreements on issues such as suppression of terrorism, food security and drug trafficking. Most of these were only paper exercises. The limited success of the organization made a Pakistani scholar to observe that the regional cooperation and understanding among the members even on agreed fronts have not been encouraging.[9] However, SAARC succeeded in creating an institutional framework for regional cooperation against all odds.

Only in the second decade of SAARC's functioning, the agenda of economic cooperation figured in discussions. Though many summits were held, special meetings of the Council of Ministers at the Foreign

Ministers level had taken place, regional economic cooperation was viewed with skepticism. Distrust and regional rivalry were largely responsible for this sorry state of affairs and these factors influenced the regionalism in South Asia. Unanimity of decision and exclusion of bilateral issues further crippled the organization. Thus initially agreed areas of cooperation did not contain vital areas of economic cooperation such as trade, investment, tariffs and harmonization of fiscal and monetary policies. It is these areas that have become the building blocks of economic growth and integration. Thus South Asia failed to experience the economic dynamism of the rest of Asia.

From the early 1990s the South Asian countries launched economic reforms, trade liberalization and opened their economies for competition. Subsequently there also began economic cooperation among the countries in the region in an organized way. The aim was to derive mutual benefits for all irrespective of levels of economic development. For the first time the role of trade was recognized as a cementing factor at the regional level in the place of distrust, suspicion and acrimonious debates over competing claims and counter claims. They also recognized the importance of low tariffs, elimination of trade barriers, according Most Favoured Nation (MFN) status and promotion of investment as trade promotion measures.

Cooperation in the core economic areas has begun with the study on 'Trade, Manufactures and Services'. The study, in fact, became the basis for many policy initiatives and practical actions in the subsequent period in South Asia. Economic cooperation among the SAARC countries is considered as an imperative for promoting all round development of the region by the study. It recommended that "as a first step all countries in the region should accord to each other at least MFN status". It is to be followed by 'a product by product' approach for extending tariff concessions on products of mutual trade interest.[10] The Council of Ministers (highest decision-making body) at its ninth session held in Male in July 1991 endorsed the study and established the Committee on Economic Cooperation comprising commerce / trade secretaries of member states with a mandate to formulate and oversee implementation of specific measures, policies and programmes to strengthen and enhance intra-regional cooperation in the field of trade and economic relations.[11]

Following this, the Colombo summit of the SAARC set up an Inter-Governmental Group (IGG) to suggest measures for liberalizing trade in the region. The IGG met twice and prepared a draft SAPTA Agreement. The agreement on SAPTA was signed on 11 April 1993 at Dhaka summit and came into force on 7 December 1995 after formal approval at the eighth SAARC summit in New Delhi in May 1995.

SAPTA envisages the creation of a Preferential Trading Area to step up trade liberalization and economic cooperation among the SAARC countries. Its major objective is to promote and sustain trade through exchange of trade concessions. Its basic principles are: 1) overall reciprocity and mutuality of advantages to benefit equitably all member states; 2) inclusion of all products, manufactures and commodities in their raw, semi-processed and processed forms; 3) special and favourable treatment to Least Developed Countries (LDCs) negotiation of tariff reforms.[12] These principles are reflected in the national lists of tariff concessions. The lists not only contain non-reciprocal cuts in tariffs on agreed products applicable but also more favourable rules of origin in favour of LDCs.

Three rounds of negotiations have completed under the SAPTA. The fourth round, supposed to be completed by 2000 – was not held due to certain political developments in the region. Under the first round tariff concessions were offered on 226 products, with India offering tariff concessions on the largest number followed by Pakistan, Sri Lanka, Maldives, Nepal and Bangladesh in the descending order. On an average India offered fifty per cent cuts while others on an average agreed for ten per cent cuts.[13] As a result of these cuts intra-regional trade increased to six per cent.[14] The gains from the first round of SAPTA are modest due to the product by product approach and the small age of products in the total trade. Further, the cuts in tariffs are not deep enough to increase the trade substantially.

The benefits from the first round made the South Asian states to move forward for greater cooperation by launching the second round of SAPTA in January 1996. The SAPTA-II, which came into force in March 1997 covered 1900 products. In this round also India offered tariff concessions on largest number of products, of which 390 offered to all and 512 were offered to the LDCs. It listed all important Non-Tariff Barriers (NTBs) with particular reference to Quantitative Restrictions (QRs). It is followed by another round of negotiations resulting in exchange of tariff concessions on 3456 items. An important feature of the SAPTA-III is that it included chapterwise negotiations on a limited basis. Further each country is required to identify existing para-Tariffs and NTBs prevailing on items on which concessions had been granted.[15]

SAPTA rounds are a modest step initiated by the SAARC countries to promote greater economic cooperation and integration. It provides a framework to encourage intra-regional trade according discriminatory treatment through tariff concessions in favour of products manufactured within the region. The agreement also provides a number of approaches to lower tariffs such as product-by-product, across the board tariff reductions, sectoral and direct measures. It also envisages trade negotiations from time to time with a view to expand SAPTA.

SAPTA, in spite of laudable principles and best intentions, could not change the existing trade pattern in South Asia. Tariff concessions failed to address the larger problems associated with the SAPTA process. The steps initiated aimed at to enhance trade coverage rather than product coverage. For instance, products imported under the SAPTA concessions translated to only fifteen per cent of total imports between the SAARC countries.[16] As a result intra-SAARC trade marginally increased. It is also observed that the SAPTA process is hampered by slow moving 'product-by-product' approach.[17] Further, it is argued that preferential treatment of imports by lower tariffs and relaxed import controls need not necessarily result in mutual trade expansion. Because governments do not trade, they only make trade easier by lowering tariffs and NTBs. In such case, trade would expand further if reduced tariffs and tariff barriers lead to lower prices for the products.[18] In the case of ASEAN, it has been shown that Preferential Trade Arrangement did not lead to any marked improvement in trade within the region.[19] It is, therefore, suggested to take the preferential trade arrangement forward to free trade area.

Theories of economic integration advocate that regional integration is a process which has to go through certain phases. They are preferential trading arrangement, free trade area, customs union and finally moving to the stage of economic union. In the early stages of their evolution the EU and the ASEAN began with the preferential trading arrangement with a common market with zero internal tariffs and a common external tariff against non-member states. From the experience of the EU it becomes clear that a region can become dynamic with increase in production, income and employment. Improving terms of trade and investment too can increase a region's competition in exports through PTA. The next stage of integration is the establishment of Free Trade Area (FTA) in a region. The advantages of FTA are that geographically contiguous countries can operate at low transaction costs because of proximity of markets, availability of infrastructure across the region and more or less similar consumption patterns. FTA also creates a large market which enhances investment climate in the region. It provides an opportunity for member states to acquire a better leverage to meet challenges of globalization.

To overcome structural limitations, weak intra – SAARC trade linkages and to further liberalize trade in the region the South Asian countries embarked upon the creation of South Asia Free Trade Area (SAFTA). It is an attempt to make economic integration irreversible.

The agreement on SAFTA, drafted by the Committee of Experts was signed on 5 January 2004 at the twelfth SAARC summit held in Islamabad. Prior to the signing, way back in 1995 the sixth meeting of the Council of Ministers agreed on the need to strive for the realization of SAFTA. To realize the objective an Inter-Governmental Expert Group is set up to identify the necessary steps. The tenth SAARC summit held in July 1998 in Colombo set up a Committee of Experts to draft a comprehensive framework for creating a FTA in South Asia taking the asymmetries in development into consideration.

The SAFTA agreement aims to promote and enhance mutual trade and economic cooperation among member countries by (i) eliminating trade barriers and facilitating the cross-border movement of goods; (ii) promoting conditions of fair competition; (iii) creating effective mechanism for the implementation of the agreement.

As per the agreement, SAFTA will be implemented through (a) trade liberalization programme, (b) rule of origin, (c) dispute settlement procedures.

Trade is to be liberalized by bringing down tariffs in the following manner:

1. The tariff reduction by the non-LDCs from existing tariff rates to twenty per cent shall be done within two years from the date of coming into force of agreement.
2. The tariff reduction by the LDCs from existing tariff rates will be to thirty per cent within two years.
3. The subsequent tariff reduction by Non-LDCs from twenty per cent or below to zero to five per cent shall be done within five years beginning from the third year.
4. The subsequent tariff reduction by the LDCs from thirty per cent or below to zero to five per cent shall be done within eight years beginning from the third year.

Additional measures include (i) simplification and harmonization of customs clearance procedure, (ii) simplification and harmonization of import licensing and registration procedures, (iii) removal of barriers to intra-SAARC investments, (iv) simplification of banking procedures for import financing, (v) transit facilities for efficient intra-SAARC trade, especially for the land-locked states.[20]

SAFTA agreement is to be fully implemented by the year 2013 for non-LDCs states and by 2016 for LDC members.

Scholars and Organizations tried to project benefits to be accrued to different nations under SAFTA. The projections are based on econometric study through simulation on different assumptions. T.N Srinivasan study covered different rates of cuts in tariffs. It concluded that unilateral trade liberalization promises substantial gains; if all tariffs on intra-regional trade are abolished, total trade increases between three per cent of GDP of India and fifty nine per cent of GDP of Nepal and in between for others. A tariff reduction by fifty per cent increases trade between one per cent of GDP for India and nine per cent for Nepal. It says the increases are much more for Sri Lanka and Bangladesh. South Asia as a region may do much better while dealing with the EU, NAFTA and East Asia.[21] Estimates made by the Associated Chambers of Commerce and Industry are that India's trade with the SAARC countries can touch Rs. 50,000 crore by 2010 and Rs. 1,00,000 crore by 2015 from the present Rs. 25,000 crore. The gains from SAFTA can be further increased by promoting intra-SAARC investment, technology transfers, joint R & D projects, joint ventures, modernizing infrastructure, telecommunications, customs clearance facilities, creating necessary institutions and connectivity, etc.

SAFTA, despite laudable principles, greater hope and excellent projections suffers from certain inherent deficiencies, numerous difficulties and uncertainty. Asymmetries and political bickerings further cast a shadow on the operations of free trade area in the region. It is these that made SAFTA negotiations to go on for almost a decade. Despite efforts for a decade, the treaty contains no specific provisions for deeper integration except defining the measures to be initiated in general terms. This makes the members not to make specific commitments. Second, the areas identified for cooperation are part of the declaration rather than part of the SAFTA treaty. It provides enough scope for members to dilute their involvement and commitment. Third, the treaty does not incorporate all components that are essential for the effective functioning of free trade regime. Fourth, the treaty has some confusing provisions and gray areas such as Rules of Origin, Sensitive Lists and Technical Assistance for LDCs in which difficulties may arise out of the inability of the member states. Similarly, differential treatment to the LDCs have not been spelt out. Fifth, the SAFTA treaty has not addressed the issue of free movement of people (labour), trade in services and improvement in physical infrastructure across the region. Sixth, trade in goods may not be encouraging as the region has a limited trade basket. All the nations maintain large sensitive lists where trade liberalization would not be applicable. Seventh, it includes concessions on commodities that countries do not produce or trade at all.

However, optimism stems from the fact that SAFTA encourages greater economic cooperation between participating countries. It includes new areas such as investments and the formation of a common energy grid for the South Asian region. In spite of reservations and apprehensions, SAFTA can become what the member countries can create out of it. Though difficulties are ahead, signatories may overcome them out of necessity and self-interest.

From Here to Where

Next stage of integration is the creation of a South Asian Union. On the realization of a Union in the region and the difficulties on the way, scholars and statesmen have commented upon and aired views for the last few years. The Group of Eminent Persons has envisaged a South Asian Economic Union by 2020 in two stages by creating a FTA by 2010 and a Customs Union by 2015. The former Indian Prime Minister, A.B. Vajpayee put forth the idea of an Economic Union for South Asia at the Islamabad summit. He also contemplated the idea of the South Asian region having a single currency. The former Prime Minister of Nepal, Surya Bahadur Thapa in his lecture in New Delhi suggested that creation of a South Asian Community is possible through greater cooperation and partnership. More important of all these is that the Islamabad declaration committed SAARC's move towards a South Asian Economic Union. Most of the statements are general in nature without offering a blueprint how it can be realized. But the Groups of Eminent Persons suggested concrete steps in the form of developing infrastructure across the region, trade facilitation measures, creating a single investment area and vertical integration of the labour market, capital flow and macro-economic policies in the region.[22] At this stage the idea may seem a difficult proposition but not an impossible task. Because in the past there prevailed political and economic coherence, administrative unity, exchange of currencies and free movement of people during Mughal period and British India.[23] The historical links and values remain strong even to this day. All these can be revived to move towards an economic union if there is a political will.

IV

The shape of things to come may be unclear, but there is little doubt that a new world is in the making. Nowhere is this more so than in Asia. Regional cooperation and economic growth are the new building blocks of the emerging global architecture in which geo-economics has been assuming a leading role. This is also the case in South Asia.

Regional cooperation is analyzed in terms of trade in goods and capital. In the emerging global scenario economic growth and regional integration are talked in terms of cooperation in the field of energy. In South Asia also energy can be a cementing factor as there are states starved of energy along with states having abundant energy potential. The sector can be harnessed and properly shared for the development of countries, increasing trade potential, inviting investment from within and outside the region and eradicating poverty in South Asia.

In Europe, Jean Monnet used the same materials that had previously divided the nations as the foundation of Europe (EEC). He was concerned about what could be done to link France and Germany, and implant a cementing factor between the two. Then the answer came: "coal and steel were at once the key to economic power and the raw materials for forging weapons of war. This double role gave them immense symbolic significance, ...To pool them across frontiers would reduce their malign prestige and turn them instead into a guarantee of peace".[24]

Can South Asia follow the same method? Perhaps, yes. But which material can be used as build block and cementing factor that divides the South Asian nations. The triggering element is Kashmir, which has been disturbing the region for half a century. The issue cannot be the 'cementing factor' because it has ideological or political flavour. There is also no agreement between the actors of the drama and none of them is sure of the role played by the other. Further, there is the two nation theory. The other issue which is contentious and yet can become a cementing factor in the near future and bring not only nations together but also help in development in pooling the South Asian waters or hydro-resources. Creating of a High Authority with the jurisdiction over the regional waters can become an experiment to be emulated by others. It would be a forward march and yet not an easy proposition. Long back the former President of Pakistan, Ayub Khan proposed improving relations with India by suggesting jointly harnessing the annual floods of the Ganges and the Brahmaputra after visiting the flood devastated area of East Pakistan (Bangladesh). In a radio broadcast in September 1964 he said: "It grieves my heart that year after year this menace of floods wipes away parts of the results of our hard efforts". Observing that India too had same problem, he added that ".... It will be possible to come to some reasonable arrangement with India and that the relations between our two countries will improve and start moving in the right direction.[25]

Ayub Khan was concerned only with managing floods. The same waters can be used for the promotion of cooperation and integration in the form of producing energy and connectivity through a South Asian energy grid. Similarly natural gas and hydro-carbon resources can be added to the hydro resources to derive optimal benefit in the region. Thus hydro resources and others can be harnessed for regional integration as well as to generate energy.

South Asia has been experiencing rapid increase in energy consumption. It has increased by fifty per cent between 1990 and 1998. India's energy demand would increase by 3.8 per cent per year through 2020 according to an estimate.[26] At the same time South Asia is an energy deficit area in spite of vast potential resources. There is a gap between demand and availability of energy. A great complementarity exists among the countries in this sector which can transform the economic future of all the countries. Greater integration is possible in augmenting region's water resources. It is estimated that only 10.57 per cent of total potential hydel power is being utilized at present.[27]

India has vast hydro and hydrocarbon resources' potential of which most is unexploited so far. Its eastern quadrant comprising eastern U.P., eastern M.P., Bihar, Orissa, West Bengal and the northeast region falls within the Ganga-Brahmaputra-Meghana basin. It is richly endowed with huge water and hydro potential resources. The region is characterized by low agricultural productivity, limited industrialization, high migration and annual flooding. The northeastern India too provides an opportunity to harness huge hydro-electric potential of over 40,000 MW. The Brahmaputra/Tsango has tremendous energy stored in the 2500 metre drop in the giant U-bend. A Japanese firm had undertaken a desktop topographical study of the power potential of the Brahmaputra U-bend. The study concluded that a 240 km tunnel from Tibet to Assam, supported by a regulating dam just South of Lhasa and another nine power dams around the horse-shoe, might have a potential of 70,000 MW, the tunnel drop alone accounting for 48,000 MW".[28] It also proposed a thirty six month pre-feasibility study with the approval of the Chinese and the Indian governments and thereafter a twenty year construction period.[29]

India's northeast neighbours, Nepal and Bhutan also have large hydro resources which can be harnessed through high dams. Hydro-power to these states is to what oil and gas are to the Gulf countries. These resources can meet the energy demand of other countries in the region. It is theoretically estimated that Nepal hydro potential is around 83,000 MW and a techno-economic potential is around 47,000 MW. So far Kathmandu could harness only 300 MW of hydro power.[30] The financial and technological magnitude make Nepal not to exploit the resources. The Pancheshwar dam (6400 MW) and a regulating dam (150 MW – 1000 MW) below it and the Sapta Kosi-cum-Kurule-Sun Kosi Diversion Project (4000 MW – 5000 MW) are to be resumed with India's assistance.[31]

Nepal has a guaranteed market for its power in India. It can also plan developing industrial parks along the Indian border to attract Indian investment. With a regional power grid, Nepal can also aim to export power to Bangladesh and even to Pakistan.

Bhutan's hydro-potential is estimated to be at 30,000 MW. India has been playing a crucial role in harnessing its hydro resources in the form of providing financial and technical assistance and buying power from Bhutan. Hydro power is considered as an engine of growth as it is financing development and economic infrastructure.[32] A vision paper published by the government of Bhutan on the silver jubilee of the monarch, King Jigme Singye Wangchuck's coronation set out to develop only 3000 MW of hydro power by 2017.[33] This is much shorter of its potential. Once the kingdom opens up its power sector for foreign investment it can lead to development, prosperity and stability of the whole region.

Availability of vast hydro resources provides an opportunity for all the countries in the region to integrate as this sector would generate wealth beyond anyone's dream. Along with wealth it brings in development and growth in the form of schools, hospitals, roads and electricity. Energy resources are non-zero sum game providing a shared opportunity in partnership.

The two-way cooperation in the utilization of hydro resources is to be seen as a forward march towards achieving energy security in the region. Once a regional energy scenario is constructed, a single energy grid connecting national grids across the region can be planned. This plan was already called as 'Energy Ring' at the twelfth SAARC summit. Regional energy trading can also increase the reliable power supply and achieve economy in the operation of power plants.

Large reserves of hydrocarbon resources too can be considered for greater integration in the era of globalization. Assam has an estimated hydrocarbon potential of about 1300 million tones of oil and 156 billion cubic meters (BCM) of natural gas. Only four per cent of oil bearing strata has been explored. Tripura is also estimated having a gas reserve of seventeen billion cubic meters.[34] India's neighbour, Bangladesh, is estimated to have large reserves of natural gas. The World Bank and the Asian Development Bank estimate the natural gas reserves to be between thirty to eighty trillion cubic feet. To exploit these reserves the country needs huge resources and technology which are available outside the country. Investment and technology can be raised only at the global level to utilize those resources for the development of the country.

So far little has been done across the region. Resources and technology are available, all that is missing is the political will. Hydro-economics should end the paradox of countries being resource rich but people remaining poor. This is possible only through cooperation across the borders and greater and greater integration in the region.

V

Integration process in South Asia is slow and could not move the way it should have. Many political and economic factors impact the process, the former dominating the latter. From the very beginning the SAARC process is affected by mutual distrust and rivalry. Political tensions and differences between India and Pakistan continue to cause periodic tremors. Territorial disputes and cross border issues continue to fester. There are also spillovers of domestic politics on regionalism. Thus South Asia is marked more by conflicts than cooperation. The King of Bhutan, Jigme Wangchuk, in 1985 observed that "In the geopolitical realities of our region, it would be unrealistic to ignore the primacy of the political factor, as in the final analysis, it will be the political environment of the region which will determine the shape and scope of regional cooperation in South Asia".[35]

The region suffers from structural limitations imposed by the SAARC charter. The charter bars bilateral issues being discussed at the summits. As a result there is no institution and mechanism to discuss contentions issues and differences arising and thereupon to resolve them. Had there been a mechanism, the separatist movements in Kashmir and North-East India, Tamil separation in Sri Lanka, Nepalese issue in Bhutan and Chakmas problem in Bangladesh could have been addressed involving neighbours with greater coordination. The former Indian Foreign Secretary, Shyam Saran observed that SAARC has shied away from undertaking even a single collaborative project. Prime Minister, Manmohan Singh, while speaking at the thirteenth SAARC summit said that SAARC process has fallen far short of expectations.[36]

The SAARC integration process also suffers from many economic and trade related impediments. Forces of demand and supply, comparative cost advantage do not govern trade, investment and macro-economic policies. SAARC as an institution merely advocates collective economic benefits. But this is less than integration. A major country like Pakistan refuses to integrate regionally by regulating its trade and refusing to accord MFN status to India. Further the region lakhs physical infrastructure, complementarities, transit facilities and common customs procedures.

Infrastructure and Transit Network

The intra-SAARC trade is very small. On an average it is less than three per cent of world trade and is about four per cent of region's total trade. This means the market is small and trade suffers from many drawbacks. One of the major drawbacks is lack of proper physical infrastructure and absence of transit networks across the region. There are few border crossings by road and they are clogged and ill maintained. It is recognized that paucity and run-down quality of infrastructure is the single largest bottleneck in the way of rapid economic growth. The development of infrastructure significantly improves intra-regional trade. Smooth movement of vehicles and commodities within the eastern region of South Asia alone, it is estimated, would increase the intra-SAARC trade to about eleven billion dollars.[37] The Expert Group of Infrastructure (for India) noted that India itself lost huge foreign exchange to Colombo and Singapore in transshipments. It noted that if desired rate of economic growth is to be achieved a quantum leap in infrastructure is required. It targeted an all India port-capacity of 390 million tones against a likely actual of around 300 million tones by 2001 and 650 million tones by 2006.[38]

Similarly development of integrated transit networks is essential pre-condition to transform South Asia into the 'take off stage'. Since some of the South Asian states are land locked, transit facilities play an important role in converting them into 'growth hubs'. At present there exist only bilateral transit agreements. A regional transit arrangement has yet to be worked out. It is observed that in the absence of transit agreement, products have to move in a circular route thus increasing their price making them unviable for customers. For instance, the Indian Cargo destined for Dhaka moves to Chittagong from Bombay via Colombo or Singapore by sea and from Chittagong to Dhaka. Moving a twenty tonne TEU by this route could cost \$ 1800-\$ 2000 as against \$ 500-\$ 600 if moved directly overland. Dyes from Gujarat used by the Bangladesh garment industry move around this route.[39] A transit agreement between India and Bangladesh would greatly reduce distance between West Bengal and Agartala by a quarter of the present all India route via Siliguri if a limited stretch in Bangladesh is converted to broad-gauge line. Similarly trade between Bangladesh and Nepal would benefit if latter's access to Chittagong port is permitted.

Article 12 of the SAPTA agreement calls on the contracting parties to grant transit facilities to accelerate trade. No initiative is taken so far in the absence of political will.

Competitive Economies

The economies of South Asian countries are more competitive and less complimentary. Most of them are basically agricultural economies with a small industrial sector manufacturing a narrow range of products. They are producing more or less similar goods and they are being traded within the region. Some of these also face competition from cheap alternative products from outside the region. For instance, India and Sri Lanka produce tea and compete each other inside and outside the region. Pakistan imports CTC tea which is not available in adequate quantities. As a result products based on agriculture and light manufacturing compete with each other in the South Asian market.

South Asian economies are less complimentary. It also appears that complimentaries have reached their limits. Goods produced on a large scale in certain SAARC countries do not meet the required demand due to inferior quality. For instance, India produces a wide range of machinery and manufactured goods but other SAARC countries find them inferior to products produced outside the region in terms of quality. Similar production base also makes trade less complimentary. Therefore, almost all the South Asian countries are having more trade with countries of North America and Europe. Even after launching diversified exports from the 1990s their main export remains NAFTA and EU. It means the SAARC countries find greater complimentaries with countries outside South Asia.

To overcome the problem it is advocated that complementarities are to be created. The Group of Eminent Persons representing the Coalition for Action on South Asian Cooperation (CASAC) looking at South Asia by 2010 advocated creating complementarities in the areas of water and energy by establishing a regional power grid.[40] It has also been suggested by a Bangladeshi scholar that India could reduce jute acreage and production in favour of Bangladesh which is having more efficient jute industry. In return India could export engineering products to Bangladesh since it has a comparative advantage. [41] Similarly CTC tea can be grown by Sri Lanka to meet Pakistani requirements. To do so modernization and restructuring of industry has to be taken up and range of products is to be widened to create greater complementarities.

Market Access

Another issue that distorts trade among the South Asian countries is limited market access for goods of other countries in the region. Market access is determined by tariffs and non-tariff barriers. Despite commitment to economic integration, South Asian states exhibit reluctance to open their markets to each other with high tariffs and non-tariff barriers. Further, their attitude to FDI is more or less negative and maintain stringent exchange controls. SAPTA and SAFTA could address tariffs to same extent but they still remain high in the form of landing charges, port charges and warehouse charges. Under 'Gujral Doctrine', India could remove non-tariff barriers on nearly 2000 products.[42] But political relations between SAARC countries had spill over effect on the trade process. The result is bilateral trade agreements to accelerate trade between the signatories.[43] Under the agreements, countries maintain a negative list with a large number of products restricting trade.[44]

Economic integration is not a smooth process in South Asia. In spite of regional agreements, bilateral political relationships to a large extent determine trade relationships. For instance, Pakistan's trade with India is affected as the former wants to find a solution to Kashmir. As the talks on the issue are not progressing in the desired direction, Pakistan dismisses India's position that trade must not be held hostage to the settlement of a long-standing problem. It also refuses to grant MFN status to India. SAFTA also could not become effective between India and Pakistan because of Islamabad's stand that its trade with India would be governed by the existing bilateral arrangements.[45] Further, it notified that the trade between the two is to be governed by the positive list which contains around 1,0000 items.[46] However, a report prepared by the Central Bank of Pakistan, the State Bank of Pakistan, observed that Pakistan would save $400 million to $900 million on its import bill if it would expand the positive list and allow imports from India. The report further says that the bilateral trade would increase by seventy nine per cent by entering into a PTA.[47] In spite of positive outcomes of greater integration, the Commerce Minister of Pakistan reiterated that his country's trade with India would continue to be guided under the existing bilateral regime. Equal treatment to India under SAFTA would not be possible "until there is progress towards resolution of some political disputes between the two countries including the Kashmir issue".[48]

Inadequate tariff cuts, protectionist policies and political distortions result in informal trade between the South Asian countries. Another feature of distortion is growing third country trade via Singapore, Dubai and Hong Kong.

Customs and Procedures

Excessive preoccupation with protectionism and regulation result in inefficient customs and immigration arrangements and cumbersome procedures in South Asia leading to slow growth in trade. A lengthy procedure for customs clearance, filling forms, delays are leading to higher costs, corruption and informal deals which in turn are resulting in evasion of laws and loss of revenue to the exchequer. An exporter from Bangladesh required to fill up twenty documents entailing 116 copies requiring fifty five signatures and costing ten per cent of the export value. In India even more elaborate procedures required to fill up twenty nine documents entailing 118 copies requiring 256 signatures, costing ten per cent of the value of the goods and engaging the services of twenty two clerks. Nepal demands more documents.[49] Absence of similar customs rules and procedures are hampering not only the opportunities for trade but also destroying whatever the chances are there for its growth. They are also contributing to states to look for opportunities elsewhere. That's why intra-regional trade more or less remains insignificant in South Asia.

To overcome barriers and to stimulate trade and to promote greater integration all the South Asian states have to wake up from inertia. To do that there is a need for technological development, improving managerial practices, higher investments not only in R&D but also in preparing regional studies and strengthening human resources.

VI

The idea of South Asia moving towards a Customs Union and an Economic Union is raised once again at the fourteenth SAARC summit. President of Mardives, Manmoon Abdul Gyoom pointed out that SAFTA is a spring board for a deeper integration of the SAARC countries. He said that SAFTA can become a platform on the journey towards a Custom Union and Economic Union. Speaking at the same summit Prime Minister of Nepal, Girija Prasad Koirala observed that members of the SAARC "should strive to take concrete and interlocking steps in an accelerated pace to operationalize the PTA....".[50] To accelerate the pace, he further said that trade facilitation measures should receive priority. For this, additional trading opportunities would be exploited by facilitating additional investment flows, technology transfers and developing human capital. Further, critical issues such as benefits from trade and distribution of the benefits of trade have to be given attention. The process of cooperation should include specific sectoral programmes. Sectoral programmes are to include emerging areas such as services, tourism and investment in addition to common issues of the region including eradication of poverty, ensuring drinking water, sustainable development and agriculture.

Services Sector

Services have come to drive the economies since the last quarter of the twentieth century. The share of the services in the GDP has been increasing due to rapid developments in technology and revolution in communications. Technological innovations are adding new services in production and processes sectors thus determining the quality and competitiveness of products in market as well as nations in a globalized economy. More employment opportunities are being generated in service sector across the borders and across the fields such as transport, banking, health, education, tourism, insurance and management services.

In recent years service sector has been significantly contributing to the economies of the South Asian countries. It figures prominently in South Asian trade. Slowly the region is fast emerging as a hub of service sector. A large number from within and outside the region are seeking different services. Nepal, Maldives and Sri Lanka emerged as major tourist destinations in recent times raising opportunities in the field. India has emerged as a major destination for health tourism, IT professionals and educational services. With the improvements in the quality of services in these sectors, the trade in services would likely to grow across the region.

The service sector integration across the region is likely to bring more benefits to all the countries in South Asia. The obstacles in these sectors are limited compared to the trade in products. Once the governments decide opening the sector for regional cooperation, the benefits will be enormous for the people.

Tourism

Tourism is one of the largest foreign exchange earning sectors. It is a highly labour intensive area and it can make significant contribution to the development of economies in the form of inviting investment and generating employment opportunities for skilled and semi-skilled people. It is also an expanding trade area in South Asia. However there exist cumbersome procedures for obtaining visas and there are foreign exchange restrictions. Once the obstacles are removed and tourism promotion measures are initiated there is a greater scope for business and trade in this sector.

Tourism is the best medium to promote understanding among people. It helps visitors to understand history and cultures of others and exchanging views across borders. Misunderstandings, mistrust and misperceptions can be minimized through constant interactions between the people and cultures. This is more so in South Asia because of asymmetries, political conflicts and mutual suspicions. Tourism can bridge the gap paving the way for continuous interaction and dialogue among people across the borders. It can also act as a confidence building measure among peoples of South Asia.

A Common Regional Identity

Regional integration also requires a common regional identity not only in economic terms but also in political, social and cultural terms to strengthen the bonds among people across borders. A common identity also brings together the elite and masses throughout the region. It minimizes the political divergences, economic disparities which help the region to move towards a community and finally to an economic Union. In Europe, the European identity remains the core value in bringing the states together for strengthening economic partnership. The common identity in the form of history, rule of law, secularism, diplomacy and culture helped the EEC to move to EU with supranational political institutions by coordinating economic policies with sectoral programmes. In Asia, the ASEAN though founded on political and security imperatives, gradually promoted economic cooperation. In the process it assumed on ASEAN identity known as ASEAN style of diplomacy in addressing regional issues and meeting the global challenges. A regional identity may be acquired through either historical process or developing a regional organization incrementally or a novel experiment that continues the cooperation at regional level.

Regionalism in Europe is a great success because it is a civilization, a culture and an idea and an evolving political and economic entity with common history, common social, political and economic institutions. In such circumstances it is not difficult to construct an identity. Whereas South Asia, as a concept, has no historical basis. It is a new construct in geographical terms emerged only in the post World War II period. The region in history, culture and civilization is either India or India and its neighbourhood.[51] India's neighbours dispute this construct and assert their own identity and separateness. The Indian scholars would like to stress the unity of the region, whereas the Pakistani, Sri Lankan and Nepalese scholars like to stress upon diversity of the region. Thus, South Asia, as a concept, brings into focus different identities.

In spite of ideational problems, there is a need to construct South Asia to bring out a common identity either as a civilization or as a socio-cultural area with similar common threads in the midst of pluralities. Because of this common identity there goes unparalled interactions among South Asian people. It is the common threads that make people to appreciate and welcome the artistic works of Mohammed Rafi, Lata Mangeshkar, Runu Laila and late Nusrat Fateh Ali Khan and Amitabh Bacchan. Cricketers like Imran Khan, Shoib Akhtar, Sachin Tendulkar, Muralitharan and Jayasuria are adored beyond national boundaries. Thus it is civilizational and cultural unity that sustains a common identity despite political divisions, threat perceptions. States, statesmen, intellectuals, media personnel, business groups, NGOs have to use these common threads in promoting an identity across South Asia. Such an effort can lead to greater cooperation and integration. Finally it may lead to move from free trade area to an economic union leading to free flow of ideas, goods, capital, technology, etc. throughout South Asia.

Conclusion

Regionalism in South Asia has began with the establishment of the SAARC. The organization is slow to embrace the concept of economic cooperation. Once it realized the importance of economic integration, it has set itself an ambitious agenda and has been making steady progress. The agenda raises high expectations. It also makes scholars to doubt whether the South Asian countries can move in the chosen path by keeping away the political differences given the history of the region. Others view that if South Asia fails to do so the price of non-cooperation is even greater. Everyone recognizes that progress on economic front is essential to lift the region from backwardness. Economic integration is the best medium to do so and it can be the best confidence building measure to promote goodwill and understanding among the people of the region.

The SAARC process is very slow in spite of leaders and officials meeting almost every day to exchange views or to discuss something or the other. It takes years to come to an understanding and finalize the issues of cooperation. It is better to hasten the process of negotiations for greater integration. Negotiations are to include not only tradable items but also services, tourism and cultural exchanges and other emerging sectors. In fact, it is the non-trade areas that may reduce tensions and promote Track-II and Track-III diplomacy and provide a common regional identity which is the need of the hour for the region.

Here one can emulate a tradition prevailing among the people of South Indian states. A music tradition has been in existence for centuries through the length and breadth of South India. The music is known as Carnatic, rendered by the Tamil artists and Keertanas and Kritis are in Telugu. The music is so popular that it cuts all the barriers – geographical, linguistic, religious, regional and touches the minds and hearts of elites and masses and brings them together. It is a base for all music compositions and songs written in all the South Indian languages. What a wonderful fusion and yet having regional identities. Why can not South Asia emulate the same? The region can have a common identity amidst pluralism. It is worth trying to achieve regional integration in South Asia.

References

1. See "Regional Integration and the Multilateral Trading System", htpp://www.wto.org and Young Jong Choi and James A. Caparaso, "Comparative Regional Integration", in Walter Carlsnaes, Thomas Risse and Beth A. Simmons, *Hand book of International Relations*, London: Sage Publishers, 2002, p. 480.
2. Bela A. Balassa, *The Theory of Economic Integration*, Homewood: Irwin, 1961, p. 2.
3. *Ibid.*, p. 961.
4. Andrew Gamble, *The Free Economy and the Strong State*, Hong Kong: Macmillan Ltd., 1989, pp. 36-38.
5. See *Asian Recorder*, 12-18 November 1981, p. 16314.
6. Y.V. Reddy, "Globalization and Challenges for South Asia", in Y.V. Reddy, *Lectures on Economic and Financial Sector Reforms in India*, New Delhi: Oxford University Press, 2004, p. 149.
7. *Ibid*, p. 148.
8. Jayanta Kumar Ray and Shantanu Chakrabarti, "Institutionalization of the Regional Space in South Asia", in Jayanta Kumar Ray (ed.), *Aspects of India's International Relations 1700 to 2000: South Asia and the World*, New Delhi: Pearson, Longman, 2007, pp. 449–453.
9. Gowher Rizvi, *South Asia in a Changing International Order*, New Delhi: Sage Publishers, 1993, p. 147.
10. See Saman Kelegama, "SAPTA and Its Future", in Eric Gonsalves and Nancy Jetly (ed.), *The Dynamics of South Asia: Regional Cooperation and SAARC*, New Delhi: Sage Publications, 1999, p. 172.

11. The Committee on Economic Cooperation over the years has emerged as the central group within SAARC addressing trade and economic related issues. It has also provided recommendations and guidance in identifying new areas of cooperation. Its functions include recommending policies and measures for promoting intra-regional trade, joint ventures, industrial complementarity and investments. Its mandate covers areas such as quality control, standards and measurements, customs cooperation, harmonization of documentations and procedures and rules of origin.
12. South Asian Association for Regional Cooperation (SAARC), *Agreement on SAARC Preferential Trading Agreement (SAPTA)*, Kathmandu: SAARC Secretariat, 1993.
13. Charan D. Wadhva, "Assessing SAARC Preferential Trading Arrangement", in Eric Gonsalves and Nancy Jetly, n. 10, p. 201.
14. I.N. Mukherjee, "South Asian Preferential Trade Agreement: India's Role", *South Asian Survey*, vol. 6, no. 1, January-June 1999, p. 26.
15. Dushni Weerakoon, "Economic Cooperation in South Asia: Challenges and Constraints" in Ȧ. Subramanyam Raju (ed.), *Reconstructing South Asia: An Agenda*, New Delhi: Gyan Publishing House, 2007, p. 194.
16. *Ibid.*
17. Nisha Taneja, *India's Informal Trade with Sri Lanka*, Working Paper No. 82, New Delhi: Indian Council for Research in International Economic Relations, April 2002, p. 26.
18. Eric Gonsalves, "Regional Cooperation in South Asia", *South Asian Survey*, vol.13, no. 2, July – December 2006, p. 200.
19. See Kelegama, n. 10, p. 178.
20. See http://www.saarc.sec.org/data/agenda/economic/safta/
21. Cited in Wadhva, n. 13, p. 196.
22. See Kalyan Raipuria; "SAARC in the New Millennium: Need for Financial Vision", *South Asian Survey*, vol. 8, no. 1, January – June 2001, p. 29.
23. Rehman Sobhan, "The Need for Economic Integration", *South Asian Survey*, vol. 13, no. 2, July–December 2006, pp. 245-252 and Gonsalves, n. 18, p. 199.
24. Cited in Claude Arpi, "Confederation for South Asia: The European Model", *South Asian Politics*, vol. 5, no. 10, February 2007, p. 12.
25. *Ibid*, p. 13.
26. "South Asia Regional Overview", The US Energy Information Administration, March 2001, http://www.eia.doe.gov/emen/eabs/sasia.html cited in Ray and Chakrabarti, n. 8, p. 472.
27. Mahendra P. Lama, "Economic Reforms and the Energy Sector in South Asia: Scope for Cross Border Power Trade", *South Asian Survey*, vol. 7, no. 1, January–June 2000, p. 9.

28. B.G. Vergheese, *Reorienting India: The New Geo-Politics of Asia*, New Delhi: Konark Publishers Pvt. Ltd., 2001, p. 161.
29. *Ibid.*
30. *Ibid*, p. 67.
31. *Ibid*, p. 68.
32. Bhutan sells its surplus power to India which constitutes 87.5 per cent of its exports. In March 2007, the Indian funded 1,020 MW power project became operational. As a result of power exports the Bhutanese economy recorded twelve per cent growth rate and GDP per person is reckoned to be $1,400. This in turn resulted in government spending twenty five per cent of its budget on health and education, which is on unusual feature in the world in the contemporary period. The growth is also providing employment opportunities for the 1,00,000 migrant workers from India. See *The Economist*, 28 April 2007, p. 36.
33. See Verghese, n. 28, p. 72.
34. *Ibid*, p. 160.
35. Cited in Bimal Prasad, "Prospects for Greater Cooperation in South Asia: The Political Dimension", in Gonsalves and Jetly, n. 10, pp. 64-65.
36. Gonsalves, n. 18, p. 198.
37. *Growth Zones in South Asia: What can we learn from Southeast Asia*, Centre for Policy Dialogue, No. 20, January 2000, Dhaka, p. 481, cited in Ray and Chakrabarti, n. 8, p. 469.
38. Cited in Vergheese, n. 28, p. 156.
39. *Ibid*, p. 171.
40. Cited in *ibid*, p. 154.
41. Rehman Sobhan, *Transforming Eastern South Asia, Building Growth Zones for Economic Cooperation*, University Press Ltd., Dhaka, 1999, cited in *ibid*, p. 177.
42. Weerakoon, n. 15, p. 195.
43. India signed bilateral trade agreements with Sri Lanka, Nepal and Bhutan. Similar agreement is proposed by Bangladesh. Pakistan also expressed its wish to sign similar agreements with other SAARC countries except India.
44. Under the India-Sri Lanka Free Trade Agreement, Sri Lanka's negative list account for over twenty per cent of India's total exports to Sri Lanka, and India's negative list account for over thirteen per cent of Sri Lanka's total exports to India. Free Trade Agreement is considered a forward step in comparison to market access granted under SAPTA. See Weerakoon, n. 15, p. 197.
45. *The Hindu*, 31 July 2006 and 29 March 2006.
46. *The Hindu*, 8 July 2006 and 4 November 2006.

47. *The Hindu*, n. 45.
48. *Ibid.*
49. Cited in Vergheese, n. 28, p. 179.
50. *The Hindu*, 4 April 2007.
51. I.P. Khosla, "Constructing The South Asian Community", *South Asian Survey*, vol. 6, no. 2, July–December 1999, p. 189.

12

Towards Building a South Asian Union

Syed Ali Mujtaba

There is a general consensus for regional peace and development in the South Asian region. However, when it comes to the idea of forming a regional block there is a tug of war between the forces of nationalism and regionalism. The skeptics want to cling on to the hard earned freedom of the nation states, while the futurists profess that regionalism could be an answer to many unresolved questions and may change their lives for better. In this tussle, some hardened nationalist may like to be convinced about the utility and purpose of a South Asian Union.

This paper intends to build an argument for a common South Asian Union and proceeds in the manner of asking questions and answering them.

Is there a South Asia?

With the Himalayan mountain ranges forming the boundary wall in the north, and the Indian Ocean on the south, the geographical frontiers of South Asia are naturally defined. It is in this geographical space, many civilizations and empires flourished and vanished. The rise of modern nation states is a corollary to post empire phase. In this sub continental landscape, it has thrown up nine countries. India occupies seventy per cent of the region and lies at its center. To its north is Pakistan and Afghanistan, the islands of Sri Lanka and Maldives are to its south. Nepal, Bhutan and Myanmar lie to east. There is a great deal of communality of norms and customs, food habit, culture, languages and traditions among the people living in this geographical landscape. The Indian subcontinent more euphemistically called South Asia is, therefore, a compact geographical entity.

Who Needs a South Asian Union?

There is a view in India that the concept of a South Asian Union does not suit its national interest. It is a poly of the smaller nations of the region to grow at the expense of India's vast resources. The perception in the neighborhood is contrary to the Indian view. They think India is more interested in a common union because it wants to dominate the smaller countries with its superior resources. These two extreme views do not take into account the challenges thrown by the market forces and globalization in the post Cold War era. A combination of domestic compulsions and external factors is demanding intra- national linkages. Therefore, a common South Asian Union is in the interest of all the South Asian countries.

Why do we need a South Asian Union?

South Asia houses nearly a quarter of the world's population. Trans-boundary disagreements have already caused disputes among the neighbouring countries. More than 240 million people lack access to safe water. Half a billion do not have proper sanitation. One child dies an average of every fifteen seconds due to lack of safe water and sanitation. All the countries of the region face the challenges of poverty, illiteracy, health, environment, potable water, energy, religious extremism, terrorism, human rights abuse, etc. Individually each of them has been grappling with these challenges but none have been able to redeem themselves. It is increasingly realized that only through common policies and programmes the entire region can be developed and in such context a common South Asian Union becomes an imperative goal.

What would we gain from the South Asian Union?

Right now the multi-ethnic societies of the South Asian nations are witnessing assertion of new group identities. Every country is gripped by forces of sub-nationalism wanting to carve out new nation states. Every country is hit by religious fanaticism. The secessionists and radical forces are asserting through violent means. Every country is reeling under the scourge of terrorism.

So we have two choices before us: either we continue to live in the geographical space with the current hardships or think how to make it a better place to live.

If we move towards a common South Asia Union, the larger grouping may provide a platform for the separatists groups to assuage their aspirations. Many lingering problems like Tamil Eelam, Kashmir, northeast separatism can be resolved in a common Union framework. The reactionary forces would be marginalized. Minorities in each country would feel safer and secure in a secular democratic South Asian Union. The common grid of water, energy and infrastructure would ensure better quality of life. It would check the lopsided growth. The resultant economic engagement would stop human migration. A vote for common South Asian Union is, therefore, a foregone conclusion.

What are the road blocks for a South Asian Union?

Having laid down the case for regionalism let us identify the roadblocks towards the evolution of a South Asian Union. There are many social, political and economic challenges that come in the way of a South Asian Union.

Since most of the states have emerged out of the long struggle against the colonial rule, it has left a deep scar on the subcontinent. Rooted in history, there is trust deficiency among the nations and each sees the neighbouring country with suspicion. The nationalist interest calls for guarding national identity that comes in the way of moving towards forming a common identity. Lack of identification of common purpose among the South Asian nations too blocks its identity formation.

Then there is the problem of unequal sizes in the region. While India's size is that of continental scale, Bhutan and Maldives are less than an average state in India. The centre and periphery problem is also glaring. Most of the countries in South Asia are on the preprimary of India.

Further regional trade is marred by several barriers blocking economic cooperation among the South Asian countries. Each country has more trade with the countries of other regions than among themselves. Almost all the countries view their national sovereignty at peril if they open their economies for free trade in the region.

The external power's relation with South Asian countries continues to block the evolution of a common Union. In the Cold War era, the horde for managing more proactive relations with world's super powers has made the neighbouring countries of the region sworn enemies of each other. This has pushed the region into a continued state of strife and conflict and stymied its growth and development. In the post Cold War era this phenomena has not receded. All the countries of the region continue to look towards the extra regional power.

The lack of political flexibility to resolve the lingering bilateral disputes over the territorial boundary left behind by the colonial rule is another road block. There are hardly any pair of states that are not affected by trans-border spilling of ethno-nationalist activities. The spilling over of intra-state conflicts into neighbouring territories causes inter-state tensions. Such issues block the process of regional integration.

Competitive military spending of the individual countries has accentuated the historically derived mutual suspicion in the region. The nuclear imbalance has magnified such suspicions. Continued spending on nuclear warheads and missiles all add to the alarming insecurity of the region. The huge amount of money spent on military establishment tends to suggest that prioritizing military security is the main concern of every nation state. The high emphasis on military security is another road block in the regional integration.

What are the launch pads for a South Asian Union?

Given the plethora of the conflict of interests among the South Asian countries it would be interesting to explore the common issues on which a mechanism of regional cooperation could be built and sustained.

There are some significant commonalties among the countries of the South Asian region. The region is geographically contiguous and shares common history. There is a great deal of cultural cohesiveness in the region. The English language remains a link for the regional unity.

South Asia is home for nearly half of the worlds poor. There are common problems of poverty, hunger, malnutrition, population, health, hygiene and epidemics. The region has low gross domestic product, low per capita income, low literacy rate, high birth and high mortality rate. The region faces acute water shortage and huge energy deficit.

In addition there is a sharp increase in environmental degradation. This has a bearing on the agricultural and industrial scene. There is massive spread of HIV/AIDs, drug trafficking and human trafficking in the region. Then there are problems related to education and employment. These issues of development generate a deep desire for regional cooperation. The cultural cohesiveness buttressed by the information technology and communication network has magnified the prospects of a common South Asian Union.

How do we progress for a common South Asian Union?

The governments and people have to view the region as a whole and not as different units while planning the strategies and activities related to development, investment and trade in the region.

A platform for regional growth can be prepared if we are successful in integrating energy, water, infrastructure, trade and communication network of the region. The regimes in South Asia may consider common policies and programmes for promotion of household hygiene and sanitation, poverty alleviation, population control, employment generation and check environmental degradations.

Such initiative efforts should be made towards common policies and programmes to build regional security. A time bound conflict resolution mechanism should be initiated to resolve the land and maritime border disputes. Once a modicum of regional stability is achieved common planning should be galvanized to develop road, waterways and railways infrastructure in the region. Common initiative should be taken for counter-terrorism, counter-narcotics, counter human trafficking, etc. There should be a calibrated shift from military security to human security.

On the economic front common policies should be formulated to encourage entrepreneurial spirit in the region. The regimes should stimulate reforms at the national level and encourage intra-regional trade. In order to share prosperity the bigger economy like India should help the other countries of the region to grow at a similar pace. In stimulating economic growth, the focus should remain on sustainable development.

Last but not the least efforts should be made to create awareness among the civil society about the usefulness of regional cooperation. The civil society should come forward and forge common linkages of cooperation through people to people approach. The participation of the civil society in decision making process should be encouraged to mandate the idea of regionalism in South Asia.

Could SAARC be the vehicle for South Asian Union?

Since 1985, South Asia is attempting to forge regionalism through SAARC. However, for even more than twenty years since its existence, SAARC is unable to achieve any thing startling. Critiques are questioning the utility of SAARC as a regional body. However, there are many limitations to SAARC's operation. The bilateral disputes are out of the preview of SAARC. In such a situation, any effort of multilateral cooperation becomes redundant because bilateral disputes come in its way. So SAARC really cannot be blamed for the slow growth of regionalism in South Asia. The very fact that SAARC has existed for over two decades suggests that it enjoys the mandate to build peace in the region.

The Islamabad SAARC summit in 2004 marks a watershed in the history of SAARC. It charted out the future direction of South Asian regional cooperation. Three landmark agreements were signed there.

(i) The SAARC Social Charter: A far-sighted document envisages removal of poverty, control of population growth, women empowerment, promotion of human rights and developing human resources, etc. It committed to implement the recommendations of the Independent Commission for Poverty Alleviation (ISACPA). It also agreed to set up a regional poverty alleviation fund.

(ii) South Asian Free Trade Area: The member countries signed an agreement for a South Asian Free Trade Area (SAFTA).

(iii) Combating Terrorism: Additional Protocol to the SAARC Regional Convention on Combating Terrorism was also signed.

The Islamabad summit committed to intensify cooperation in a number of other areas that include:

1) Reiteration of the commitment for the creation of a South Asian Economic Union;
2) Energy cooperation;
3) Strengthening transportation, transit and communication links across the region;
4) Harmonization of standards and simplification of customs procedures;
5) Public and private sector cooperation through joint ventures;
6) Setting up a South Asia Development Bank;
7) Cooperation among Central Banks;
8) Development of tourism within South Asia; and
9) Discussing and adopting common positions at multilateral forums.

The resolutions adopted at the Islamabad SAARC summit suggest that South Asian states are realizing the importance of regional cooperation much more than before. The obvious deduction from it is that SAARC is acquiring a momentum of its own. The growing importance of SAARC can be ascertained by the fact that China and Japan have acquired observer's status in SAARC. The US and South Korea too have shown keen interest to join the SAARC as observers. Afghanistan was included as SAARC member country at the Dhaka summit in 2005. There are hopes that Myanmar at some stage may also be brought on board of SAARC. This would complete the geographical matrix of a South Asian Union.

What should be the future agenda of South Asian Union?

If regionalism is the answer to meet future challenges then it is imperative for the political leadership and intelligentsia to shed the past and search for creative strategies to build peace and prosperity in the region. Here is some loud thinking in this context.

1) Create Awareness about regionalism: The first and foremost task of the regimes in South Asia should be to create awareness among its people about the wisdom of regional cooperation.
2) Dialogue between civil societies: Promoting a dialogue between civil societies in the region.
3) Emphasis on human security: The South Asian regimes should consider shifting their focus from military to human security.
4) Explore the hydroelectric potential of the Himalayan region: The hydroelectric potential of the Himalayan region can be developed by collectively exploring the vast water resources of India, Nepal, Bangladesh and Bhutan.
5) Improve economic and trade relations: SAARC member countries have to set aside their disputes and strive to improve their economic and trade relations. The Indo-Sri Lanka trade agreement could become a model how difference could be subordinated to the goal of progress.
6) Common South Asian Market: The focus should be on creating a common South Asian Market.
7) Fee trade area: The region should be made a free trade area.
8) Customs Union: Work towards a common customs union.
9) Economic Union: Moving towards an economic union

What are the prospects of a South Asian Union?

The deepening cooperation among the member countries has a cascading effect. Here is some loud thinking on the prospects of a common South Asian Union.

1) The Free Trade Area could evolve into a Customs Union with a common tariff barrier with the rest of the world. The Customs Union could lead to a common exchange rate policy and eventually a common currency.
2) Energy cooperation could evolve into a common energy grid across the region with integrated electricity and gas systems.
3) Transport cooperation would lead to an integrated transport infrastructure which permits uninterrupted travel from Peshawar to Chittagong and from Kathmandu to Colombo.
4) Investment cooperation would culminate in regional corporations with production facilities located across the region within vertically and horizontally integrated production systems. Shares

of both national and regional companies would be quoted in the stock exchanges across the region as capital flows without hindrance across national boundaries to underwrite investment in any part of South Asia.

5) Within such a framework of cooperation, the goal of poverty reduction enunciated by ISACPA would eradicate poverty across the region.
6) The deepening cooperation would ultimately lead to integrating of the labour market in the region. People can move across national boundaries to seek work anywhere in the region. Such scenario undoubtedly requires a complete transformation of the prevailing social, political and economic realities.

Conclusion

To wrap up the discussion the mechanism to build a common South Asian Union may have to structure around some broad principles. These are redefining the goals, institutionalization of redefined goals; building comprehensive security, building people's stake in peace and a common South Asian policy. These processes have to be operationalized incorporating conflict moderation initiatives along with peace building initiatives at the same time.

Redefinition of Goals: The conflicts in South Asia emanate from goals of territorial nationalism and the monotheistic concepts of nation-building. If these goals are redefined and focus is shifted from territory to people, the regional insecurity spectrum may undergo a sea change.

Institutionalization of Goals: The goals have to be integrated into the institutional structures within the state mechanisms and upgraded at the regional level. Institutionalization of goals could be worked out through SAARC by changing the terms of its reference. It will help overcome problems centered on adhoc initiatives, vulnerability to political conveniences and individual perceptions, etc.

Building Comprehensive security: The institutionalization of the goals would shift the territorial model of security to a comprehensive regional model of security. It will lead to diffusion of intra-state conflicts, inter-state tension and the challenges posed by the forces of globalization.

Building people's stake in peace: The comprehensive security framework can provide a security blanket to the civil society and involve them to participate in the regional planning. Setting up of co-operative mechanisms in security, trade, sharing of scarce resources can build people's stake in the peace process.

A South Asian policy: A common South Asian policy based on the principle of multilateralism and multiculturalism is required for a common South Asian Union. An integrated approach by looking at the multi-dimensional components of the issues of discord is required to manage the differences. Through multi-lateral arrangements linkages in technology, capacity building and intelligence sharing could be built to ensure the sustainability of the vision of a common South Asian Union.

13

Ethnicity and the Operation of Social Processes in the South Asian Societies

V. Sreemannarayana Murthy

South Asia is an abode for numerous ethnic stocks of people. Most of the societies are plagued with ethnic problems which if remain unresolved would hinder the progress of the nations however diligent and sagacious the economic policies may be. The economic programmes aimed at the welfare of the people must be designed, with an eye on the social structure of the country. This would help resolve the contentious issues, to make the economic programmes more meaningful. It is pertinent to define the terms ethnic group and ethnicity before dwelling upon the subject.

The Origins of the term Ethnicity

The term ethnicity according to Thomas Hylland Eriksen (1993) was derived from the Greek word ethnos which in turn was derived from another Greek word ethnikos. This meant Pagan or heathen. This meaning continued in English until around the middle of the nineteenth century when it started being used as an alternative to race. However, Eriksen observes that in modern anthropology and sociology an ethnic group is seen as being culturally rather than physically distinctive. J. Milton Yinger (1981) distinguishes the difference between physically defined and socially defined races. He observes that physically distinct races may exist theoretically but practically the boundaries between physical races have become so blurred that humans with a distinct phenotype are difficult to distinguish. Yinger points out that biological races are of relatively little concern to the social scientist, though they form a subject to the biologist and physical anthropologist. Socially defined races consist of ethnic groups who are seen by themselves or others as having distinct biological characteristics whether they form a distinct biological group or not. According to Yinger, "an ethnic group exists in the fullest sense when a section of a larger society is viewed by others as different in some combination of the following characteristics – race, religion, language, and ancestral homeland with its related culture; the members also perceive themselves in that way; and they participate in shared activities built around their (real or mythical) common origin or culture".[1]

According to Michael E. Brown, six criteria must be met for a group to be identified as an ethnic group:

1. The group must be identified with a name.
2. They must trace their origin to a common ancestor.
3. They must have shared beliefs of their collective past. These beliefs could often be mythical.
4. They must share a culture which is generally passed on through a combination of religion, language, laws, customs, institutions, dress music, crafts, architecture, even food.
5. The must have a sense of attachment to a specified territory.
6. Finally, members of the group must be aware that they constitute an ethnic group.[2]

Social processes are 'any identifiable and repetitive patterns of social interaction'. They are – Associative Processes and Dissociative Processes. The Associative processes are Accommodation, Cooperation, Acculturation, Assimilation and Integration while the Dissociative Processes are Competition and Conflict.[3]

The South Asian Association for Regional Cooperation (SAARC), a regional block formed to derive collective benefits, is beset with a host of problems of which the paper concentrates on ethnicity in the seven SAARC Countries. The paper also examines how the social processes in these countries are in operation.

Broadly, the causes for the problems are identified as relative deprivation and alienation. Since prevention is better than cure, the state should strive to establish social equilibrium by exploring an effective mechanism.

Social processes in India

When India witnessed historical waves of migration with the hordes of Central Asian Tribes making inroads into its society, the dissociative process of conflict was set in motion. Conflict as such does not continue for long. Hence, it transformed into accommodation or ceszation of hostilities which is an associative process. It further leads to cooperation when the rival groups recognize mutual benefits. Steadily it could lead to acculturation where certain cultural practices which were reckoned to be useful are exchanged by the distinct groups. It could ultimately lead to Assimilation or Integration. Assimilation stands for absorption of a smaller group into bigger one, or merger of two groups into one, while integration stands for peaceful coexistence of different groups which continue to maintain their respective cultural identities.

Post-independent India adopted a constitution with democratic and secular principles. The Constitution was the result of a great deal of mutual accommodation, compromise and wide ranging consensus. The makers of the Constitution realized that it was necessary to grapple with multiple pulls and pressures of various ethnic diversities, to transcend them or to subsume them under the overall Indian national identity. The government has been endeavouring to bring in different backward ethnic groups to the main stream of the society. Special provisions have been made for the emancipation of the tribes and other backward sections of the society. Their cultural identity is respected. There is state sponsored mobility in the name of 'protective discrimination'. Despite movements in different parts of India by certain ethnic groups either due to deprivation or identity crisis, India survives as a united nation and a functioning democracy which shows the inner strength and resilience of the people.[4] The Indian constitution is vibrant enough to resolve them. The Indian society is in a state of accommodation and integration despite certain inevitable pinpricks.

Sri Lanka

In Sri Lanka, the ethnic, religious and linguistic distinctions are essentially the same. Three ethnic groups, namely Sinhalese, Tamils and Muslims constitute the vast majority of the country's population. The Sinhalese alone account for nearly three-fourths of the people. The Tamil segment comprises of two groups – Sri Lankan Tamils who are long-settled descendants from southeastern India and Indian Tamils, the recent immigrants from southeastern India, most of whom were migrant workers brought to Sri Lanka during the British rule. Slightly more than one-eighth of the total population belongs to the former group. Muslims, who trace their origin to the Arab traders of the eighth century, account for about 7.5 per cent of the population. Burghers, a community of mixed European descent, Parsis immigrants from western India, and Veddas who are regarded as the aboriginal inhabitants of the country constitute less than one per cent of the population. The Sinhalese are numerically preponderant in the southern, western, central, and north-central parts of the country. In the rural areas of the wet zone lowlands, they account for more than ninety five per cent of the population. The Sri Lankan Tamils are concentrated in the Jaffna Peninsula and in the adjacent districts of the northern lowlands. Smaller agglomerations of this group are also found along the eastern littoral where their settlements are proximate to those of the Muslims. The Muslims are mainly concentrated in the eastern lowlands. In other areas, like Colombo, Kandy, Puttalam and Gampaha, Muslims form a small but important segment of the urban and suburban population. The Indian Tamils, the vast majority of whom are plantation workers, live in large numbers in the central highlands.[5]

Sri Lanka was earlier ruled by the Portuguese and the Dutch before it became a colony of the British in 1815. It was granted independence in 1948 with the power passing into the hands of the Sinhala majority.

The first constitution of Ceylon was adopted by an Order in Council rather than by a Constituent Assembly. It was known as the Soulbury Constitution which remained in force until 1972. The origin of the Sinhala – Tamil conflict may be traced back to the 15 November 1948 Citizenship Act and the laws of disenfranchisement which deprived the Tamils of Indian origin and those in the hill country (plantation workers), of the right to select their representatives to the parliament. More than a million plantation Tamil workers became stateless. In 1956 'Sinhala Only Act' was proclaimed and thus Sinhala became the only official language of Ceylon (as Sri Lanka was formerly called).

On 26 July 1957 the Banda-Chelva pact was signed between Bandaranaike, the Prime-minister and Chelvanayagam, the leader of the Tamil Arasu Katchi (Federal Party). This agreement was based on a quasi federal system devolving certain powers to the Tamils in the North East provinces. Within a week of its signing, the pact was unilaterally repealed by the Prime Minister Bandaranaike due to fierce protests staged by the United National Party (UNP), Buddhist clergy and the Sri Lankan Freedom Party. Consequently in 1958, clashes ensued between Sinhalas and Tamils and many Tamils were plundered and killed.[6] In 1964 the Srimavo-Shashtri pact was signed for the repatriation of the Tamil people of Indian origin who were denied citizenship and the franchise through the 1948 Citizenship Act. They had lived in the island for over 115 years. On 22 May 1972 Ceylon became a Republic and it was officially renamed as the Republic of Sri Lanka. The United Front government adopted 'Republican Constitution' which made Buddhism the state religion. State's prejudice against Tamil students' admission to Universities was marked by the introduction of 'Standardization'. University admission based on merit was abandoned. This step deprived the Tamil students of their entry into the Universities. In the same year the 'Tamil New Tigers', which was rechristened as the Liberation Tigers of Tamil Eelam (LTTE) in 1976, was formed by Velupillai Prabhakaran. In July 1977, Tamil United Liberation Front (TULF), contested the parliamentary elections and won the mandate to establish the Right to Self-determination of Tamil Eelam in the North East. J. R. Jayewardene of the UNP became the Prime Minister, with a five-sixth majority in the parliament. The TULF became the major opposition party in the parliament. The UNP failed to honour its manifesto promise[7]

In 1978 a new Constitution was adopted and Jayewardene became first Executive President of the country. The phrase Republic of Sri Lanka was rephrased as Democratic Socialist Republic of Sri Lanka. Sri Lankan security forces started perpetrating atrocities against Tamil youths. Counter activities of Tamil militant organizations were also on the increase. In July 1983 anti-Tamil violence took place. The victims of ethnic holocaust were not only the Sri Lankan Tamils but also the estate workers of Indian origin.[8]

In 1987, the Indo-Sri Lankan accord was signed as per which Colombo agreed for devolution of power to the provinces and India was to send a Peace keeping force to Sri Lanka. This arrangement fizzled out as the LTTE was reluctant to lay down arms.[9]

Several military operations conducted by the Sri Lankan army against the LTTE proved futile. The Norwegian peace mission also did not yield a solution for the decades old strife.

In December 2006 the 'Majority report' of the Sri Lankan government's multi-ethnic experts' panel has recommended maximum devolution of power with the province as the unit of devolution and the appointment of two Vice-Presidents from communities other than that of the President. The report said though the country was multi-ethnic and multi-religious, the crisis had arisen due to the numerically smaller ethnic groups not having their due share of state power. This has resulted in alienation of the minorities from the Sri Lankan state, as initial efforts to redeem this situation by power-sharing mechanism failed. To make the devolution meaningful, it is recommended that the majority of the subjects and functions be categorized as belonging to the national sphere or the provincial sphere with a concurrent list consisting of a minimum of subjects and functions. It was recommended that subjects such as defence, national security, foreign affairs, immigration/citizenship, communication, national transportation, international commerce/trade, maritime zones, and shipping and navigation, be reserved for the Centre. It was also recommended to establish an autonomous Zone Council to address the concerns of the Tamils of Indian origin.[10]

The peace process continues and a great deal is expected from the government's side to create confidence in the Tamils of opportunities on par with the Sinhalas in order to transform the conflict into accommodation. History bears testimony to the fact that the government retracted its commitment on several counts. Hence it must adopt necessary measures to win the confidence of the Tamils.

Maldives

Maldives is a cluster of Islands in the Indian Ocean. It gained independence from the British in 1965. The earliest settlers were said to be from southern India. Indo-European speakers followed them from Sri Lanka in the fourth and fifth centuries BC. In the twelfth century AD, sailors from East Africa and Arab countries came to the islands. The only distinct ethnic minority is found in Male among the trading community of Indians, who settled there in the 1800s. Several hundred in number, they are also a religious minority, belonging to the Shia branch of Islam. In addition, a small number of Sri Lankans have come to Maldives in recent years to work in the tourist resorts because Maldivians, as devout Muslims, refuse to work in facilities serving alcoholic beverages. Today, the Maldivian ethnic identity is a blend of these cultures, reinforced by religion and language. Originally Buddhists, Maldivians were converted to Sunni Islam in the mid-twelfth century. Islam is the official religion of the entire population.[11] Maldives is undergoing a process of integration under the influence of Islam as a common religion.

Pakistan

Pakistan is a multi-ethnic and multi-lingual country. The majority (nearly two thirds) of the population is Punjabi. Other major ethnic groups include the Sindhi, Pathan, Baloch, and Muhajirs. The Rajputs and the Jats are the most numerous of the Punjabi castes. In the area of the delta and the lower course of the Indus River are Sindhi peasant tribesmen. In the north and northwest are the warlike nomadic and semi nomadic Pathans (pashtuns). The Balochi live in the vast western part of Pakistan and are divided into twelve major tribes, some of them are purportedly of Dravidian origin. Native speakers of Urdu, the Muhajirs are refugees, or descendants of refugees, from pre-partition India. They are well represented in the cities. Language is an important criterion of ethnic identity. Among the more than twenty spoken languages in Pakistan, the most common ones, Punjabi, Sindhi, and Urdu as well as Pakhtu or Pashto, Balochi, and others, belong to the Indo-Aryan branch of the Indo-European language family. Additional languages, such as Shina and other northern area languages are related to the Dardic branch of Indo-European and the early Dravidian language family. Brahui is one such language; it is spoken by a group in Balochistan.

Forty eight per cent of Pakistanis speak Punjabi. The next most commonly spoken language is Sindhi which is spoken by twelve per cent, followed by the Punjabi variant Siraiki with ten per cent speakers, Pakhtu or Pashto – eight per cent, Balochi – three per cent, Hindko- two per cent, and Brahui – one per cent. Native speakers of other languages, including English, Burushaski, and various other tongues account for eight per cent. Although Urdu is the official national language, it is spoken as a native tongue by only eight per cent of the population. Generally people who speak Urdu as their native language identify themselves as Mohajirs. A large number of people from educated backgrounds and those who aspire for upward mobility speak Urdu, as opposed to their native languages.[12]

The regional assertion based on the ethnic identities came to the fore in more pronounced ways in the 1990s. Ethnic discontent was brewing in Baluchistan and North West Frontier Province (NWFP) since the 1970s. Similarly, the Mohajirs of Pakistan were emerging as an important ethnic group with the growth of Mohajir Quami movement since the 1980s as a major force in urban centres in Sindh, especially in Karachi and the twin city of Hyderabad. The Sindhi assertion has all along been there since 1950s.

The assertion of regional identities can be attributed to the dwindling resources too. Economic growth is sluggish in Pakistan. Apart from gross mismanagement by the ruling elite – the army-bureaucracy-landlord troika – the nuclear engagement with India has taken its toll. The Constitution of Pakistan is silent on the issue of ethnicity and only addresses this question indirectly. Islam is the official religion of Pakistan and this is enshrined in its Constitution. The basic argument against ethnicity is that since the country was formed on the basis of religion or the two nation theory, it cannot subscribe to a concept which divides people on the basis of race or culture.[13] Since the political history of Pakistan is dominated by military rule, a healthy democracy which represents the aspirations of the people and addresses ethnicity must take root otherwise the social turmoil or the intermittent conflict in the society would continue.

Bhutan

The people of Bhutan can be divided into three broad ethnic categories – Ngalops, Sharchops, and Lhotsampas. The Ngalops make up the majority of the population, living mostly in the western and central areas. The Ngalops are thought to be of Tibetan origin, arriving in Bhutan during the eighth and ninth centuries A.D. and bringing Buddhism with them. Most Ngalops follow the Drukpa Kagyupa discipline of Mahayana Buddhism.

The Sharchops, living in the eastern section of Bhutan, are said to be the descendants of the earliest major group to inhabit Bhutan. The majority follow the Ningmapa discipline of Mahayana Buddhism. Sharchop is translated as 'people of the east'. The Ngalops, Sharchops, and the indigenous tribal people are collectively known as Drukpas and account for about sixty five per cent of the population. The national language is Dzongka, but English is the language of instruction in schools and an official working language for the government. The Lhotsampas are people of Nepali descent, currently making up thirty five per cent of the population. They came to Bhutan in the nineteenth and twentieth centuries, mostly settling in the southern foothills to work as farmers. They speak a variety of Nepali dialects and are predominantly Hindu.[14] In the late 1980s the Bhutanese ruling elite became deeply concerned over their threats to the national identity. In 1988-90, there was Nepalese uprising in southern Bhutan. The King promulgated an edict prescribing Driglam Namzha (traditional etiquette) to strengthen Bhutan's cultural identity. The government forced them to adopt the Bhutanese religion dress and customs. Though there are reports of the sufferings of ethnic Nepalese, the government claims that ethnic discrimination in employment is not a problem as ethnic Nepalese hold twenty two per cent of government jobs which is a little less than their proportion of the total population.[15]

Traditionally a decentralized theocracy and, since 1907, a monarchy, Bhutan is evolving into a constitutional monarchy with a representative government. The country must evolve a healthy democracy and adopt a constitution which accords equal treatment to all its ethnic groups to end the conflict and work towards accommodation.

Bangladesh

Bangladesh has ethnic homogeneity to certain extent only in cultural terms. The Bengali Muslims constitute about eighty six per cent of the population followed by Bengali Hindus who are about thirteen per cent. The tribal people constitute nearly one per cent of the population. They are divided into several tribes of which the four largest are the Chakmas, the Marmas (Maghs), the Tippers (Tipras) and the Mros (Moorangs). They speak Tibeto-Burmese rather than Indo-European languages. Though every tribe has adherents of more than one religion, the Chakmas and the Marmas are dominantly Buddhists, while the Tipperas are Hindus. Baptist, Roman Catholic, and Seventh Day Adventist missions have been able to win converts from all the tribes with some of the smaller tribes being dominantly Christian. The Mros are considered to be the original inhabitants of the Chittagong Hill tracts, the district with concentration of tribal population, while the rest of them are presumed to have migrated from India and Burma. Though 'Marma' means Burmese, they are believed to be of Thai origin or tribals from Thailand having come through Burma to the Hill Tract after their ancestors were expelled from China.[16]

Though Bangladesh was declared a secular nation since its emergence, it changed to Islamic Republic in 1988. The process of Islamization is resisted by the Hindu minorities and the Muslim secularist parties. The Buddhist Chakmas also fear Islam being foisted on them. The frequent atrocities against the minorities reflect a situation of conflict.[17] There is demand for autonomy for the Chittagong Hill tracts with its own legislation and the recognition of the right to self- determination. Though they are provided with quota in employment and education institutes, their demands persist.[18] Bangladesh is passing through political turmoil A great deal remains to be done by a stable government in making suitable constitutional amendments in order to instill confidence in the minorities to set in motion the associative processes.

Nepal

Nepal reflects a great ethnic hetrogenity. On the basis of race or descent, the three-fold categorization of the Nepalese people into Mongoloid or Tibeto-Burman, Indo-Aryan and Austro-Asiatic groups has blurred because of the intermixing of racial groups. So also is the case with religion, which cannot be the exclusive criterion for determining the boundaries of all ethnic groups, as is evident from the confluence of Hindu-Buddhist and non- Hindu religious beliefs, customs, and practices among several ethnic groups like the Newars, Magars, Tamangs, and Gurungs.

The non-Tarai Hindus are the largest in number, comprising about half the population, with the Tarai Hindus accounting for one-fourth. Next in numerical terms are the Tamangs with the Kiratis, Newars as well as

Tharus accounting for about four per cent of the total population. The ethnic groups such as the Muslims, Gurungs, Sherpas, Magars, are small in number and account for one to three per cent each of the population.

The Tarai and non-Tarai Hindus share the same religion and have certain cultural features in common, e.g., goods, festivals, and a body of Sanskrit literature. Also, the Tarai Hindus by and large speak one Hindi dialect or the other, while the non-Tarai Hindus speak Nepali. Thus, the cultural affinity of the Tarai Hindus appears to be towards the adjacent states of Bihar and UP (India), while that of the non-Tarai Hindus seems to be more specifically towards the hill valley culture which has synchronized two cultural streams of Buddhism from the north and Hinduism from the south. The Newaris are believed to be an autochthonous group, while the Muslims migrated from the south at various times. Excepting the Tharu tribe, which is concentrated in the forest belt of the Tarai, the other ethnic groups belong to various tribes, having the main Mongoloid features.[19]

Religion has a prominent place in Nepal. According to the 2001 census, Nepal is about eighty one per cent Hindu. Buddhists account for about eleven per cent of the population. The interim constitution promulgated on 15 January 2007 declared the country a 'secular state'. Buddhist and Hindu shrines and festivals are respected and celebrated by many. The government celebrates most Hindu and some Buddhist holidays. Nepal also has small Muslim and Christian minorities. The Madhesi movement began recently in the Terai area of Nepal. It demands an end of discrimination against the Madhesi people. Nepal has a chequered political history and establishment of a healthy democracy is the need of the hour otherwise the social turmoil or the dissociative process of conflict situation would continue.

Conclusion

All the states must be pragmatic in their adherence to the principles of secularism which could transcend the cultural distinctions. Healthy democracy which represents the aspirations of the people must evolve. The grievances of the ethnic minorities must be addressed to establish accommodation. Otherwise the state must spend its resources in quelling the movements or the insurgency. Relative deprivation would one day or the other lead to a social movement; the state should be on its guard to bring forth social equilibrium. It is not characteristic of the people or groups to remain hostile or in conflict perpetually. The government of the respective country is a stakeholder in resolving the conflict. Hence it must come out with a viable and abiding solution to set in motion the Associative Social Processes.

References

1. Michael Haralambos, R.M. Heald, Martin Holborn, *Sociology: Themes and Perspectives,* U.K: Collins, 2000.
2. *Ibid.*, p. 234.
3. David Jary & Julia Jary, *Sociology*, Glasgow: Harper Collins, 2000.
4. Subhash C Kashyap, "Ethnicity and Constitutional Reforms", in Iftekhar Ruzzaman (ed), *India in Ethnicity and Constitutional Reforms in South Asia,* New Delhi: Manohar, 1998, pp. 28-46.
5. Urmila Phadnis, *Ethnicity and Nation- building in South Asia*, New Delhi: Sage Publications, 1990.
6. S.D. Muni, *Pangs of Proximity*, New Delhi: Sage Publications, 1993.
7. *Ibid.*, p. 44.
8. *Ibid.*, p. 50.
9. *Ibid.*, pp. 90-119.
10. *The Hindu*, 7 December 2006.
11. *Ibid.*, Phadnis, n. 5, pp. 43-44.
12. *Ibid.*, pp. 37-39.
13. Moonis Ahmar, "Ethnicity and Constitutional Reforms: A Pakistani Perspective", in Ruzzaman (ed), n. 4, pp. 108-127.
14. *Ibid.*, Phadnis, n.5, pp. 39-40, and see www.nationsencyclopedia.com
15. Naveen Mishra, Sudhir Kumar Singh, *Status of Minorities in South Asia*, Delhi: Authors Press, 2002, pp.27-36
16. *Ibid.*, Phadnis, n. 5, p. 39.
17. Lok Raj Baral, *Regional Migrations, Ethnicity and Security, The South Asian Case*, New Delhi: Sterling Publishers, 1990.
18. Mohammad Humayun Kabir, "The Problems of Tribal Separatism and Constitutional Reform in Bangladesh", in Ruzzaman (ed), n. 4, pp. 10-24.
19. *Ibid*:, Phadnis, n. 5, pp. 40-42, and see www.nationsencyclopedia.com

PART IV

SAARC – CHINA, ASEAN AND BIMSTEC

14

China's Interactions with South Asia: New Beginnings

Srikanth Kondapalli

China's desire to be part of the South Asian Association for Regional Cooperation (SAARC) was fulfilled in April 2007, its interactions with the seven South Asian countries provides for a fascinating study of not only for the sharp shifts in its policy but also for its expanding role in the region to make it perhaps the third largest external factor in the policies of these countries next only to the United States and the Soviet Union. With the gradual decline and disintegration of the Soviet Union, China expects to reap strategic opportunities in the region. While during the Cold War, China followed a policy of building close relations with Pakistan, currently new policies are being implemented towards South Asia. Stabilising its peripheries with the recently launched Western Development Campaign, coming to grips with rising India, nuclear stability in the region, counter-terrorism measures, exploration of markets for its burgeoning exports, raw materials and exploring ways to secure sea lines in the Indian Ocean for sustainable supplies to fuel its economy characterise the new features of China's interactions with the South Asian region in the recent period.

The People's Republic of China (PRC)'s policy towards South Asian countries in the region have been influenced by its overall foreign policy goals, emphasis on pursuing national interests [*guojia liyi*] and its position towards the then superpowers. China's relations with the South Asian countries are rooted in history, though the current state-to-state relations have emphasised aspects of territorial boundaries, sovereignty issues and trade and non-traditional security issues given the geographical proximity of most of these countries. Another broad feature of this interaction is the bouncing back of aspects of the Panchsheel principles in the Chinese foreign policy as a guiding philosophy, after its birth in the mid 1950s and the 1955 resolve of the PRC to build close links with its neighbours. After a brief review of the bilateral relations between China and South Asian countries, this paper has outlined below several new factors influencing the Chinese policy in the region. These include China's Western Development Campaign in its north-western regions, the success of which would be crucial not only to the balanced geographical development of the country and internal security but also in influencing China's relations with the region. A stable environment across its western and south-western borders would not only lead to security in Xinjiang and other regions but also focus on economic development. In a post September 11 counter-terror global trends and given the festering of the Xinjiang Uighur 'separatist' movement, China is poised to take more than a cursory interest in this region.[1] Other new influences on China's policy include coming to grips with rising India, nuclear stability in the region, exploration of markets for its burgeoning exports, raw materials and exploring ways to secure sea lines in the Indian Ocean for sustainable supplies to fuel its economy.

China and India

Several major policy adjustments are taking place in China's policy towards India in the recent period from 'cooperative and constructive' security strategy in the 1980s to the 2005 'strategic partnership and cooperation.' Increase in the Indian economic growth figures, military modernization efforts and its growing links with the US are said to be the triggers in Chinese policy changes.

China's relations with India have undergone a sea change in the last decade and a half after Prime Minister Rajiv Gandhi's visit to Beijing in late 1988. The bilateral relations that reached their peak during the 1950s "*Hindi-Chini*" bonhomie nose-dived after the two countries fought a war in 1962 on the borders. Subsequently, though diplomatic relations were restored in the late 1970s, the border war left a lasting imprint on the relations.[2] The basic considerations of China in its interactions with India are as follows:

- curbing efforts of the Tibetans in 'splitting' China;
- 'balancing' India with other South Asian countries (viz., Pakistan, Bangladesh and Bhutan);
- stability in the South Asian region in the aftermath of the nuclearization, counter-terror measures and efforts at its Western Development Campaign;

- energy security in the Indian Ocean region; and
- joining the multilateral SAARC processes.[3]

From an Indian perspective, major issues in bilateral equations are related to the

- unresolved border problem;
- Sino-Pakistan ballistic and nuclear weapon cooperation;
- China's active military and political assistance to the South Asian countries against India;
- China's support to Kashmir issue in the 1960s which has changed by the 1980s;
- China's 'string of pearls' strategy of building up facilities in the Indian Ocean region; and
- 'rise' of China.

Despite having concerns in the bilateral relations, both India and China have also been cooperating at the multilateral fora in the fields of

- Multipolarity through trilateral cooperation between Russia, India and China (of which seven meetings between the three leaders took place till 15 February 2007)
- Non-traditional security issues like environmental and energy issues,
- World Trade Organization and the like.

At the broader policy level, India during Rajiv Gandhi's visit in 1988 undertook a 'constructive cooperative security strategy' with China. While China is to recognize the *autonomy* of Tibet, India declared that Tibet is a part of China. To recall, during Nehru's time in 1954, India signed an agreement with China agreeing that Tibet is an integral part of China. Currently, there is also a perceptible change in the Chinese position on Kashmir, from its previous position of supporting the self-determination movement in the valley and in the Northeast India. However, successive Indian positions expressed concerns on Chinese strategic and conventional weapons sales to India's neighbours, specifically Pakistan. Chinese active nuclear and missile cooperation with Pakistan, support to the UN Security Council Resolution of 1172 calling for the roll back of Indian nuclear programme in the aftermath of Pokhran II tests in 1998, India identifying China as 'potential number one' enemy, Vajpayee's letter to Clinton, etc., marked tensions in bilateral relations.[4] Subsequently, relations between the two improved and the 2003, 2005 and 2006 high-level political visits marked a significant change towards 'strategic partnership.' In the backdrop of the growing Indo-US relations in economic, technological and military spheres, China is aware of such implications. Relatively greater role for India in the East Asian Summit (in December 2005 and January 2007 meetings), Shanghai Cooperation Organization meetings were part of the November 2006 joint formation 'for cooperation in Asia.' China considers nuclear stability as important to its own national interests in these bordering areas and has conducted at least three talks on such issues in addition to two strategic dialogues with India in 2005 and 2006.

More critical, however, is the unresolved nature of the border issue between the two countries.[5] To tackle the border issue successive governments of India and China have conducted eight border talks between 1981 and 1987 and established Joint Working Groups and Expert Groups. Fifteen Joint Working Group meetings have been conducted from 1989 to 2006. After 2003, these were elevated to the 'Special Representative' level of which nine rounds of discussions were held till November 2006. In 1993, during Narasimha Rao's visit to Beijing, the famous Peace and Tranquillity agreement was signed. President Jiang Zemin's visit in December 1996 and the treaty concluded with India raised confidence-building measures across the border. Withdrawal of troop concentrations, no-fly zones and local military contacts across the Line of Actual Control (LAC) and so on contributed to the relative calm on the LAC after the Samdurangchu Valley incident in 1986. While India wants the border dispute to be settled before full normalization of relations, China argued for a 'comprehensive' improvement in economic, political and cultural contacts.

The bilateral economic relations of India and China are carried out through the traditional border trade and the more recent trade through ports.[6] Though border trade existed between the two countries for centuries, it came to a standstill after the 1962 war, only to resume in the 1990s. Following the first-ever visit of Indian pilgrims through the Indo-Tibetan side after twenty two years in 1981, Chinese officials expressed their hope that the Tibetan border town of Taklakot would become a thriving border trade post in the region.[7] During Premier Li Peng's visit to New Delhi in December 1991, an agreement between the two countries on the resumption of border trade was signed.[8] Subsequently in the 1993 Joint Working Group meeting it was decided that border trade points in Himachal Pradesh (Namgya) and Tibet (Zhuba) are to be opened. In mid–2000 the Indian side pointed out that more border trade points should be opened on both sides. Nathu La in Sikkim was opened in 2006 while plans are afoot to open one more border post at Demchok in Ladakh.

Overall bilateral trade, however, was not affected due to problems in political relations (after May 1998 nuclear tests). Indeed, bilateral economic trade between the two countries gradually increased to about $ 1.2 billion by this period, increasing to about $ 3 billion by 2001, about $ 5 billion by 2002, $ 6.5 billion by 2003 and more than $ 20 billion by 2006. Though these figures are a miniscule in proportion to the overall trade that the two countries conduct with others, several long-term investments are on cards. In the backdrop of infrastructure development in Tibet, China considers burgeoning trade with India marks a new phase in its commercial diplomacy in the region as compared to its trade with other countries in South Asia, although its proposal for a free trade agreement was not acceptable to India so far.

China and Pakistan

More concrete are China's relations with Pakistan given the latter's geographical proximity to the Islamic world,[9] as a counter to the growing power of India,[10] as a source of western military technology and other factors. Surprisingly, China's perceptions about Pakistan have undergone a change from worse, as in the late 1950s when the latter was a part of the US-led security apparatus, to the recent building of an 'all-weather' relationship.[11] In fact from 1957 to 1960, Pakistan followed a policy of antagonism with China on the core issues of Taiwan Tibet, PRC's UN membership and the like, though deterioration of the Sino-Indian relations quickly led to their coming together on agreeing on the boundary issue including portions of the disputed Pakistan-occupied Kashmir.

Ever since the 1960s the Sino-Pakistan cooperation in several fields such as cooperation in the international arena, conventional, and later strategic, weapons programmes, industrial and science and technological aspects and trade have improved.[12] Even though Chinese official positions on several issues have undergone some change including in areas close to the Pakistani positions like the Kashmir issue (on which its own problems related to the ethnic movements in its Xinjiang region may have contributed towards such change), the 'all weather' relationship between the two countries has stood the tests of the changing times. Despite the 1996 tour of Jiang Zemin in which he reiterated the value of *all* South Asian countries to the Chinese in consolidating its socio-political and economic situation into the twenty first century, the Kargil conflict in mid 1999 has indicated the close relationship between China and Pakistan and the Chinese resolve to open another possible armed front against India, bringing back to its position in 1971 Indo-Pakistan war.[13] That is, in other words, the Sino-Indian rapprochement of the late 1980s and 1990s have had their own limitations in the Chinese calculus, though Pakistani support to the Taliban in Afghanistan and through the latter to the Xinjiang Uighur Muslims could pose problems for the Sino-Pakistan relations. With serious concerns a rising on possible linkage between Al Qaeda and the Uighur separatist movement in Xinjiang, China has conducted counter terrorism exercises with Pakistan in August 2004 at Taxkorgan area west of Tibet and at Pak-Afghan borders in November 2006. This is considered to be a major security issue for China.

China's relations with Pakistan have been more beneficial, in concrete terms, in the military field. In fact, most of the Pakistani inventory is based either on the Western equipment or of those made in China. More beneficial is the strategic weapons transfers from China including its cooperation in the making of the nuclear weapons in Pakistan from the 1980s and transfers of short and intermediate-range ballistic missile (M9 and M11) covering entire north Indian territories.

Bilateral economic and trade contacts are also not negligible with more than $ 4 billion in trade, though as a proportion of China's trade with other Asian countries, including India and North America, compare to be very small in volume. In this context, China has established a number of infrastructural projects and provided aid to these ventures in basic engineering plants at Taxila, textiles, electrical products, energy, highways and the like. While the balance of payments on the bilateral trade is still in China's favour, in the recent period, the gap has been decreasing. China plans to expand its infrastructural projects in Gwadhar, Northern areas, etc for trade and strategic considerations.

China and Bangladesh

Like its relations with Pakistan, China's conduct of its policy with Bangladesh also went a drastic change from hostility and even non-recognition after the latter's liberation in 1971 to a closer pragmatic association from about the 1980s. Diplomatic relations were not established until October 1974 between the two countries after Zia Rehman took over the reigns. The first visit of the Chief Executive of Bangladesh Zia to the PRC indicated the choices of the then regime. During this visit, Zia thanked the Chinese "for supporting Bangladesh to safeguard its national independence and in the issue of sharing of Ganges water."[14] Subsequently, during the Ershad's tenure, the Sino-Bangladesh relations were further strengthened. In the five visits that Ershad undertook in China, a 'solid foundation' was laid since both the countries faced 'common targets and interests.' During President Li Xiannian's visit, Bangladesh government was praised for "safeguarding peace and stability in the region of South Asia and Asia as a whole."[15] The 2005 visit of Premier Wen Jiabao was considered to be significant not only because of the nuclear agreement but also for elevating ties to the 'comprehensive and cooperative partnership' levels.

In more concrete terms areas of mutual interest include Bangladeshi acquiescence to the 'One China' policy, position on Tibet, support to China in international organizations on human rights issues, membership/partnership in areas even far away from the Chinese shores such as Indian Ocean Rim Association for Regional Cooperation,[16] SAARC[17] and sub-regional groupings within South Asia as a countervailing force to India, etc, though China refused to join the single regional currency idea in May 2000.[18] Benefits for Dhaka in cooperating with Beijing appeared to be too many to ignore. These included elevation in bilateral relations, investments in infrastructure projects and military supplies. Through the December 2002 defence cooperation agreement, Bangladesh expected to 'institutionalize' defence relationship with China. Quietly, conventional arms have been flowing from China to Bangladesh in its army, navy and air force inventories. Nevertheless, some complain about the poor combat quality of military equipment that China sold to Dhaka at 'friendship prices', although these are essential for Bangladeshi troops. Such transfers to Bangladesh so far have been mainly made on 'very easy financial terms'; credit purchases and 'spread out' payments to the Chinese give certain political mileage in the bilateral relations. Also, given the high cost of such weapons in the Western or Russian arms bazaars, 'cheap' Chinese products are an attractive proposition to the Bangladeshi government.[19] For expanding cooperation, both these countries are also pursuing mutual high-level military contacts. Further, in October 2005 Bangladesh was admitted, along with Pakistan, into the Chinese-led Asia-Pacific Space Cooperation Organization in Beijing. Through this process, Bangladesh is entitled to receive cooperation in space technology.

Sino-Bangladesh bilateral trade volume has increased over a period of time. As both countries celebrated a 'Year of Friendship' in their thirtieth anniversary of establishment of diplomatic relations in 2005, Bangladesh saw China replacing India as its largest trading partner, thanks to China's surge in its exports of textile fabrics, capital machinery and dyeing chemicals. The Chinese trade with Bangladesh indicated favourable balance of trade for China.[20] In 2005, of a bilateral trade of less than two billion dollars, Bangladesh exported goods valued at about a mere forty five million dollars to China. China's major imports from Bangladesh are: jute, leather, tobacco, fertilizer, tea, etc. and major exports are: pig iron, dyestuff, chemical products, machinery, scientific and medical equipment, coal, textile, local and livestock products, light industrial products, hardware, medicines, high-speed diesel, fire-proof materials, road-building equipment, billet, electric meter and its elements and the like. Such an imbalance in trade has led to a severe criticism from Bangladeshi trade bodies.[21] Investments in the infrastructural projects have been undertaken by the PRC agencies in the fields of electricity generation, constructing bridges, laying gas pipeline, telecommunications, chemicals, etc. China eyes a large portion of the potential sixty trillion cubic feet of natural gas that Bangladesh reportedly possesses. Indeed, the Bangladeshi government has granted exploration rights to China and Begum Zia has invited China, during her visit to Beijing in August 2005, to develop gas fields. China is currently exploring gas explorations and possible construction of gas pipelines. Construction of 1,250-kilometer pipeline from gas fields in Myanmar to its Yunnan province is being considered. This may be connected with Bangladesh in future. Reports indicate the Chinese interest in acquiring container port facility at Chittagong and other military facilities in Bangladesh. Also, the Kunming-Chittagong road through Myanmar is under negotiation with the concerned countries. Besides, China is exploring the first coal mine and constructing the coal-based power plant in Barapukuria and, in November 2005, the first 125×2 MW power plant was put into production. China built the Bangladesh-China Commercial Town with 500 Chinese shops at Kanchpur built at a cost of about six million dollars from April 2005. This would further give a boost to the entry of Chinese goods into Bangladesh.

China and Nepal

China's foreign policy objectives vis-à-vis Nepal are several. At a minimum, these objectives emphasise the security of Chinese interests in Tibet as that region is dependent on the neighbouring countries for border trade. Additionally, given the regular flow of thousands of Tibetan refugees into Nepal and India every year, Chinese objectives emphasise on nullifying any negative fallout of Tibetan refugees from these countries. Related to this objective is Chinese measure to counter the spread of Maoists influence in Nepal. This factor has assumed significance in the recent period as Nepalese Maoists have increased their influence in more than two-thirds of Nepalese territory. For China, if Maoists succeed in capturing state power in Kathmandu, there is always a prospect of increasing Maoist influence not only in other parts of China but also in Tibet. Any Maoist long march on Lhasa not only disturbs Chinese hold over Tibet but also has the prospects of questioning and undermining Chinese Communist Party's legitimacy to rule over the country.

China's (and Tibet's) relations with Nepal in history have exhibited a more state-to-state character than the case with other South Asian countries. While China had historical contacts with all other countries in the region, thanks to the Buddhist monks' visits, Tibet and Nepal fought wars on the question of territories and trade aspects in the eighteenth century, though Nepal lost the war in 1791 and signed a treaty. The 1856 treaty with Tibet provided Nepal with certain trade and other rights in the former though these were abolished in 1950s.[22]

After the diplomatic recognition of China in 1955, Nepal signed an agreement in 1956 that allowed it to 'establish trade agencies at Shigatse, Kyerong and Nyalam' on reciprocal basis. The border trade between Nepal and Tibet were thus maintained though the former has acknowledged that Tibet is a part of the PRC. For the traditional Tibetan link to the region has been one of the most decisive ones for the socio-economic aspects of Tibet. Thus, then, the objectives of the PRC in Nepal have been influenced by the Tibetan factor, including whether the 10,000 and odd refugees play a destabilizing role from Nepal, to secure Nepal as a buffer, as an *independent* actor away from the 1950 Indo-Nepal treaty (the implications of which surfaced in the late 1980s when Nepal tried to procure $ 200 million worth of arms from China and India responded by blockade and once again after China supplied $ 13.7 million worth of arms in 2005 to Royal Nepalese army), support to Zone of Peace proposal and Himalayan regional grouping and the like.

Towards these objectives, the PRC has extended cooperation to Nepal in terms of aid in constructing several highways including the Kathmandu-Lhasa route, leather factories, textiles, paper mills, sugar factories and other such projects.[23] The total trade volume between China and Nepal is miniscule, although within this China enjoys a favourable balance of trade position.[24] In March 2006, visiting state councillor Tang Jiaxuan agreed to bridge the unfavourable trade by agreeing to provide duty free treatment to about 1,550 Nepalese goods to China.

China and Sri Lanka

Though the Sri Lankan government has recognized the PRC in 1950 full diplomatic relations started only from 1957. Nevertheless, a Rubber &

Rice Pact was signed between the two countries in 1952 in the difficult years of trade embargoes against the PRC. Also, Sri Lankan position on Taiwan, and more importantly, given its predominantly Buddhist orientation, Tibet and human rights are crucial for consolidating the PRC's national interests.[25] The Joint Communiqué issued by both the governments during the 1972 Bandaranaike's visit clearly identified the status of Sri Lanka in the region. The Chinese government, in this document, supported Sri Lanka's policy of 'independence, peace, neutrality and non-alignment' and backed the Sri Lankan proposal for declaring the Indian Ocean as a Zone of Peace in the backdrop of the UN Resolution in 1971. For China, Sri Lanka's position on colonial struggles, moral support to the Indo-Chinese peoples, Palestinian movement and the like have provided ammunition for its ideological dispositions. More pertinently, the 1972 communiqué also reflected on the South Asian region in the immediate aftermath of the Indo-Pakistan war of 1971 and the liberation of Bangladesh. It stated:

> The two sides expressed their concern over the present tension in the South Asian subcontinent and reiterated that the outstanding issues in the region should be settled through peaceful negotiations on the principled basis of complete equality, mutual respect for national independence and unity, territorial integrity and sovereignty, mutual non-aggression, non-interference in each other's internal affairs and mutual benefit and accommodation, and without resorting to the use or threat of force.[26]

In the subsequent period, the bilateral relations have been expanded to include mutual areas of interest including in the regional and international arenas, trade, economy and military-related support.[27] In the mid-1990s the Sri Lankan chose to elect China as its first destination outside despite the fact that the Chinese premier did not pay a visit to the island for almost a decade till the 2001 visit of Zhu Rongji.[28]

Nevertheless, the Sino-Sri Lankan cooperation is reflected partly in the arms transfers to the latter to fight its insurgency problems relating to the LTTE. Apart from Israel and other countries, China formed one such principal supplier of the much needed weapon systems. The China North Industries Corporation (NORINCO) carried out most of such transactions, though even in this sphere they are not without controversies related to corruption, etc.[29]

More concrete results were achieved in economic and trade areas. The Joint Trade Committee, established between the two countries in 1982, formed the nodal organization to pursue economic cooperation in several fields. In the early 1990s this organization was amalgamated with another to form the Joint Commission to look after trade and economic issues. From 1957 to about 2000 China had provided Sri Lanka with economic aid to the tune of about Yuan 702 million to carry out various infrastructural and joint ventures in piggery and poultry, toy-making projects, deep sea-fishing, chaff-processing and pencil-making and the like. Bilateral trade between the two countries, in addition to the traditional items like rice and rubber, included Chinese imports of red tea, precious stones coconut oil and main exports to Sri Lanka include rice, light textile products, medicine equipment, metal fittings, machinery tobacco sugar and so on. The bilateral trade increased gradually over a period of time to about $458 million in 2000, with $445 million in export and $12.85 million in import on the Chinese side.[30] In 2003 trade amounted to $524 million with Chinese exports of $504 million. In 2004, this increased to $717 million. Clearly the trade figures showed a heavy imbalance at the cost of Sri Lanka.[31] It is in this backdrop and Sri Lankan displeasure at the negative balance of payments, that the PRC was compelled to invest in joint venture projects. Nearly 300 contracts were signed between the two countries worth about $400 million for cooperation in textile, electric power, water conservancy, highways, communication, fishing industry and agricultural sectors of Sri Lanka.[32] The 2007 joint statement between the Presidents of the two countries indicate to the development of the Hambantota Development Zone, including a harbour in near future.

China and Bhutan

Though China and Bhutan do not have diplomatic relations, the border problem between the two has been one of the factors in maintaining contacts. From 1984 to 2002, China and Bhutan have held sixteen rounds of talks on the boundary question based on the traditional pasturage rights and tax collection. During the twelfth round of talks on boundary questions held in 1998 in Beijing, China and Bhutan signed an agreement on Maintenance of Peace and Tranquillity in China-Bhutan border areas. This forms some kind of official document between the two countries.[33]

China and Maldives

Chinese entry into Maldives has been relatively late, if we discount the traditional and historical contacts of the yore. This explains partly to the delay in diplomatic relations between the two only in 1972. Mutual high-level visits have also been very few and far between with the first visit made in 1980 by the Maldivian Foreign Minister Fathulla Jameel. Later in 1981 Foreign Minister Huang Hua visited. In 1984 Maldivian President Maumoon Abdul Gayoom paid a state visit to China, followed by Jameel's visit in 1993 and Foreign Minister Qian Qichen in 1994.[34] More significant, however, was Premier Zhu Rongji's visit in May 2001 in which it was reported that the PRC has signed an agreement with the Maldivian government to construct a naval base for the Chinese navy at Marao, 40 kilometres from the capital Male.[35] No progress in this project is, however, reported from the area. The Sino-Maldivian trade volume in 1998 totalled $590,000, with Chinese exports amounting to $540,000 and imports of $50,000. In 2000, bilateral trade volume reached $1.358 million with Chinese exports totalling $1.338 million and import $20,000. In 2003, total bilateral trade amounted to $3.351 million with Chinese exports at $3.342 million. In 2004, this increased to $8 million. The 2006 trade figures indicate to a similar picture of unfavourable balance of trade position for the Maldives, with the exception that gradually Taiwan lost out to China in this country.

Conclusion

China's interactions with the South Asian countries in the last five decades provide some broad generalizations. The concept of modern nation-state, which is new import for all these countries, has led to opportunities to improve relations as well as problems in adjusting with each other. One dominant feature that emerges in these interactions is the PRC's effort to dislodge or at least reduce the influence of the dominant powers like US, Russia or India in the region. To an extent it has been successful in some of the major indicators like the level and influence in the bilateral relations with the South Asian countries. More importantly, from its national interests perspective, China has initiated several new features in its South Asia policy, viz.,

- Western Development Campaign of opening up its interior western regions bordering South Asia and making efforts to link the infrastructure facilities,
- following a re-adjustment in its previous policy of supporting Pakistan towards coming to grips with rising India with which it intends to evolve a 'strategic partnership' while reportedly demoting Pakistan from strategic to regional spheres (as reported during President Hu Jintao's visit to Islamabad in November 2006),[36]
- adjusting towards a policy of outright opposition to the Indian nuclear programme (as in 1998) towards talks with India while

taking measures with Pakistan and the US so that the nuclear materials do not fall into the non-state actors and ushering in nuclear stability in the region,

- counter-terrorism measures primarily aimed at securing its position in Xinjiang and curbing evolving relations with the Uyghur's and Al Qaeda networks,
- exploration of markets for its burgeoning exports and raw materials through greater economic engagement and proposals for free trade areas and
- exploring ways to secure sea lines in the Indian Ocean for sustainable supplies to fuel its economy.

Another feature that emerges out of this brief comparative study is the economic and trade issue – that is the balance of payments is largely in favour of China with South Asian countries. To overcome this problem the PRC has either invested in the joint venture projects in these countries or as foreign aid at simpler interest rates or has tried to reduce the economic burden with arms transfers under 'friendly' rates. Nevertheless, while the Chinese infrastructural development in several South Asian countries in the fields of highways, bridges, industrial ventures, etc. is commendable, some of these may have been built with a strategic perspective. China intends to link these projects to the Arabian Sea or the Bay of Bengal so that its interior provinces could access to the Indian Ocean in the longer run. The so-called China's 'string of pearls' in the Indian Ocean region comes into the picture, albeit in defensive terms at this point of time. In 2006, China imported about 145 million tonnes of oil, with about eighty per cent of this passing through the vulnerable Straits of Malacca's. Again, Chinese transfers of technology to the region indicates that its investments are generally in low or medium-technology areas in which China has been already undergoing transformation towards high-tech areas in its modernization drive from the late 1970s. Even in this joint venture nature of projects, the local Chinese companies (which are mainly state owned enterprises as compared to the local private entrepreneurs in the South Asian countries) have time and again insisted on compenzation for the devaluation of the local currencies and often created problems to their local participants. Although China has amassed the largest foreign exchange reserves in the world today (about $1 trillion) it is not clear whether these resources could be put to use for Asian- or South Asian – reconstruction purposes. It needs to be seen whether China will take any new initiatives after the fourteenth SAARC summit in April 2007 in this regard.

References

1. For the policy shifts of China towards this region and the factors behind them, see Han Hua, "China and South Asia" in K Santhanam and Srikanth Kondapalli (eds), *Asian Security and China 2000-2010*, New Delhi: Shipra Publications & IDSA, 2004, pp. 290-300. See also Cheng Ruisheng, "Sino-Indian relations after India's nuclear tests" May 20-22, 1999, http://lxmi.mi.infn.it/~landnet/NSA/cheng.pdf.
2. Wang Hongwei, *Qimalayashan qingjie: Zhongyin guanxi Yanjiu* (*The Himalayas Sentiment: A Study of Sino-Indian Relations*, Beijing: Zhongguo Zangxue Chubanshe, 1998 (hereafter *Qimalayashan qingjie: Zhongyin guanxi Yanjiu)* and Zhao Weiwen, *Yinzhong guanxi fengyunlu 1949-1999* (*Record of stormy India-China Relations, 1949-1999*, Beijing: Shishi Chubanshe, 2000); and Liu Xuecheng, *The Sino-Indian Border Dispute and Sino-Indian Relations*, Lanham: University Press of America, 1994.
3. See *Zhongguo Waijiao, China's Diplomacy* (various yearbooks), Beijing: Ministry of Foreign Affairs.
4. Li Yanan, "India Dreaming to be a Military Super Power", *Liberation Army Daily* (Beijing) 12 June 1999. On the Indian nuclear tests conducted in May 1998 see Chang Ya-chun, '*Yindu hezi shihuo yu zhonggong wei lilun*' (The Indian nuclear tests and the Communist China's Threat) *Zhongguo dalu yanjiu, Mainland China Studies*, Taipei, vol. 41 no. 5 May 1998, pp. 1-2; and Zou Yunhua, *Chinese Perceptions on the South Asian Nuclear Tests*, Stanford: Centre for International Security and Cooperation, Stanford University, 1999.
5. This is based on Srikanth Kondapalli, "Negotiating Borders or Bordering on Negotiations? Predicaments in Indian and Chinese Policies" in P.Sahadevan (ed), *Conflict and Peacemaking in South Asia*, New Delhi: Lancer Books, 2001, pp. 308-45
6. For an account of the economic relations between India and China see Yan Shijing and Chen Jidong, *Zhongguo Xinan dui Yindu Maoyi wenti yanjiu* (*Studies on Problems Related to Trade Between Southwest China and India)*, Chengdu: Sichuan University Publications, 1997 and Institute of South Asian Studies, Sichuan University and Embassy of India (ed), *Zhongyin Jingmao Zhinan* (*Sino-Indian Economic Cooperation and Trade-A Guidebook*), Chengdu: Sichuan University Press, 1998.
7. "China to Resume Border trade", *The Statesman*, 23 October 1981.
8. See Ma Jiali, "Striving to build a constructive and cooperative partnership with India", *Contemporary International Relations* (Beijing), vol. 10, no. 3 March 2000, p. 4.
9. Samina Yasmeen, "Sino-Pakistan Relations and the Middle East", *China Report*, vol. 34, nos. 3 and 4 1998, pp. 327-43. For the geo-political link with Pakistan see Lin Liangguang, et.al 2001, p. 114.

10. See John W. Garver, *Protracted Contest: Sino-Indian Rivalry in the Twentieth Century*, New Delhi: Oxford University Press, 2001; Mohan Malik, "The China factor in the India-Pakistan Conflict", *Occasional Paper Series*, Asia-Pacific Center for Security Studies, Honolulu, November 2002; Shao Zhiyong, "India's big power dream", *Beijing Review*, 12 April 2001 p. 10.
11. At one point of time the Pakistani establishment reportedly collaborated with the American agencies in covert operations in Tibet in the 1950s. See, for instance, "Dhaka airstrip used by CIA for covert operation", *Independent*, 23 April 1999.
12. For a comprehensive account of the Sino-Pak relations, though dated, see Anwar Hussain Syed, *China and Pakistan: Diplomacy of an Entente Cordiale*, Amherst: University of Massachusetts Press, 1974 and Yakov Vertberger, *The Enduring Entente: Sino-Pakistani Relations, 1960-1980*, New York: Praeger, 1982.
13. Indeed during PM Sharif's visit to China amidst the Kargil events, Jiang not only indicated China's moral and political support to Pakistan but also reportedly decided to conduct military exercises in Tibet. See "What is meant by China's military exercises", *Ausaf*, 1 July 1999 in *BBC SWB FE/ 3577 A/5*, 3 July 1999.
14. See "China and Bangladesh", http://www.fmprc.gov.cn/eng/4311.html.
15. For implications of the Sino-Bangladesh cooperation for India see Padmaja Murthy, "Bangladesh-China relations: Implications for India's policy", paper presented at Institute for Defence Studies & Analyses, New Delhi Fellows Seminar, 14 July 2001.
16. "UK, China as dialogue partners", *Independent*, 24 January 2000.
17. It was at the thirteenth SAARC summit at Dhaka that China's candidature for observer position was accepted reportedly under Bangladesh, Pakistan and Nepal's pressure, while India wanted China first to sign bilateral MoUs with respective South Asian countries.
18. "Asian clearing union thinks of single currency", *Independent*, 21 May 2000.
19. "Dhaka considering Chinese offer of F-7 MB jets", *Daily Star*, 28 December 1999; "MiG deal made with absolute transparency, says PM", *Independent*, 23 March 2000; "Bangladesh to acquire eight Chinese fighter planes", *Daily Star*, 8 April 2000.
20. See "China and Bangladesh", http://www.fmprc.gov.cn/eng/4311.html and *Zhongguo Waijiao 2006* (China's Diplomacy 2006), Beijing: MFA.
21. For these discrepancies in Sino-Bangla trade, "Exporters of raw jute to China facing problems", *Bangladesh Observer*, 28 January 1998. A similar problem arose when the China National Water resources & Hydropower Engineering claimed compenzation for currency devaluation of the Taka

in April 2000. See "Chinese Co claims compenzation for devaluation of Taka", *Bangladesh Observer,* 11 April 2000.

22. This is based on Narayan Khadka, "China's foreign policy and foreign aid in Nepal" in his *Foreign Aid and Foreign Policy: Major Powers and Nepal,* Delhi: Vikas Publishers, 1997, pp. 249-310.

23. See Ramakant, *Nepal-China Relations,* New Delhi: Abhinav Publications, 1976; TR Ghoble, *China-Nepal Relations and India,* New Delhi: Deep Publications, 1986; Shashi Bhusan Prasad, *The China factor in Indo-Nepalese Relations, 1955-72,* New Delhi: Commonwealth Publications, 1989 and Shiva Bahadur Singh, *Indo-Nepalese Relations: Discord and Harmony,* Varanasi: Ganga Kaveri Publication House, 1994.

24. "China and Nepal", http://www.fmprc.gov.cn/eng/4402.html and *Zhongguo Waijiao 2006* (China's Diplomacy 2006), Beijing: MFA.

25. While Sri Lankan trade with Taiwan was not a problem for the PRC, no diplomatic relations were allowed due to its "One China" policy as reiterated again during Foreign Minister Kadirgamar's visit to Beijing in 1995. See for details, "China seeks Sri Lanka support at human rights meet", *Sunday Times* (Colombo), 26 February 1995 and "Business with Taiwan despite one-China policy", *Island* (Colombo), 3 March 1995. For the displeasure of the Tibetan community at the refusal of the Sri Lankan government to allow the Dalai Lama, see "Refusal to okay Dalai Lama visit to Lanka decried", *Sunday Leader* (Colombo), 15 August 1999.

26. See the "Joint Communiqué between the People's Republic of China and the Republic of Sri Lanka (1972)", http://www.fmprc.gov.cn/eng/4989.html.

27. For a broad study of the phases in the Sri Lankan foreign policy towards China see V. Suryanarayan, "Sri Lanka's China Policy-Legacy of the past and prospects", paper presented at the Department of Chinese & Japanese Studies, University of Delhi, 17-18 September 1993.

28. The bilateral relations nose-dived not only when Sri Lanka supported Indian nuclear tests in 1998 but more specifically when China's Xinhua correspondent Jin Wei was asked to leave the country for his reportage. The Chinese Ambassador Cheng Defu even went to the extent of boycotting fiftieth anniversary celebrations of Lankan independence in March 1998. See "Cancellation of Xinhua scribe's deportation averts row", *Sunday Times,* 8 March 1998.

29. See "Sri Lanka's main military equipment deal under cloud", *Sunday Times,* 20 August 1995; "Armed forces acquiring equipment to meet Tiger threat", *Island,* 13 September 1995; and "Rs 2.5 billion Sino-Lankan arms deal", *Sunday Times,* 17 September 1995.

30. For details see "China and Sri Lanka", http://www.fmprc.gov.cn/eng/4437.html.

31. By the mid-1990s, the adverse trade balance against Sri Lanka stood at Rs. 8 billion according to the Sri Lankan Trade Ministry's statistics. See "Commerce minister leads trade team to China", *Daily News*, 26 March 1996.

32. See "China assures credit to Sri Lanka", *Daily News* (Colombo), 27 February 1995; "Biggest trade fair from China from April 5", *Sunday Observer*, 2 April 1995; "Singer, D.Samson sign up with 3 Chinese companies", *Sunday Observer*, 23 April 1995; "China grants Rs. 1 billion as economic aid: Accords signed", *Daily News*, 24 April 1996.

33. See for an excellent study on the subject, Surjeet Mansingh, China-Bhutan Relations", paper presented at the Seminar on *China and South Asia in the Post Cold War* at Department of Chinese and Japanese Studies, University of Delhi, 17-18 September 1993 and "China and Bhutan", http://www.fmprc.gov.cn/eng/4316.html.

34. See, "China and Maldives", http://www.fmprc.gov.cn/eng/4388.html.

35. See, AB Mahapatra, "China acquires a base in Maldives against India with some help from Pakistan", 27 July 2001, http://www.indiareacts.com.

36. This is based on interviews with Chinese experts at Beijing in late November 2006.

15

Prospects of India's Partnership with ASEAN and BIMSTEC for the Development of Landlocked Northeast India

A. Lakshmana Chetty

One of the spectacular features of India's foreign policy during the post-Cold War period has been India's growing association with the regional and trans-regional cooperative frameworks such as Association of Southeast Asian Nations (ASEAN), Bay of Bengal Initiative for Multi-sectoral Technical and Economic Cooperation (BIMSTEC), Mekong-Ganga Cooperation (MGC) and Kunming Initiative at a time, when new Asia had been emerging as a 'centre of gravity' in the global economy, despite hazards like tensions between China and Japan, the rising level of terrorist menace, the grim scenario of energy security and the increasing dependence of Asia's economies on the US. The region's prospects have been brightened, thanks to India's robust economic growth, and the rising global significance, China's phenomenal economic growth and ASEAN's emergence as a geopolitically vital and economically vibrant region. In moving closer to the regional groupings, India was guided among others, by its deep concern for the development of its Northeastern Region (NER), which was admirably placed to serve as a 'land bridge' between India and Southeast Asia. This paper examines the various development models tried out as part of India's strategy to bring about peace, prosperity and all-round development in the states of NER and the advance made thereof besides probing into India's burgeoning partnership with the regional outfits and its impact on the growth and development of NER.

NER and its Integration with Rest of India

NER which comprises Arunachal Pradesh, Manipur, Meghalaya, Mizoram, Nagaland, Tripura, Assam and Sikkim, enjoys a unique place in the political, economic and cultural landscape of India. It is a paradox that the region is rich in developmental potential, but remains least developed. NER's strengths include fertile land, diverse agricultural resources, educated manpower, rich energy resources, proximity to the Southeast Asian markets, rich potentials of tourism and a conduit between India and the countries in its neighbourhood. NER's weaknesses include lack of local entrepreneurship, poor infrastructure, high cost of logistics, lack of local markets, landlocked location and governance of low standard. Following the partition of India in 1947, NER became 'virtually landlocked surrounded by inhospitable neighbours'. Even with mainland India, the link is only twenty two kms. through the tenuous 'Siliguri Corridor' or 'Chicken's neck' which stands in sharp contrast to its international border stretching 4,500 kms.[1] In the absence of the traditional road and river transportation routes, alternative routes turned out to be uneconomical circuitous routes. For instance, the distance between Agartala and Kolkata port is 1,700 kms, in contrast to the earlier one of about 375 kms. across Bangladesh.[2] NER is far removed from India's chief centres of economic activity. It is proximate to Dhaka, Yangoon and Bangkok than to Delhi, Mumbai and Chennai.[3]

Early attitude of Government of India towards NER

Government of India (GOI) began evincing interest in NER, only after the Chinese invasion in 1962. GOI focused on security, rather than on economic development. The North Eastern Council (NEC) created in 1971, also remained a security-oriented one. Absence of economic development gave rise to despair and dejection which in turn led to growing problem of insurgency. The invasion by the illegal migrants confounded the situation in the region.

NER and the Look East Policy

The traditional links of a glorious antiquity between India and Southeast Asian countries drifted along the cross currents of the Cold War towards a dusty twilight. Nonetheless, the launch of Look East Policy (LEP) by India in 1992, marked a new dawn in the relations with its eastern neighbours. As the Prime Minister Manmohan Singh has pointed out, LEP was not merely an external economic policy, but also a strategic shift in India's vision of the world and India's place in the evolving global economy. Most important, it is all about the reaching out to India's civilizational neighbours in East and Southeast Asia.[4] India, therefore, initiated the process of building blocks with the countries of the region through free trade and economic cooperative mechanisms.

LEP's chief focus, thus, has been on diversifying India's external economic relations with the countries of Southeast Asia, in particular. India, hence, made conscious effort to promote regional and trans-regional trade and economic cooperation. NER, which enjoyed the locational advantage by virtue of its closeness to Southeast Asian markets, became 'economic bridge-head' to Southeast Asia. Commercial exchanges were expected to 'galvanize growth and development' in the NER. In other words, the development of NER constituted a significant feature of LEP. Rajiv Sikri, Secretary (East), Ministry of External Affairs, described the LEP as the one which "envisages the Northeast region not as the periphery of India but the Centre for a thriving and integrated economic space linking two dynamic regions with a network of highways, railways, pipelines, transmission lines crisscrossing the region". He expressed the fond hope that one day trains and buses would carry "millions of tourists, pilgrims, workers and business in both directions".[5]

LEP's key elements in so far as NER was concerned, were:

- To create supportive environment to the economic development of NER and its emergence as a thriving economic hub;
- To help the region to integrate itself with rest of India; and
- To enable NER to become gateway to Southeast Asia

Accordingly, P.V. Narasimha Rao government (1991-1996) constituted a committee to probe into the problems of NER. In 1996, Northeast Finance Corporation (NFDFI) was set up with a corpus fund of Rs.100 crores. The very next year, Northeast Industrial Policy was unveiled offering a number of sops to the industries in the region. In 1996, Premier Deve Gowda (1996-1997) announced a Rs.100 crore economic package to develop infrastructure. The Vajpayee government (1998-2004) announced various infrastructural projects including transport corridors, hydropower projects, introduction of airlines and extension of broad gauge railway to the region, besides launching peace initiatives with the Naga outfit, NSCN (I.M.), and with the Bodos. In 2001, India completed 144 km. road, connecting Tamu in Manipur with Kalemyo (near Mandalay in Myanmar), which facilitates people-to-people contacts, exchange of goods and services between NER and the countries of South and Southeast Asia. In 1998, Vajpayee announced a package of Rs.10,217 crores to boost the region's development. Steps were initiated to earmark at least ten per cent of the budget of Central Ministries/ Departments for the development of NER. The BJP government also created a Non-lapsable Central Pool of Resources (NLCPR) by mobilizing the unspent balance of the budgets of Central Ministries/Departments concerned, for hastening the development of the infrastructure in NER. The creation of the Department of Northeastern Region (DONER) in 2001, which replaced the NEC, made it clear that the emphasis was not on security, but on development. The NDA government started the practice of holding Northeast Business summits every year with the participation of business leaders and policy makers for the speedy realization of an all-round development in all the eight states of NER.

The incumbent UPA government led by Manmohan Singh, upgraded DONER to a full-fledged Ministry in May 2004. Of the various steps taken by Manmohan, the establishment of road links with the Southeast Asian countries; an initiative to set up Brahmaputra River Valley Authority/Northeast River Valley Authority to find a lasting solution to the recurring flood problem; and the exploration of sources of energy are a few to name. In September 2005, the UPA government announced the launch of a high way development programme for NER with an outlay of Rs.12,000 crores.[6] Commenting on the financial packages announced by the successive Prime Ministers, Jairam Ramesh, M.P., and Secretary of the Congress Economic Affairs Cell, observed: "The Government of India contributes heavily towards the expenditures of eight states (the seven sisters and Sikkim). The total expenditure of these eight states is Rs.30,000 crores a year for the population of roughly thirty two million or thereabout– 10,000 rupees per person per year is not a small sum."[7]

India's Economic Interaction with Regional Groupings

ASEAN

Though political gap kept India from a meaningful interaction with ASEAN for two and a half decades, both India and ASEAN felt the need for starting a new era of friendship and cooperation for mutual benefit in the changing global scenario. ASEAN, hence, offered India Sectoral Dialogue partnership in 1992. Subsequently, India was accorded Full Dialogue Partnership in 1995, membership of ASEAN Regional Forum (ARF) in 1996 and Summit Dialogue status in 2002.

The major thrust of India-ASEAN partnership was on strengthening economic linkages. Thanks to the improved economic ties, the bilateral trade shot up from $ 3.1 billion in 1992, to $12 billion in 2002. The share of NER in this annual trade was around twelve per cent. There is vast scope for increasing the volume of this trade further.[8] Commenting on this,

Suvrokamal Dutta, the renowned Foreign Affairs and Economic Expert, noted: "Looking into the political, strategic and economic angle of this, Look East Policy of India towards ASEAN and East Asia can be gold mine for North East India in the long run and solve her age-old political problem and economic backwardness."[9] In order to reinforce business and industry links, India and ASEAN Business summits are being held since 2002. The singular achievement in this sphere of economic interaction is the conclusion of an agreement to establish India-ASEAN Free Trade Area by 2011. By the end of March 2007 senior officials of India-ASEAN were scheduled to hold what may turn out to be an 'almost make or break' talks for finalization of long-stalled free trade agreement. Meanwhile, India has signed free trade agreements with Thailand, Singapore and two more with Malaysia and Indonesia are in the pipeline. The historic 'agreement of ASEAN-India Partnership for Peace and Progress and Shared Prosperity' signed in November 2004, mapped out a multi-pronged action plan for boosting the trade and investment. All these economic engagements have facilitated the realization of the targeted India-ASEAN trade turn over of $30 billion by 2007. The ASEAN-India Car rally from Guwahati to Indonesia in November 2004 was designed to draw attention to NER's proximity to the Southeast Asian countries. Speaking on the eve of Car rally, Rajiv Sikhri hoped that NER would get a good opportunity to showcase itself.[10] Flagging of the first ever Car rally Manmohan Singh said, "We are now rediscovering the age-old relations."[11]

President Abdul Kalam's state visit to Myanmar, during 8-10 March 2006, had much to do with the advancement of the interests of NER: energy security, infrastructure projects, counter insurgency, counter narcotics, development of economic linkages between NER and ASEAN region.[12]

BIMSTEC

Two years after securing Full Dialogue Partnership of ASEAN, India, joined by Thailand, Sri Lanka and Bangladesh, founded a trans-regional cooperative framework which, after the subsequent admission of Myanmar, Nepal and Bhutan, was called BIMSTEC. Of the seven members, two represented Southeast Asia and the remaining five hailed from South Asia. Being 'a bridge between South Asia and Southeast Asia' BIMSTEC aimed at "rapid economic development through identification and implementation of specific cooperative projects in the sectors of trade, investment and industry, technology, human resource development, tourism, agriculture, energy and infrastructure and transportation."[13] Bringing out the significance of BIMSTEC for India, Prime Minister

Manmohan Singh said, "We consider our participation in BIMSTEC as a key element in our 'Look East' policy and long standing approach of good neighbourlyness towards all our neighbours – by land and sea. The challenge before us is to transform the richness of our human and natural resources into cooperative regional activities promoting development, enhancing prosperity and the well-being of our people, and ensuring our collective security in all its multifarious dimensions."[14]

BIMSTEC accorded top priority to the development of different modes of transport, particularly the Trans-Asian Railway and Trans-Highway networks, which were imperative for achieving connectivity among member countries to promote the movement of goods and people.

By virtue of its size and level of development, India has been in a unique position not only to influence and to shape the policies but also to boost its economic cooperation with other members. India's membership of BIMSTEC supplements New Delhi's initiatives at strengthening its economic cooperation with the ASEAN countries and the member countries of SAARC, except Pakistan.

India's major trading partners (in exports) in the BIMSTEC region are Bangladesh, Thailand, Sri Lanka and Nepal and with respect to imports are Thailand and Myanmar. India's trade with Nepal and Bhutan is through over land by road and with Myanmar, Sri Lanka and Thailand through sea routes. India's trade with BIMSTEC members in 2002-03 was of about six million tons. One half of this was through overland and the remaining half through sea.[15]

According to the report of EXIM Bank published in 2004, since the inception of the BIMSTEC, India's trade with the group has been rising from $2.2 billion in 1997-98 to $3.7 billion in 2002-03. India has been maintaining a significant trade surplus with all the BIMSTEC members with the sole exception of Myanmar which enjoys a fairly favourable balance of trade. Among the BIMSTEC members, Bangladesh provides the largest market for India's exports there by accounting for thirty nine per cent of India's total exports to BIMSTEC in 2002-03, followed by Sri Lanka, Thailand and Myanmar.[16]

The signing of the framework agreement for the BIMSTEC Free Trade Area (BIMSTEC-FTA) by the members of BIMSTEC minus Bangladesh in February 2004 was a major step in the direction of economic integration of the grouping. A study by RIS, (New Delhi-based Think-Tank) in 2004 finds the trade creating potential of BIMSTEC-FTA between forty three billion dollars and fifty nine billion dollars a year.[17] BIMSTEC was given further boost in 2004 when its first ever summit was held. Since the development of infrastructure topped the agenda, BIMSTEC members decided to take up the Trans-Asian Highway project linking Saurashtra to Singapore through NER. A major initiative has been launched by the railways of India and Myanmar to work on 315 km. 'missing rail link' to ensure cross-border travel and freight movement. In a statement made on 22 March 2007 Railway Board Chairman, J.P. Batra, who also happens to be the Chairperson of the International Union of Railways, said, "Both sides have agreed to work towards forging this new relationship to complete the missing link of 315 km. We are taking up construction of 100 km. of the link on the Indian side and the rest will also be completed in due course of time. It is likely to cost around Rs.1100 crore."[18] Prime Minister Manmohan Singh perceived BIMSTEC as a great boon to NER. Addressing a press conference after the BIMSTEC summit, Manmohan said, "The North-Eastern Region of India faces considerable handicaps because of the high cost of transport. The BIMSTEC initiative opens up the possibilities of making more effective arrangements for transportation of goods and services to other countries of Southeast Asia through land routes, making use of roads, railways and ports that would certainly help to promote the development of North-Eastern Region."[19]

At the BIMSTEC summit meeting in 2004, a decision was taken to set up a Joint Working Group to counter terrorism. The member nations were unanimous in refusing to allow their territories to be used by terrorist groups for launching attacks on friendly countries. This was a welcome step from the perspective of NER which is plagued by border terrorism.[20]

Kunming Initiative

On 17 August 1999, Yunnan which 'enjoys a special status' in the Peoples Republic of China, officially undertook the initiative to organize a conference on the regional cooperation and development at its capital, Kunming, in which academics, businessmen, professionals and even officials from India, Bangladesh, Myanmar and China participated. This Track-II initiative, also known as Kunming Initiative or Bangladesh-China-India-Myanmar (BCIM) forum, aimed at accelerating the development of direct commercial, economic and cultural ties between the South Asian and the Mekong basin countries, by developing road, rail, waterway and air links. Yunnan and Sichuan, China's southwestern provinces, were keen to reach out to the markets of NER, West Bengal and Bangladesh through Myanmar and the Indian Ocean. This initiative which amounts to the revival of the ancient southern Silk Route trade and travel between Assam and Yunnan, had the distinction of seeking to involve the two Asian giants in the first ever institutional economic cooperative framework. The BCIM forum failed to take off chiefly for two reasons: India's apprehensions about China's economic domination and spread of influence over the disaffected people in the NER and the conditions of insecurity prevalent in India's northeast, bordering on China, Bangladesh and Myanmar.[21]

Mekong-Ganga Cooperation (MGC)

While the dominant factor in India's participation in ASEAN, BIMSTEC and Kunming Initiative was economic cooperation, India's association with yet another regional grouping called MGC, had economic as well as cultural dimensions. On 10 November 2000, MGC was formally launched in Vientiane, the capital of Laos, by India, the riparian country of the Ganges and the five ASEAN member nations who happen to be the riparian nations of Mekong, namely, Myanmar, Thailand, Laos, Cambodia and Vietnam. By participating in this forum, India "extended its footprints into the ASEAN region under the geostrategic backdrop."[22] MGC supplements the India-ASEAN relationship. The chief objective of the MGC was to promote cooperation in diverse areas including tourism, culture, education, transport and infrastructure, as well as cooperation in science, technology and human resource development between India and the five Mekong basin countries. It was hailed as India's major cooperative venture in Southeast Asia, after the BIMSTEC. MGC offers immense scope for India's private sector to make a foray into the region. Highlighting the salient features of the MGC, the Minister of State for External Affairs, Ajit Kumar Panja, said in a statement in Lok Sabha, "This initiative aims at promoting cooperation among six countries in the areas of Tourism, Culture, Education, Transport and Communications. Cooperation in these sectors among the six countries opens up business and economic opportunities for Indian companies and also interaction and exchanges between India and those countries."[23]

Similar sentiments were aired by the Minister of Foreign Affairs of Myanmar, in an interview, given to the journal, *World Affairs*, "This project is aimed at strengthening the links between India and the Mekong basin countries especially in the areas of tourism, education and culture. It will improve communication links between India and the Mekong region and include such projects as Trans-Asian railway line. The project would also provide an impetus to strengthening political ties with ASEAN."[24]

Unfortunately enough, this benign move made by India for all drawing inspiration from its civilizational bonds with its Southeast Asian neighbours, was misconceived and misinterpreted by certain sections of the international press, as an initiative, chiefly directed against China which was not associated with the grouping. As the Laotian Deputy Prime Minister, Somsavat Lengsavad clarified that the MGC was not a military grouping against anybody and on the contrary it was mainly designed to assist the countries of the region, to promote economic development.[25] Jaswant Singh, the then Indian Minister of Foreign Affairs, also sought to clear up the misapprehensions. He stated categorically that the "initiative was not aimed at China, nor a means of increasing India's power projection." He described the project as "an affirmation of historical, cultural and geographical ties."[26] China, however, welcomed the MGC project.[27]

As a follow up action to deepen the cooperation among the six member nations, the second MGC Ministerial meeting held in Hanoi on 28 July 2001 came up with what is called 'Hanoi Programme of Action' which focused on four areas of cooperation, namely, tourism, culture, human resource development and transportation and communication among member nations.[28] Vietnam expressed the hope that the successful cooperation of this 'programme' would help fortify other already existing cooperation arrangements between India and ASEAN.[29] Responding to the plea of the third MGC Ministerial meting held on 20 June 2003 at Phnom Penh for money required for MGC's proceedings, India offered $ 100,000.[30]

The MGC serves as a mechanism in addition to the ones already in place, namely, ASEAN, BIMSTEC and Kunming Initiative, to the acceleration of the economic growth of the NER. The MGC would also facilitate India's playing of an effective role in helping bridge the gap between the less developed and developed nations of ASEAN through activities in the spheres of tourism, education and culture. Striking a note of optimism about the MGC, Nguyen Dy Nien, Minister of Foreign Affairs of Vietnam, said, "The Mekong-Ganga Cooperation can make use of common traditional and cultural values of all countries and help turn this sub-region into a region of sustainable development and prosperity. It, therefore, can be a very good mechanism that supplements the existing cooperation between India and ASEAN. Participation in the Mekong Basin Sub-region could also help reduce this gap."[31]

It is an acknowledged truth that India lagged behind China in fostering ties with the Southeast Asian nations. Still, India enjoys the advantage, thanks to its civilizational bonds – characterized by fruitful cultural and commercial interaction – to enlarge its 'strategic footprint' in Southeast Asia, certainly not through military cooperation in the form of joint military exercises, but by expanding ties in the areas of trade and commerce in particular. The regional cooperative initiatives like ASEAN, BIMSTEC, Kunming Initiative and MGC are mainly designed to harness the natural resources of the countries of South, Southeast and Northeast Asia. India could avail itself of these forums, to exploit the richness of our human and natural resources, to transform the growth profile of its own in general and the NER and its eastern neighbours in particular.

Factors Impeding NER's Development

Even though the Central government has been spending huge sums for the rapid development of NER, "the desired result is not commensurate with the money spent."[32] Pouring out his anguish over the sorry state of affairs, Prime Minister Vajpayee said in his inaugural address at the second North East summit on 1 January 2004, "We are particularly determined to attend to the developmental needs of our states in the North-Eastern Region.... However it is a matter of deep concern to us that slow economic growth has implied lesser opportunities of employment and progress for its people. The resultant discontent is exploited by certain extremist organizations to foment violence and divisiveness."[33]

However, the fact remains that various factors have contributed to this conundrum.

Disturbing Security Scenario

One of the major challenges of NER is violence and conflicts among various ethnic groups. It is common place that various underground groups have divided the highway into their own exclusive territories to extort money.[34] Believing that "security of our people and their property is of prime importance" and also holding the same sense of security as "a prerequisite for fresh investments to come in and for enterprises to flourish," the Union government has developed an elaborate and expensive security apparatus. This line of approach has been subjected to criticism. Sanjib Baruah stated that the prism of security through which Indian policy-makers viewed the NER was likely to remain a major factor inhibiting serious investment of resources – intellectual, political and material – to make the region, India's gateway to Southeast Asia.[35] Indiresan, a columnist, made impassioned pleas to reduce expenditure on security forces and spend more on infrastructure. He cautioned that

"The harsher the government has tried to impose its authority, the more bitter have the people become."[36]

Closure of Borders

Since the Chinese aggression of 1962, government of India had banned the cross-border trade for two reasons: first, security concerns in the troubled NER and second, the prospect of Chinese goods flooding the Indian markets which would adversely affect local producers with the result that the local economies are hit hard and the trade routes linking NER to China and Southeast Asia have 'rotted with disuse'. India has only one border trade point opened with Myanmar while China has three. Trade with the rest of India through Siliguri corridor has not been flourishing. Pallavi Iyer has pointed out that the secessionist violence continues to wreck the region and the tribal people remain marginalsed.[37] Yeo Jiannong, head of the Development Strategy section of the Yunan Development Research Centre (VRDC), made out a strong case for keeping the borders open, "If we press ahead seriously and open up direct overland routes between Northeastern India and Yunnan, it could reduce transport costs, by over 30 per cent not to mention the slash down on transport time.[38]

It was for this reason that the Kunming Initiative has been harping on the issue of the repair and reopening of historical Stilwell Road which is the shortest one, between NER and Southeast Asia.

Lack of Good Governance

As in the rest of India, NER is also victimized by bad governance. As long as this deplorable state of affairs continues, the issues of poverty eradication and the dawn of prosperity are ruled out. Jayanta Madhab has pointed out that the states of NER with the exception of Sikkim and Tripura, suffer from poor governance. Despite the subsidization of eighty to ninety per cent of their budgets (except Assam) by the Central government, their record of the growth of GDP, anti-poverty measures, human development indices and corruption level, are appallingly bad.[39] Bijoya Chakravarthy, the representative of NER in the NDA cabinet, regretted that "The Vajpayee government has virtually gone overboard to help the North East. While the region has only 8.3 per cent of the country's population, it has been allocated 10 per cent of the funds from every department. Yet the state governments in the region have failed to take advantage."[40] In its harrowing report, *The Sangai Express* revealed that the Central funds were diverted to pay salaries of state government's employees and to maintain jumbo-sized ministries or used in lining pockets of those in power.[41] The best way to overcome the problem of bad governance is to make the governments of the states of NER to account to the Central government for every rupee the latter invested in the development of the former.

Hostile attitude of Bangladesh

Bangladesh with which India shares the longest border of well over 4000 kms. constitutes a serious challenge to the integration of NER with the rest of India and the rest of Asia. Dhaka harbours fear about India, based on India's relative size and geographical location. As Rajiv Sikri has pointed out the transit from the rest of India to the NER across Bangladesh or for the NER for regaining its traditional access route to the sea via Chittagong port has been a sensitive political issue.[42] Dhaka which has fostered deep interest in the strategic partnership with Beijing was under no compulsion to provide the transport corridor to the states of NER. Even though Myanmar was prepared to supply gas to energy hungry India across Bangladesh, the recalcitrant Dhaka stalled the move. As India was exploring two options – a (far more expensive) pipeline bypassing Bangladesh through Mizoram or shipping the gas by converting it into LNG – the Yangon government informed New Delhi in March 2007 that it would supply gas to China and not to India.[43]

Some of the Indian leaders like Jairam Ramesh and diplomats such as Rajiv Sikri and C.V. Ranganathan, former Ambassador to China and one of the chief promoters of regional cooperation, believed that the multilateral cooperative frameworks rather than bilateral negotiations would ease the attitude of Bangladesh citing Dhaka's consent at the tripartite meeting of energy Ministers of Myanmar, Bangladesh and India held in Yangon during 12-13 January 2005 to allow the construction of a cross-border gas pipeline which would carry natural gas from Myanmar to India through Bangladesh. But Dhaka subsequently came up with a list of demands which India could not meet. Under this pretext, Bangladesh withheld its permission to gas pipeline. Therefore, even the multilateral forums could not bend the adamant Bangladesh. Dhaka's intransigence represented a serious challenge to India's 'Look East policy'. However, the Bangladesh's caretaker government headed by Fakruddin Ahmed has begun sending positive signals. Bangladesh's Foreign Affairs Advisor, Iftekhar Ahmed Chowdhury stated in Dhaka, on 9 March 2007, that the new government was keen on cultivating a close relationship with New Delhi after trying to 'bury past misunderstandings.' It has to be seen whether the new government in Dhaka, after the elections, would pursue the same positive line.

Conclusion

The failure of different development paradigms pursued by the government in the NER in the last four or five decades to deliver goods triggered the quest for viable alternative models to bail out the hapless people of NER caught up in a morass of despondency, poverty, ethnic strife and insecurity despite the fact that there "is one armed personnel for every ten northeasterners."[44] The need of the hour is an integrated approach to NER which has been an issue that is a real conundrum for the government. The political, economic and cultural reinforcement of NER demands integration with the rest of India to make it a 'solid springboard' for the globalization process;[45] development of highways and railways linking the states of NER to each other and to the rest of India and to the countries in the neighbourhood of NER, which is imperative for the region to emerge as the hub of economic activity; and the Indian political and security establishment to shed the fear of China's economic domination of the region by accepting the challenges from China as opportunities. Moreover, improvement in India's ties with Bangladesh – which had caused immense damage to the interests of India and which 'landlocked the Northeastern region' with attendant problems – should be accorded top priority. The success of this multi-pronged strategy calls for paying due regard to the local initiative. Instead of dealing with the northeastern states as a regional entity, the individual states of NER should be encouraged to come out with their own solutions to a myriad of problems confronting them and to evolve strategies to integrate themselves with the economies of the nearby Southeast Asian countries for mutual benefit. Treating the states of NER with too much kindness and protection would be counter productive. The people of NER would feel that their self respect was at stake. The government of India, while reducing its involvement to the barest minimum, should encourage the state governments of NER to shoulder the responsibility to beef up the politico-economic-strategic landscape of their respective states and even to hold negotiations with insurgent groups. The government should realize that there is lot of wisdom in jettisoning its practice of thrusting its own policies which smacked of utter disregard for the ground realities on the states of NER. It would not be inappropriate to mention here the freedom the Beijing government has given to Yunnan province in forging closer relationship with its neighbours in South and Southeast Asia. Projects might be more acceptable if they are initiated locally than externally. Already there is a widespread resentment against the government of India that the benefits of their programmes did not reach the common man in the region. Disregard of the local initiative might further widen the chasm between the Union government and the people of NER.

'Old habits die hard'' as the saying goes. But time has come for the government of India to abandon its worn out policies and embrace strategic approaches in dealing with the individual states of NER.

References

1. Jayanta Madhab, "Unbounding the Frontier: Enabling the North East", *Dialogue*, January-March 2006, pp. 63-64.
2. *Ibid,* p. 64.
3. Rajiv Sikri, *Press Release,* http://199.236.117.161/pressr/march19 04.html.
4. Manmohan Singh, "India has come to terms with globalization", See http://in.rediff.com/money/2006/march18asoc.htm.
5. Sanjay Baruah, "The Problem", see http://www.manipuronline.com/North-East/ November2005/theproblem232.htm).
6. Madhab, n. 1, pp. 67-68.
7. Jairam Ramesh, "Northeast India in a new Asia", see http://www.india-seminar.com/2005/550/550%20jairam%20ramesh.htm#top.
8. Suvrokamal Dutta, "Look East Policy Could be the Kohinoor for North East India", see http://www.indolink.com/display Articles.ph.?id=010707060358.
9. *Ibid.*
10. Nitin A. Gokhale, "Look East Policy? The Farce-sighted", see http://www.tehelka.com/ channels/coloumns/columntehelka/08182005.asp?ename=Nitin20%.A..
11. Dutta, n. 8.
12. *The Hindu,* 10 March 2006.
13. See http://www.mofa.gov.bd/bimstec_back-html.
14. Web: meadia 2004 a.
15. RIS, *Future Directions of BIMSTEC,* New Delhi, 2004, p. 42
16. EXIM Bank, *BIMSTEC Initiative: A Study of India's Trade and Investment Potential with Select Asian Countries,* Mumbai, July 2004.
17. RIS, n. 15, p. 2.
18. *The Hindu,* 23 March 2007.

19. *Strategic Digest*, September 2004, p. 1260.
20. *Ibid.*
21. See Sudhir Devare, *India & Southeast Asia: Towards Security and Convergence*, New Delhi, 2006, pp. 141-142; and B.H. Vergheese, *Reorienting India: The New Geo-Politics of Asia*, New Delhi, 2002, p. 136.
22. Chandran Irom, "Whatever happened to India's Look East Policy? The Mekong-Ganga Cooperation", see www.manipuronline.com/Features/January2002/mekongganga19htm.
23. http://www.meadev.nic.in/govt/parl-ga/loksaha/Dec6-2741/htm.
24. Interview "*Myanmar enters the New Century*", *World Affairs*, April-June 2001, p. 16.
25. Amit Baruah, "Mekong project aimed at economic development", *The Hindu*, 10 November 2000.
26. *The Hindu*, 9 November 2000.
27. Amit Baruah, "Look East", *Frontline*, 8 December 2000, pp. 49-50.
28. See http://www.mfa.go.th/web/882.php.
29. Nguyen Dy Nien, "ASEAN-India Dialogue Relations: Present and Prospects", in RIS, *India-ASEAN Partnership in an Era of Globalization: Reflections by Eminent Persons*, New Delhi: RIS, 2002, p. 136.
30 See http://www.mfa.go.th/web/882.php.
31. Nien, n. 29.
32. Madhab, n. 1.
33. See http://pib.nic.in/relese/release.asp?relid=754.
34. Gokhale, n. 10.
35. Baruah, n. 5.
36. P.V. Indiresan, "The Kuomintang Initiative", *Frontline*, see http://www.hinduonnet. com/fline/fl1707/17070980.htm.
37. Pallavi Iyer, "Yunnan Model", *Frontline*, http://www.hinduonnet.com/fline/fl2321/stories/20061103000306300.htm
38. *Ibid.*
39. Madhab, n. 1, p.72.
40. *Sangai Express*, "Arrested Development",
see http://www.manpuronline.com/ Editorials/April2002/april07 3.htm.
41. *Ibid.*
42. Sikri, n. 3.
43. *The Hindu*, 22 March 2007.
44. Ramesh, n. 7.
45. Dutta, n. 8.

16

Strengthen BIMSTEC to Revitalize SAARC

Y. Yagama Reddy

If the phrases like Greater India, Farther India, India-Southeast Asian Ethnic Enclaves and India-Extra Ganges had obviously kindled a sort of enchantment and nostalgia in the protagonists of Indian culture, the regional initiatives like BIMSTEC and Mekong-Ganga Cooperation do definitely testify to the age-old spirit of India's cooperative approach that has never subscribed to the tendencies like political domination and economic exploitation. The Indian cultural legacy was a glorious chapter in the cultural history of Southeast Asia, until the Southeast Asia began to get slipped off into the European colonial rule, which was obviously meant for economic exploitation. It was in tune with the historical legacy of inclusiveness that India expressed its solidarity with the nationalist movements in Southeast Asia and also extended the possible economic assistance and cooperation to the newly independent countries in Southeast Asia. The theme that "we are of Asia and the peoples of Asia are nearer and closer to us than others" was the unequivocal expression of Pandit Jawaharlal Nehru. To quote him further: "we have many problems in common, especially in the Pacific and in the Southeastern region of Asia, and we have to cooperate together to find solutions."[1]

Given the proven track of India being identified as the messiah of its neighbours, the newly independent Southeast Asian countries too expected India to provide a basis for developing regional cooperation among themselves as well as between them and India. But, differential estimates of security risks in the context of Cold War, India's reluctance to participate in the regional security pacts, India's indifference to the ASEAN formation and its obsession with the South Asian politics have widened the gulf all through the period of Cold War. With the termination of Cold War geopolitical rumblings and the economic imperatives of new global order gaining ascendancy, India and Southeast Asia sought to move onto the stage of convergence of interests. India's Look East Policy besides enabling its integration with the ASEAN process, facilitated India to get itself associated with several initiatives for trans-regional cooperation through Mekong-Ganga Cooperation and BIMSTEC. At the base of these trans-regional initiatives lie not merely the compulsions of circumstances, but the underlying commonalities and complementarities that could meet the demands of common concerns and interests. Thus, this paper makes an attempt to analyze the commonalities (based on the physical attributes like geology, climate, landforms, soils and biotic life) and the complementarities (as being the product of historical processes and geographical factors) that could sustain the spirit of regional cooperation through BIMSTEC, which in turn shall rejuvenate the emancipated SAARC.

Conceptualization of Region-Forming Factors

There are different approaches pursued for the delimitation of regions. Various region forming factors based on historical legacy, political development, cultural semblance, economic pattern and physical similarity would invariably plead for a degree of homogeneity in delimiting the regions. In this process, the areal extent has been so much varied as to find some regions as being very small and some others becoming quite unwieldy and thereby losing the functional character. This fallacy in the region-forming efforts has given credence to the remarks that the 'regions are good servants, but bad masters.'

Political regions, as is known well, are the artificial creations owing "only to the hazards of geography and history".[2] Austrian empire and the Soviet Union are the classical examples of this category. In yet another form, regionalization process on political considerations tends to bring in cleavages in the already existing regional framework, as testified by the emergence of loose-regional security alliances. Hence, many geopolitical and geostrategic regions do hardly possess the spirit of regional cooperation, as in the case of the Indian Ocean region. Historical developments, on the other hand, tend to eclipse the cultural linkages, as in the case of partition of countries into several nation-states. About the same, the cultural regions, like Greater India, tend to ignore the intrinsic realities undermining the basic character of several regions included in it. Therefore, there have been attempts made at identifying natural regions, as could be found from various studies on the regional geography of the world. Even in this process, many regions are climatic–oriented, eclipsing other basic features. Nonetheless, the regions based on physical attributes do have a greater degree of homogeneity, unlike the cultural, conceptual (geopolitical) and ill-demarcated (political) regions.

Thus, regional identity should be primarily based on the semblance within a given physical environment which tends to sustain economic linkages. Such macro-regions, which Cohen elucidated, tend to become relatively homogenous if they are associated more with common concerns than with the compulsions. Cohen, while delimiting the macro-regions, felt that "few communities are destined to have closer political, cultural and economic ties with some communities than with others; and the macro-regions (so evolved), would get united on account of complementarity in their outlook / behaviour and would exhibit potentialities for further integrations".[3]

It is in this background that the BIMSTEC is to be reckoned a logical regional entity, the spatial homogeneity of which is not pleaded in terms of more geometrical location (geographical proximity), but on the lines of geometric symmetry. It is also a justifiable agreement that certain historical developments manifesting in complementarities have been predisposed to geographical factors, what it is to be understood as geographical determinism on historical momentum.[4] The regional framework of BIMSTEC is characterized by geographical contiguity and hence broad correspondence in the physical setting and socio-cultural milieu. An understanding of this spatial phenomenon would help the reader make an estimate of the functional viability of this nascent regional grouping.

Geology, River Systems and Landforms

If the collision of the two grand landmasses – Gondwanaland and Angaraland – resulted in the emergence of the tertiary folds of Himalayas in the form of a series of parallel mountain ranges, further northward movement of Gondwanaland produced syntaxial bending of the Himalayas in the western and eastern sectors. As a result, Brahmaputra has swerved its course by making a 'U' turn, as if to drain the northeastern region of India, to a tune of 19.5 million hectors of land, accounting for thirty four per cent of total basin area of Brahmaputra. It is for the same geological phenomenon that the Himalayan series run southwards as Arakan Yoma and Pegu Yoma in Myanmar and further down as the Main Range through Thailand and Malaysia, and then as an arc of mountains through Indonesia.

The mountainous topography, which manifest in pronounced variations in the form of steep and rugged mountain slopes and deeply dissected inter-montana valleys, has imposed restrictions on the prospects of regional transport and communication networks; and hence there have been limited human contacts. Young folded mountains are also identified with a negative phenomenon in the form of occasional tectonic disturbances like earthquakes, besides frequent incidents of land sliding and subsequent erosional hazards. On the other hand, Korat Plateau (of Thailand) is comparable to the Indian Deccan plateau (of pre-Cambrian age), known for stability and hence the development of subdued landforms and azonal soils in the lowland region, as opposed to the zonal soils formed in the mountainous terrain regions known for geological instability.

Like the great rivers of Ganges, Indus and Brahmaputra draining northern India, the rivers of peninsular (mainland) Southeast Asia are of perennial in nature, because of their origin in the snow-capped Himalayas, besides demonstrating similarity in hydrography. Thus, the two great rivers of Myanmar – Irrawaddy and Salween – flow through the inter-montane valleys. Though the rapids in the upper courses of the Himalayan rivers impinged on the prospects of navigation, the multipurpose projects are now offering multitude of benefits like irrigation, electricity, fishing, flood control and tourism.

Since the mountainous terrain, as pointed out, remained detrimental to wide range of human contacts, it could only offer scope for the scattered settlements of several ethnic minorities. Thus, heterogeneity in human environment of such terrain is markedly ethnic diversity and demographic imbalance; and terrace and shifting cultivation, food gathering and hunting form the main sources of livelihood. On the other hand, wet rice cultivation dominates the agricultural landscape of the alluvial flood plains developed by Irrawaddy and Salween rivers. Thus, the lowlands have through out the history emerged as the centres of economic and political activity.

Climatic Semblance

Same latitudinal position has its bearing on the prevalence of same bioclimatic types/ zones in the BIMSTEC region, with the exception of some changes owing to altitude. Thus, in a broader sense, the tropical subtropical and temperate climatic zones are as much commonly noticed as the tropical evergreen/deciduous and temperate/coniferous forest types.

a) Monsoon Rhythm

Of much significance is the prevalence of similar monsoon rhythm characterized by the pronounced spatio-temporal variations in rainfall often in the form of floods and droughts, due in large part to the alignment of mountains across the monsoon winds. Further the entire Bay of Bengal region experiences wet (rainy) summers and dry winters as well as cyclonic storms. The history of maritime contacts across the Bay of Bengal did only testify to the sailing routes being much in accordance with the direction of monsoon winds.

b) Climate and Spread of Indian Culture

The historical developments were predisposed to geography needs can be exemplified. The southward extensions of Himalayas in the form of Arakan Yoma and Pegu Yoma had virtually prevented the overland movement of people and goods between the geographically proximate regions of northeastern India and Myanmar. On the contrary, Bay of Bengal, which is considered as a gift of 'Mother Nature', posed no major climatic obstacles to the early navigators. All along historically the trade, the Indianization process was accomplished and sustained for over 1500 years from the beginning of the Christian era. The spread of Indian culture was of tremendous historical significance of cultural geography in as much as all the successive waves of migrants of Mongoloid stock of Southern Chinese origin got themselves attracted to the facts of Indian culture, based on Hinduism and Buddhism or Islam at a later stage. Thus, BIMSTEC is a mosaic of religions having their roots extended far and beyond, and hence a discernible broad semblance in the socio-cultural milieu.

Coastal Plains

The vast stretch of coastal plains in Sri Lanka, India, Bangladesh, Myanmar and Thailand tend to portray a degree of semblance in geomorphology and economic developments based on farming and maritime pursuits. Thus, the costal plains have emerged as the centres's political and economic activity. The modern period of Western domination, in particular, has accomplished the process of pre-modern capitals getting overshadowed by the commerce-oriented port cities. Bangkok, Yangoon, Kolkata, Chennai and Colombo have all gained such prominence. Barring the landlocked states of Nepal and Bhutan, the littoral states, irrespective of the length of coastline, has made them stake overlapping claims on the maritime boundaries and exclusive economic zones. The emergence of trading ports all along the coast of Bay of Bengal is a testimony to the maritime trade of international importance. The long coast line and the insular realm of Andaman & Nicobars of India and the insular character of Sri Lanka have led to the building of naval capabilities either for territorial protection or maritime surveillance.

Agricultural Pattern: Both Semblance and Complementarity

The tropical monsoon rhythm and edaphic conditions in the Bay of Bengal littoral states led to the adoption of similar agricultural practices (typology) and emergence of subsistence farming system. If crop diversity signified the upland ecology, preponderant monoculture of rice in the lowlands has assumed significance as a source of economic power for building up the political base all through the premodern times. Besides developing rice cultivation on commercial lines, colonial period witnessed the agricultural economy evolving on to the stage of exportation, through the introduction of rubber, oil palm, tobacco, coffee and indigo. Obviously, agricultural economies have become complementary in nature, with least susceptibility to commodity-competitiveness. Thus, for all the broad semblance in crop structure, there are crop specializations identified with each of the member states of BIMSTEC. For instance, sorghum cultivation is preponderant in India and Thailand; groundnuts, cotton, potatoes, onions, pulses, apples and millets in India and Myanmar; jute in Bangladesh; tea, coffee and rubber in Sri Lanka; teak and forest resources in Myanmar.[5] This bears significance in the context of little prospects for intra-regional trade among the ASEAN or SAARC member states, because of the similarity in agricultural economies.

Inherent Complementarity and Imminent Cooperation

For all the parallels among the Bay of Bengal countries, there are pronounced regional variations subscribing to complementarity, which in turn, testifies to interdependence owing to surplus or deficit of goods. Besides remarkable variations in geographical size and demographic characters (population size, density, growth rate, life expectancy and literacy levels) and human development, there are significant disparities in the arable land, cropland, crop production and yields. Further, BIMSTEC countries are very much at variance with each other in their mineral resources and exploitation as well as in industrial production. The similarities in the physical environment besides the linkages in the human environment shall enable India to understand more about BIMSTEC than any other country external to BIMSTEC region. The set of complementarities also paves the way for the application of symbiotic modality based on mutual interests and common concerns that would ultimately promote 'business opportunities' and 'linkages' in the region.[6] Foremost of all, India shall derive benefit through transfer of technical know-how essentially required for the countries in need of it. The resource potentialities of India's northeast region shall be harnessed for accomplishing the much-delayed development.

BIMSTEC countries have assumed specific responsibility of focusing on the identified core areas of cooperation, like transport & communication and tourism (India), energy (Myanmar), trade and investment (Bangladesh), technology (Sri Lanka) and fisheries (Thailand). BIMSTEC also accorded importance to cooperation in such other areas as education, public health, human resource development, agriculture, environment and disaster management, peace and security. In addition to trade & investment, scientific & technological collaboration among BIMSTEC countries became imminent. In pursuit of multi-dimensional cooperation, BIMSTEC summit meeting (held on 31 July 2004 in Bangkok) rechristened the grouping as Bay of Bengal Initiative for Multi-Sectoral Technical and Economic Cooperation through the admission of Nepal and Bhutan, albeit the acronym remains unchanged. The summit also decided to accord priority to the projects and to streamline procedures for making BIMSTEC more efficient and output-based.[7] The ninth BIMSTEC Ministerial meeting (held on 9 August 2006 in New Delhi) reiterated its commitment to enhance cooperation for accelerating the economic and social growth and each of the member countries offered to lead a particular aspect.[8] But, like SAARC, BIMSTEC is carrying the stigma that it has not accomplished substantial progress, except envisaging targets at various meetings. BIMSTEC is, in fact, characterized by new regionalism laying emphasis on export-oriented industrialization, as opposed to the import-substitution manufacturing of the old regionalism order. Having experienced disenchantment with SAARC, India looked upon BIMSTEC as an integral part of its Look East Policy, though not as an alternative to SAARC. Instead, BIMSTEC, in the words of the Indian Prime Minister, Manmohan Singh serves as "a bridge between the ASEAN and SAARC countries".[9]

Northeast Region of India as the Fulcrum of BIMSTEC

India's Northeastern region (NER), which had been in the moribund backwaters all through the period of Indian history, has assumed paramount significance, because of its strategic location sharing international borders with as many as four countries (Bangladesh, Bhutan, China and Myanmar). The overland route connecting NER through Myanmar with other MGC countries was viewed as an opportunity for developing trade and industry in Brahmaputra valley and thereby the development of NER.[10] The road link (144 Km) from Tamu (Manipur) to

Kalemyo (near Mandalay in Myanmar), successfully accomplished by India in April 2001, has become functional for felicitating the exchange of peoples, goods and services between the South Asian and Southeast Asian countries.[11] This road link has served as a cue for a prospective trilateral project of road of over 1400 km (northeastern India-Central Myanmar-Thailand). The regional transport links entailing the proposed transcontinental highway would make BIMSTEC a truly functional region. About the same time, Mekong-Ganga Cooperation, which was conceptualized as part of India's Look East Policy, becomes not merely "a bridge of continuity for the affirmation of historical, cultural and geographical ties"[12] between India and ASEAN, but also enables the entire northern tier of BIMSTEC to gain access to China. What deserves much appreciation is the Kunming Initiative that has also envisaged a Growth Quadrangle for the development among the geographically contiguous regions of northeastern India, Bangladesh, Myanmar and southwestern China (Yunnan province),[13] through opening of the historic World War II Stilwell road over a distance of about 1000 km. Thus, for all its geopolitical isolation, NER shall become a gateway or corridor to ASEAN and to China as well. Furthermore, all the SAARC members in the BIMSTEC and Myanmar which do not have direct access to the Pacific Ocean shall be well connected with the Pacific rim countries, if a canal across Kraisthmus is fructified. Of much significance is the glorious past of the Kraisthmus when it acted as a transit between the tenth degree channel and Gulf of Siam. This proposed canal like the Suez and Panama canals shall reduce the distance between Indian sub-continent and South China Sea, besides relieving naval traffic congestion in the narrow constricted Malacca Straits.

Percolation of SAARC Bickerings into BIMSTEC

Though BIMSTEC is a natural region/entity to be reckoned with, it is not altogether free from certain contradictions, mostly inherited from SAARC. Except Pakistan and Maldives, all other SAARC members by virtue of being in the littoral zone of Bay of Bengal have logically become the members of BIMSTEC. But their behavioural pattern has not been transformed altogether, rather tends to transcend into the nascent regional grouping of BIMSTEC. Besides the unresolved Farakka barrage and border dispute between India and Bangladesh, the illegal cross-border migration from Bangladesh into an Indian territory is a contentious issue. Bangladesh, which had earlier accepted in principle for Myanmar, Bangladesh-India oil pipeline, has put the project on tenterhooks. Nepal could not desist from its dubious policy of exploiting its buffer status between India and China. The issue of ethnic Tamils in Sri Lanka still remains a nuisance in the Indo-Sri Lanka bilateral partnership. India, though unwittingly, carries the stigma of having assumed big brother role among its South Asian neighbours. It is high time that all these South Asian brothers are relieved of their bickerings in order to sustain the spirit and purpose of BIMSTEC.

Much Needed fillip to BIMSTEC for Revitalization SAARC

What is more skeptical about BIMSTEC is its status as sub-regional grouping even after a decade of existence. Given the geographical situation and its structural character spanning over SAARC and ASEAN, it ought to have been considered as a trans–regional organization, but not as a sub-regional grouping, as has been depicted unlike SAARC which is limping even after two decades of existence, BIMSTEC accomplished its expansion as well as its activities. Thus, it is to be identified as a regional entity. In fact, further structural expansion as to include the two other Bay of Bengal littoral states–Malaysia and Indonesia –would give credence to the concept of 'extended neighbourhood' what is then to be known as Bay of Bengal community. All said and done, BIMSTEC needs to evolve an action plan for getting itself strengthened, without much lapse of time. The emboldened BIMSTEC shall then act as a stimulus to SAARC's vitality.

References

1. For full text of Jawaharlal Nehru's speech at the Asian Relations Conference, see, *Asia Relations,(Report of the Proceedings and Documentation of the First Asian Relations Conference*, New Delhi, March – April 1947), New Delhi: Asian Relations Organization, 1948, p. 22.
2. Isablle Cordinnier, "Asia Revisited: What for, How, Whither?", *Strategic Analysis,* vol. 20, no. 5, August 1997, pp. 651-664.
3. Saul B.Cohen, *Geography and Politics in a Divided World*, London, 1964, p. 62.
4. For a comprehensive understanding, see Y. Yagama Reddy, "Geographical Cauzation in Southeast Asian History," *Journal of contemporary Asia and Europe,* vol. 1, no. 2, 2004, pp. 81-97.
5. This analysis is based on the crop statistics compiled from the recent Yearbooks of *Far East and Australia.*

6. H.P. Roy and S.K. Chakrabarty, "Calcutta Port Forging Synergic Ties with Southeast", *Journal of Indian Ocean Studies,* vol. 9, no. 1, April 2001, pp. 33-41.
7. BIMSTEC Summit Declaration: Bangkok, 31 July 2004, see http://www.moa.gov.bd /bimstic/ d_f_summit.html
8. Joint statement of the Ninth BIMSTEC Ministerial Meeting, New Delhi, 9 August 2006, see http://www.mofa.gov.bd/*bimstec / js_fm_speech.htm*
9. See news indiamart.com/new-analysis/bimstec-summit-a-mi-7074.
10. G. Parthasarathy, "India's Look East Policy: Need for Addressing New Dimension," see, http://www.Meadev. Nic.in/opn/2000 dec/20trb.htm.; also see *The Hindu,* 11 April 2002, p. 11
11. G. Parthasarathy, "The Road to Mandalay",
see http://www.rediff.com/ news/2000/Dec./20gp.htm.
12. Amit Baruah, "A new Get-together, says Jaswant", *The Hindu*, 11 November 2000; also see *The week*, 26 November 2000, pp. 48-49.
13. See the report on "The Kunming Initiative for a Growth Quadrangle between China, India, Myanmar and Bangladesh, 14-17 August 1999," *China Report,* vol. 36, no. 3, 2000, pp. 417-24.

Contributors

I. P. Khosla, Former Secretary, Ministry of External Affairs, New Delhi.

Shibashis Chatterjee, Senior Lecturer, Dept. of International Relations, Jadavpur University, Kolkata.

Sulagna Maitra, pursuing her Masters in International Humanitarian Action at Uppsala University, Sweden.

Gopalji Malviya, Professor, Dept. of Defence and Strategic Studies, University of Madras, Chennai.

Noman Sattar, Senior Research Officer, Area Study Centre for Africa, North & South America, Quaid-i-Azam University, Islamabad.

Rajpal Budania, Reader, Dept. of Political Science, Allahabad University, Allahabad.

T. Nirmala Devi, Professor & Director, Centre for SAARC Studies, Andhra University, Visakhapatnam.

Som P Pudasaini, UN Resident Coordinator & UNFPA Country Director, Maldives.

Adluri Subramanyam Raju, Associate Professor, Centre for SAARC Studies, Andhra University, Visakhapatnam.

Nalini Kant Jha, Professor, Rajiv Gandhi Chair in Contemporary Studies, Allahabad University, Allahabad.

M. J. Vinod, Professor, Dept. of Political Science, Bangalore University, Bangalore.

J. Laxmi Narasimha Rao, Reader, Dept. of Political Science, Osmania University, Hyderabad.

Syed Ali Mujtaba, Journalist, Chennai.

V. Sreemannarayana Murthy, Assistant Professor, Centre for SAARC Studies, Andhra University, Visakhapatnam.

Srikanth Kondapalli, Professor, Jawaharlal Nehru University, New Delhi.

A. Lakshmana Chetty, Professor & Former Director, Centre for Southeast Asia & Pacific Studies, Sri Venkateswara University, Tirupati.

Y. Yagama Reddy, Professor, Centre for Southeast Asia & Pacific Studies, Sri Venkateswara University, Tirupati.

Index